Living on Less

Living
on Less

Classics From

Mother Earth News

Edited by John Vivian and the Staff of
MOTHER EARTH NEWS
Illustrations by Will Shelton

MOTHER EARTH NEWS • Arden, NC

Dedicated to the memory of Scott and Helen Nearing…
who showed the way.

Printed in the United States of America on recycled, acid-free paper
by McNaughton & Gunn, Inc.

Designed by Stefan Killen
Illustrations by Will Shelton
Cover Design by Lisa Marie Giordani

Published by
MOTHER EARTH NEWS
Sussex Publishers, Inc.
P.O. Box 129
Arden, NC 28704

ISBN: 0-9660494-0-3

Contents

Forward to the Second Edition

Living On Less first appeared in 1983, compiled from reader-written articles featured during the first 15 years of MOTHER EARTH NEWS, America's Original Country Magazine.

In this second edition, we have changed as little as possible, seeking to retain the sense of youthful innocence and back-to-the-land enthusiasm of MOTHER's early days. You'll find a few 1970s attitudes almost quaint, many then-contemporary references dated, prices and income figures unbelievably low, and inflation and interest rates alarmingly high.

Ideas, products, and techniques that are common knowledge now are presented as if they'd just been discovered...which was the case when these real-life accounts were first recorded. Also, you may find the writing a bit labored; often as not, it was based on a long letter, hand-written by lantern light in the wood-heated kitchen of a log house during brief rest periods between chores.

What endures, however, is the solid value of the commonsense advice offered by MOTHER's first readers ("them that's doin' it" in the hip language of the times) as they bring alive the timeless appeal of a life of sturdy independence on the land, in harmony with nature and using a minimum of the earth's finite resources.

Truly, living (better) on less.

⚘

CHAPTER 1

Personal Economics

They Couldn't Afford to Keep Their Jobs

Back in the 1950s, "The American Dream" was defined as a split-level suburban home, humming with automatic appliances, a big lawn, and a two-car garage bulging with Detroit iron. Conveniently ignored was the 30-year mortgage, the high-interest auto and houseware loans, and a lifetime of commuting twice a day to a 9-to-5 city job to finance it all.

The cost of the dream—spending their lives working in some dreary office to repay money borrowed to buy status symbols—proved too high for one young couple.

Both had good jobs in the city, he with a large corporation, she as a teacher. The pay was good enough, but the work was repetitive and stressful, and commuting to their suburban home left them exhausted most evenings, and frantic for diversion on weekends. Life had become a tedious cycle of of bills, bosses, and the "Monday Morning, Back to the Rat Race Blues."

Then they subscribed to a new magazine called Mother Earth News that contained readers' stories about finding new freedom in country living. The couple began dreaming of a place of their own where they could live a life of sturdy self-reliance on the land and raise a family in the clean country air of a wholesome community, free of both the rattle, smog, and violence of the cities and the conformist pressures of suburbia. They could also live in a way that reduced their contribution to pollution and energy waste, and they could follow a new and growing ethic: Environmentalism.

In the early years of their marriage, they'd saved every cent and had even accepted family help to raise a down payment for their suburban dream home. But, now somehow, they could never quite find enough money to pay all the bills—to say nothing of saving up for a down payment on a piece of country property. Everything they earned seemed to be spent in advance, and they were getting more and more into debt.

Running the Numbers: Feeling terminally broke one evening, the wife decided to analyze the true economics of her job. She didn't understand how they couldn't seem to get ahead. The hard, cold figures showed that most of her check was spent before she got it—largely on what she needed to earn the money in the first place. Here is where her income went before any savings, investment, personal, or recreational expenses:

Salary		$18,000
State and federal taxes	$3,000	
Car payment ($270/month)	3,240	
Gasoline for commuting ($160/month)	1,920	
Auto repair, tolls, miscellaneous	480	
Auto insurance and registration	700	
Working wardrobe, repair, cleaning	1200	
Total work-related expenses	$10,540	
Net disposable income		7,460
Less Credit Payments		-2,000
Net free income		$5,460

She decided that if she had to spend more than two and a half dollars in work-related expenses for every dollar she kept…and then, was spending half of that to pay off revolving credit bills, leaving her just a little more than four hundred dollars a month to enjoy life with…it was time to quit.

So she did!

The credit accounts were canceled, and she began to trade on a former hobby—a lifelong love of horses. Years of riding instruction and ring-competition in her youth, combined with her classroom teaching experience, qualified her to instruct youthful riders. The pay wasn't much—but her commuting days were over, and she earned more than enough to pay down the credit-account debt in short order, begin accumulating a gardening library, and have some money left from each paycheck to go into savings. Work hours were easy: after school and weekends plus summer-camp sessions. The work was stress-free, rewarding, and afforded plenty of healthful outdoor activity as well as the leisure time to develop handy home gardening skills that helped to further stretch the money she did bring home.

The riding stable was near home, eliminating the need for a second family vehicle, so (following a new idea they read about—barter) they began reading the local auction circulars and swap columns and were able to trade her car and a little cash for several acres of remote country property.

They quit the health club, canceled the charge account at the fancy wine store, and began spending weekends on their land—clearing brush, digging up a garden, learning to cut down trees...and washing off the good sweat in the river at the bottom of the hill. They used plans they found in a book to build a privy...that took almost a summer of weekends, as they were learning carpentry the hard (and fun) way—by learning from their mistakes.

Just being there and knowing they owned it outright, the land began to lure them—who cared if it was on a dirt road, and there wasn't a telephone pole or electricity for a mile and a half? On close examination of the husband's earnings, they realized that the idea of simply packing up and trying to make do in a rural location wasn't too farfetched at all!

The following figures demonstrate how nearly all of the husband's income was going to maintain a suburban lifestyle they found increasingly empty:

Salary		$40,000
State and federal taxes	$4,500	
Mortgage payments ($800/month)	9,600	
Property taxes	1,200	
Electricity ($75/month)	900	
Telephone ($40/month)	480	
Oil heat	2,000	
Truck payment ($207/month)	2,568	
Gasoline ($ 100/month)	1,200	
Truck repair, miscellaneous	700	
Vehicle insurance and registration	800	
Food ($250/month)	3,000	
Credit Cards	2,500	
Clothing	1,000	
Total living expenses	$30,448	
Net disposable income		$9,552

With the siren song of their country land in their ears, they took a (first) really hard, honest look at the way their mortgage, car loans, and revolving credit payments broke down. They were paying almost double to use other people's money to finance their keep-up-with-the-Jones' lifestyle.

All but a few dollars of their house payment was lost forever in interest; their equity would not begin to build for 20 years! The truck loan and the appliances bought on store credit cost double their ridiculously high original prices over the loan periods. And, they would never get the credit accounts paid off; the monthly payment was almost all high interest charges; the credit accountants only reduced the face value of the loan by a dollar or two a month. They realized that revolving loans were designed to keep them perennially in debt!

Faced with those facts, the couple made the decision to abandon their suburban way of life. They put their house on the market and began to scrimp and save again, investing free cash in how-to books and tools. Weekends over the next winter became invigorating work rather than a search for temporary escape as they converted the garage to a workshop and prefabricated a small cottage from mail-order plans, scrounging lumber at building sites and paying strictly cash for new materials.

That spring, they arranged with a new country-neighbor-to-be to build a simple concrete-block-pier and landscaping-timber foundation on their land. Then they loaded the panels of their new cottage on a rented truck, hauled them up-country, and during weekends and vacation time that summer (with welcome help from new neighbors), they erected the structure.

When their suburban house sold (quicker than they expected) they used the recovered down payment money and their pitifully small amount of added equity to pay all their debts (including money borrowed from parents who weren't exactly happy about their change of life plans). What was left went to finance the move into their paid-for home on their paid-for country acreage.

The first winter was hard as body and mind acclimated to living without city services. Hauling water from the river got to be work, and there was a period the following summer when cash ran out and they had nothing to eat but fresh produce from the garden (poor them). But they were out of debt, out of the city, and free. They never looked back.

Living Cheap: They cooked (and heated in an emergency) on an old range they bought for $15, and burned bottled gas that cost all of $20 a month. Light (when they weren't so pleasantly weary from honest, hard work that they stayed up past dusk) came from economical kerosene lanterns. A small barrel stove replaced the suburbanite oil furnace, and wood gleaned from the woods and bartered for temporary busy-season work in the cordwood dealer's yard provided fuel. Their handy-man neighbor helped them tap a flowing spring up their hill and run a gravity feed to the little sink they got for nothing at the town dump.

The pickup truck was sold, and the loan paid off. The truck was replaced with a used camper van, which was a little rusty in places but economical, reliable, and paid for.

Both took on seasonal and occasional jobs: working farm fields, housekeeping, and waiting tables at a local resort, and working the diner counter, pumps, and cash register at an all-night truck stop just off the interstate. Their complete time-flexibility let them work nights and off-hours for higher hourly rates, but it was still menial work for low wages. But they no longer needed big money to pay for a split-level dream house with wall-to-wall bills, a new car every few years, fancy clothes and fancy French wine, and ever-increasing income and Social Security taxes.

In time, their annual budget looked more like this:

Total joint income:		$14,800
Rent/mortgage	$ 0	
Car payments	0	
Electricity	0	
Heat	0	
Income and Social Security taxes	1,240	
Property taxes	500	
Telephone (occasional use of pay phone)	200	
Bottled gas and kerosene	240	
Gasoline (errands and travel to occasional cash work)	600	
Vehicle insurance and registration	800	
Grocery (non-food items, plus staples to supplement the garden	2,800	
Garden, homesteading, and building tools and supplies	2,500	
Clothing (leaving city jobs really reduces this expense)	500	
Total living expenses	$9,380	
Net free income		$5,420

Their change of lifestyle left over one third of their income available to spend or save—many times what they had when earning over three times the gross income back in suburbia.

Without employer pensions or medical insurance, they began to save rigorously—first, to build up a four-figure "untouchable" savings account to pay unexpected bills such as a major auto repair or $1,000-plus to cover the big deductible before their inexpensive "Major Medical" insurance policy took over.

Because both were free of the 40-hour week, their time was their own to devote to building a barn and stable, growing food, hunting and fishing, community activities, and budget travel. Their recreational expenses had actually increased since their move to the country. They rented their cottage one summer for enough cash to buy a fresh engine for the camper, pay the year's taxes and insurance, and keep the gas tank and lunch basket full while they explored Alaska. After three months on the road, with expenses totaling $2,900 for 12,000 miles of unforgettable travel through some of the most spectacular country on earth, they took off-season jobs as caretakers of a fishing camp on the Alaskan coast. There, they feasted on salmon and crab, and watched the seals, whales, and bald eagles while they continued to expand their country-living knowledge and skills.

These folks are back in the "lower 48" now—though they did spend one "Europe on $5.00-a-day" year walking the hostel circuit. And they continue to

Mortgage Calculator:
How Much Can You Borrow

Most of us borrow as much as our monthly pay check will allow. The bank decides how much that is by taking the lower result from the following pair of calculations.

1. Add up monthly gross pay (total before income taxes and other deductions are subtracted) of all parties to the mortgage. Say, $4,000
2. Multiply by .28   x .28
                                                                                1120
3. Subtract a month's projected real estate tax and insurance   -400
4. What you can spend/mo. on principal and interest $720
   OR
1. Take the same combined income $4,000
2. Subtract tax and insurance on the new house   -400
3. Also subtract all monthly credit payments: auto loan, revolving
   charge, etc.   -1000
                                                                                2600
4. Multiply by .36   x.36
5. What you can spend each month on principal and interest: $936

Free income of $900 to 1000 /mo. will indenture you for 30 years to pay back $160,000 at 6 %...$120,000 at 8 percent...$100,000 at 10%. Or, for a fifteen year term, the same income will get you $112,000 at 6%, $100,000 at 8% or $88,000 at 10%. ■

---

live their dream—thanks to their courage to break free from a life they thought they couldn't afford to leave.

Until they faced the facts and figures, they'd never acknowledged that the heart of their lives—age 30 to 60—was indentured to earning the cash to borrow the capital to buy the status symbols to sustain a suburban lifestyle that they found wanting. Hooked on the "enjoy-it-now-and-pay-for-it-later" credit mentality, and burdened with high living at high prices, their free time, free cash, and the energy to enjoy either were always in short supply. But they've learned how to place money and money-making in perspective—as the means to live the way they really want to.

Now, they are planning for a family, and need to add a room or two to the cabin, a solar-electric plant, and a septic system...plus expanded life and health insurance. For the needed cash they have made a temporary compromise. The wife teaches riding at a nearby private school three days a week during the school year plus a full summer-camp schedule, and the husband works as local-news reporter for the nearby city newspaper and spends every free second he can muster establishing his own computer-based home business. For now, the garden is smaller, and they are considering joining their neighbors in having electricity run up the mountain.

For them and perhaps for you too the solution to money problems was not in earning more, but in simplifying life so as to require less.

The transition from city or suburbia to a low-cost country life does take time, planning, and money. How much income you'll need will depend on your skills, determination, desired lifestyle, and current assets. How you'll earn what you need depends on your earning potential at country skills and country wages or your ability to commute (physically or electronically) to wherever higher-paying work is.

You may have to sell valued property, and, since you will surely deplete your personal savings, you'd best start building them up well before you make the move. It is good to sell the TV and golf clubs and devote spare time to learning a transferrable skill to bring in the income you'll require, and to learning the skills necessary to live the good country life.

But, however you shuck those "Monday Morning, Back to the Rat Race Blues," you will be investing in yourself rather than banks and automakers, mall stores, and escapist recreation.

Mortgage Calculator:
How Are Monthly Payments Calculated?

Monthly Payment for Each $1,000 Borrowed (P & I only; tax and interest not included).

Borrowing $48,000 at 8% for 30 years will cost you $352 per month ($7.34/thousand/month x 48 thousands). ■

	Term Of Loan		
Interest Rate	15 yrs	20 yrs	30 yrs
6%	8.44	7.16	6.00
6.5%	8.71	7.46	6.32
7%	8.99	7.75	6.65
7.5%	9.27	8.06	6.99
8%	9.56	8.35	7.34
8.5%	9.85	8.68	7.69
9%	10.14	9.00	8.05
9.5%	10.44	9.32	8.41
10%	10.75	9.65	8.78

Mortgage Calculator:
How Much Cash Do You Need?

The down payment (dp) is the cash you have to produce "on closing." The bank figures that if you have a substantial sum locked up in the house you are less likely to default on the loan. A typical dp figure is 20% of the house value. Let's say you are after a loan to buy a $120,000 home. The dp should be $24,000 (20%) and the mortgage $96,000 (80%).

1. Add up total savings, investments, money from home and other cash resources, plus equity in currently owned home.
    Say you can get hold of: $40,000
2. Calculate cash you'll need at closing.
    — "Closing costs": lawyers fees, title registration and etc.,
      averaging about 5% of mortgage.   -4,800
    — "Points": a bribe to the bank of 1% to 6% of mortgage, say
      2% of $96,000   -1,920
    — Escrow, where bank pays your taxes and insurance—charging
      you 1/12th of the cost each month and holding it in an
      escrow account. You need the first year's cost. Say,   <u>-2,000</u>
                                                                      -8,720
3. Subtract cash costs from your savings: $31,280
4. Hey, you made the $24,000 dp with a few thousand to spare.

Bankers and realtors will offer you their congratulations. Lucky you...you just qualified to borrow $96,000 for 30 years at 8%...and get to spend the rest of your earning life paying $704/month for 360 months...or $254,000. That's nearly 2 1/2 times the loan. The bank looks forward to income of $160,000 over the next generation. The realtors go home with their 8% commissions, or $9,600. The lawyers keep $5,000 for a few hours work. And you are in hock for principal, interest, taxes, and insurance till you reach your 60s. Who deserves the congratulations? ∎

CHAPTER 2

❧

Your Own Country Place

How One Family Achieved Self Sufficiency

Dan Taylor and his wife, Mary Lou, felt that the true cost of living in our technology-based society failed to reflect the damage that was being done to the environment. They were convinced that the price of fossil fuel and food in the supermarkets would eventually rise to reflect its true cost, which could very well force a return to the self-sufficient way our forebears lived. They resolved to establish a life for their young family that was independent of the conventional food supply cycle and nonrenewable sources of energy.

In 1973, the senior Taylors and their young sons, Mark and Brad, pulled up their urban roots and settled in the Arkansas Ozarks. They invested 10 years of savings to buy an old, but livable house on 160 acres (120 wooded hillside and 40 bottom land) of mountain land where they determined to supply most of their own needs for food, energy, and shelter in a manner harmonious with nature and the environment. After four years on their farm in the hills, the Taylor family had achieved a great deal of the self-sufficiency it sought and agreed to share the secrets of their success.

The Land: In 100 years the land had been farmed to exhaustion producing corn, cotton, sugar cane, and small grains. Getting anything at all from the rocky soil was a struggle. But the family produced almost all its own food, primarily because in the early days they were willing to eat whatever they had. They lived on little but canned black-eyed peas and green beans their first winter, and as a result those legumes still have a special place in their affections.

Foraging: Foraging food from the wild was very important to survival when the family first moved to the farm, and four years later it still provided

a significant portion of their diet. A big bowl of crisp watercress mixed with tiny wild onions is hard to beat in the spring, long before the first lettuce is ready to pick from the garden. Black walnuts and hickory nuts are real staples, and the Taylors canned 50 quarts of wild blackberries in their third year in the Ozarks. They also harvested elderberries, huckleberries, gooseberries, grapes, persimmons, and other wild vegetables and fruits.

Milo maize was a real lifesaver for them the first couple of years. It grows in extremely poor soil and produces in even the hottest and driest summers. In a typical year, the family plants 5,000 feet of row with two pounds of seed and harvests 300 pounds of the grain.

They reaped the milo by cutting the plants' heads off with a pocketknife, then beating out the grain, grinding it fine, and using it just like cornmeal. The ground grain makes a good pan bread, and when cooked in milk, an excellent hot cereal.

By plowing and replowing their garden three or four times during the first winter, working large quantities of manure and limestone into the soil over the years, and sowing a mixture of winter vetch and rye grain on the area each fall and plowing it under as green manure the following spring, the Taylors were able to build their vegetable patch into a fairly fertile piece of land.

Planning: Homegrown fruits and vegetables made up a substantial portion of their diet, and the Taylors approached their gardening activities in a well-planned systematic way. They rotated crops for maximum utilization of soil fertility and for control of diseases and insect pests. They spread manure heavily and used a certain amount of mulch. Both standard and hybrid seeds were sown, and in other ways these homesteaders took a middle road through all the "miracle, cure-all gardening methods" that the "experts" seem to be constantly pushing.

Their best advice to the beginning gardener is to start slowly with the old cultivation systems, such as plowing, discing, harrowing, or rototilling, that have already proven effective. Experiment with new ideas a little at a time, and beware of the agribiz industry's claims that any and all problems can be solved now and forever by the application of some magic chemical. Prepare your seed bed as well as you can, and stir the soil around your plants as they grow. Plant across the slope, and grow cover crops during the off-season to keep the ground from eroding. Learn what to expect from your soil and climate before you begin to test new theories and ideas, and then test such "breakthroughs" cautiously and a little at a time.

The Taylors found that Jerusalem artichokes are a true survival food. A few roots from a neighbor are all the start you'll need, and after the first year or two, the plants should become so prolific that they'll need to be thinned for better tuber production.

The roots of this plant store themselves in peak condition in the ground right through the winter, and they can be dug and eaten at almost any time. They're good raw in salads or prepared any way that potatoes are cooked. The Taylors also used Jerusalem artichokes as supplemental feed for their hogs, chickens, and rabbits.

Animal Protein: When the garden was in full production, the family was vegetarian. During the vegetable patch's off season, however, they ate about 2-1/2 pounds of meat a day. For one year, this broke down to: 300 pounds of pork (two 150-pound hogs), 110 pounds of rabbit (44 fryers averaging 2-1/2 pounds), 96 pounds of Muscovy duck (24 four-pounders), 60 pounds of Bantam chickens (60 one-pound fryers), 24 pounds of Khaki-Campbell ducks (eight, weighing three pounds each), and 20 pounds of wild squirrels, rabbits, and groundhogs. Grand total: 610 pounds of meat for the four of them.

The Taylors kept two sows to raise feeder pigs (weaned young pigs for buyers to raise to slaughter weight) for market and to produce pork for homestead use. The feeder pig business is very labor-intensive, and a lot of study was needed to learn the ropes. When the market is reasonable, however, the sale of feeder pigs can substantially boost a small farm's income even when it's necessary to buy feed.

Rabbits are an indispensable source of meat for the small homestead, but the inexperienced owner must be willing to spend some time studying the animals and to give them regular and adequate care. When properly housed, a trio of two does and a buck requires only a few minutes of care a day, yet in an average year will produce 110 pounds of meat for the table.

The Taylors got their start in poultry by purchasing day-old baby chicks from a hatchery. They ordered 25 Light Brahmas, 24 Araucanas, and 10 Bantams. The Brahmas and Araucanas eat a lot and lay very little most of the year, though in the late winter and early spring, they overwhelm the family with eggs.

The Bantams, however, were not a mistake. They lay reasonably well, they make excellent setters and mothers, and they forage for most of their food. The Taylors plan to butcher everything but the Bantams, add a good laying breed such as White Leghorns, and then set both Bantam and White Leghorn eggs under the Bantam mothers.

They got into the goose business on a small scale by setting two Toulouse eggs under their hens. The chickens didn't mind incubating the large eggs but rejected the large goslings, so that the Taylors brooded the two youngsters, one a goose and the other a gander, in the house, and the two birds quickly became pets.

Geese are easy to keep and inexpensive to feed. In the Ozarks climate, they prefer no shelter, they eat grass, and the only grain they get is the little they snitch from the hog trough. They should be a very efficient source of meat and eggs.

A neighbor gave the family a pair of Muscovy ducks in return for help around his farm, and the female sets at least twice each season. As clumsy as she appears to be, she handled the job all by herself, and in 1975, she successfully raised 25 ducklings. When butchered at about five months of age, these birds provide meat that is exceptionally tasty and tender as well as plenty of fat that makes good cooking oil or (cooked with potash water from rain-soaked wood ash) a strong, soft laundry soap.

The family also raises some Khaki-Campbell ducks, which, according to a USDA pamphlet, have been known to lay 365 eggs per year. The Taylors' ducks weren't nearly that productive, but they did lay well in the spring and were easy to care for. Khakis forage constantly, although they do require some grain, particularly during their laying season.

Guineas Are Foul Fowl: The family felt their guinea fowl were a glaring failure. The guineas certainly are excellent foragers. Indeed, they are too good, since their favorite foraging territory was the garden. Young seedlings seem to be quite a delicacy in the guinea diet, and the birds have a particular affection for any kind of peas, beans, and squash. Guinea fowl can also spot and peck out the tiniest speck of pink on a green tomato.

These birds nearly destroyed a hive of bees by standing in front of the hive to catch the pollen-laden insects as they landed.

Guineas are poor mothers, and the Taylors found that contrary to popular belief, they have little value as "watchdogs," as they screeched all the time. The birds are extremely wary, and after you've killed one, the only way to ever harvest the rest is with a rifle. Also, guineas like to sleep in trees, where they are easy prey for owls. All in all, the Taylors felt guineas weren't worth the effort.

The family acquired three mixed-breed cows that were bred to calve at four-month intervals. The idea was to have one of the three coming fresh and producing between three and four gallons of milk per day early in her lactation on a regular enough schedule to give a steady supply of milk the year-round. They figured that each new calf could have one gallon a day, and the other two would be for them.

And that's just the way everything worked out…until one cow dropped twin heifers, leaving only a gallon of milk for daily household use.

Beating the Bugs: Flies are a nuisance to livestock left in the open during Ozark summers, but the Taylors found that pennyroyal made an effective and inexpensive repellent. A large handful of the mint is boiled for a few minutes in water, and then the liquid is mixed with mineral oil and a couple of drops of dish washing detergent. The mineral oil extends the effective life of the repellent by helping it stick to an animal's hair, and the detergent helps the oil and water combine into a useful emulsion when the container's shaken vigorously.

The Taylors freely admit that their goal of self-sufficiency in the purest sense was unattainable. They feel they could never, for instance, produce the iron in a plow or manufacture the implement in their backyard. For this reason, they are willing to accept what they call "durable technology" such as a tool that uses only renewable sources of energy as its driving force, has a relatively long life—say on the order of a human lifetime—and when damaged or worn, can in almost every instance be repaired right on the farm.

They first tried farming the land with an old tractor, but it was impossible to operate one of the machines in their rough woodland and on the small patches of land they cultivated. Besides that, they didn't like the expense of pouring gasoline through such a piece of machinery.

Attempts at using horses proved equally frustrating. Real draft horses were few and far between and very expensive. The horses and mules that the Taylors could afford were usually of the saddle type and too small to do significant amounts of work.

The family felt that horses have at least three other major drawbacks. They must be fed large quantities of grain when they're working, their harness is expensive, and some horses become excited in a confusing or tight situation and immediately make a gigantic lurch or jump. The invariable results of this action are a broken set of harness, expensive repairs, and delays.

Gentle Oxen: So they turned to oxen and found that, especially when hand-fed from birth, the beasts are calm, steady, and forgiving. When confronted with an unfamiliar situation, they tend to stop and think things over.

This is an ideal response, since it gives the teamster a chance to gather his thoughts too.

Oxen are not unduly expensive or hard to find, and they're not difficult to train. None of the family had ever seen another team of the animals work before, but they soon had their pair working together beautifully.

Also, it doesn't take a lot of money to harness a span of oxen. Following directions received by mail, the Taylors made a sliding yoke with just the crudest of tools. The only expense was a few cents for having the yoke's beam sawed out and a few dollars for nuts and bolts.

Oxen are sure-footed and work well in brush and other tangles. Their simple gear is much harder to foul than the harness on a team of horses. The animals can get by reasonably well on no grain at all if they're allowed all the forage or hay they can eat. The only drawback is that they must be yoked and exercised every day to remain fit and remember their training.

The Taylors' span pull a mold board plow, disc harrow, spring tooth harrow, standard tooth harrow, row cultivator, two-row planter, mowing machine, hay rake, and hay wagon. "Bigun" and "Mawry" are also invaluable for dragging logs out of the woods and hauling firewood on a cart, and for two years they turned the sweep on a homemade irrigation pump that could move 1,000 gallons of water an hour 15 feet uphill from the Little Buffalo River to the garden.

The oxen complete a classic sun-energy cycle. Grass in the Taylors' pasture and the trees in their woods gather the sun's energy and store it for later use. The oxen then consume the grass and use the energy derived from it for draft work. The family cuts the wood and burns it in their stoves, steam engines, and food dryer. Even the nutritional value of the things they eat from the garden, orchard, and woodland and the animals they butcher originally come from the sun.

Solar Power: During the summer, when heat from a wood burning cook stove would make the house intolerable, many meals were prepared in a homemade solar oven. In addition, the oven saved the work and time that the family would otherwise have spent in cutting wood for summertime cooking.

Cooking is slower with the solar rig than with the cook stove, but the Taylors felt that stews and casseroles, yeast bread, pan bread, potatoes, meats, and most foods but fresh vegetables taste better when cooked slowly.

Because of the labor and expense of pressure canning 1,300 quarts of food on a wood cook stove as the Taylors did in 1975, they tried drying some of their food. They tried sun-drying garden produce several times, but thanks to the heavy dew every night throughout the summer in the Arkansas Ozarks, it was completely unworkable for them even when they covered the food or took it inside each evening. Electric dryers were too expensive to operate and use nonrenewable energy, and the Taylors didn't care for oil-fired units because the fumes from their fuel always seemed to taint the produce.

So they built a dryer that radiates clean, controlled, smoke-free air at any temperature up to 150° Fahrenheit through anything they want to preserve. This dryer was heated by the renewable fuel the family cut from their 120 acres of woodland. It worked like a charm, and by disconnecting a single length of pipe so that the smoke from the fire went up through, rather than around, the drying chamber, the rig also served as a meat smoker.

Steam Power: The Taylors also bought two old but still serviceable steam engines that were so simple to work on that they put back into working order with minimal effort. One weighed only 100 pounds and put out five horsepower. The plan was to set it on wheels with a small boiler and pull it around from the irrigation pump, to a washing machine, to a battery charger (for household lights, a car radio for news and weather reports, and an electric fence), to a grain thresher, to a concrete mixer, and so on.

The other power plant served for larger jobs, such as driving a cordwood saw, thereby freeing the family from using the gasoline-eating chain saw.

The Taylors planted 80 Chinese chestnut seedlings and gathered their first 10 pounds of chestnuts three years later. They hoped that these trees would eventually produce 100 pounds of nuts per tree. That's 8,000 pounds of food with a protein content roughly three times that of corn, or the equivalent of 24,000 pounds of corn. Pipe dream or not, they expected to feed most of the chestnuts to the livestock in place of grain. Such tree culture has been done by other people in other lands, and the family liked the idea. Once established, the crop requires no annual replanting and cultivation, and the trees protect and hold the soil better than more conventional forms of agriculture.

While the Taylors found that their newfound lifestyle was viewed askance by some of their friends and relatives, they felt quite comfortable with their homesteading experience. They felt that while they were enjoying a heavily self-sufficient way of life, they had not retreated from the world and were still an integral part of modern society, hardly immune to economic, environmental, or social problems.

Indeed, they were well prepared to help others work toward individual or community self-sufficiency should the need or desire arise for whatever reason.

Finding a Country Place That Is Right for You

Perhaps you've decided to leave the crowded city life and make the move to a place in the country. Living peacefully in a quiet hollow where you can raise your own garden and tend your own livestock might sound appealing, but it can turn into a most unpleasant experience if you impulsively flee to a section of the country or a piece of land that's wrong for you.

Finding the right country property isn't difficult; it just requires a bit of forethought and a lot of research and patience. People who leap into farm life without giving proper consideration to the part of the country where they'll be at home, or who buy their land without gathering the information, facts, and figures needed to make a calculated decision, stand a good chance of winding up back in the city, licking their wounds and feeling resigned to living elbow-to-elbow with thousands of others.

There are several matters to consider before even looking at farm and property listings in the real estate catalogs. Among these are the climate and topography you prefer, the distance you want to be from friends and relatives, what you can afford to pay for property, and whether you want a remote location or one with access to a large metropolitan area.

You'll need to decide whether you want four distinct seasons or year-round sunshine. Do you prefer hills and mountains to flatlands...the dryness of the desert or a certain amount of rainfall? Have you always yearned to live near the ocean or a lake?

If price is a factor, as it is for most people, look at population shifts to see which areas of the country have stable or declining populations. Land prices are most likely to be lower in these locations, and property is probably more readily available.

Realtors: Once you've decided which type of land and climate are most suitable, contact the country-property arms of the national real estate chains that maintain directories of farms, acreage, country homes, and even small businesses for sale all over the United States. You'll get a good idea of the land prices, the geography, and the types of farming practiced in various parts of the country.

The next step is to find out more about the specific areas that interest you and to try to narrow the field to a single state. The public library is a good place to find information you need. Talking to people and ordering government publications can also be helpful.

When you have chosen a state, write to the state's land grant university for the address of the agricultural extension service. Ask them for publications on soil, climate, farming, wildlife, poultry raising, beekeeping, and gardening.

Next, break the state down into counties and get the address of every county seat. Then, order a map of each county and write to inquire about proposed highways, industry, and other developments. This should narrow your search to a handful of counties.

Address letters to the chambers of commerce of small towns in the areas that interest you most. Ask about schools, churches, libraries, recreational facilities, clubs, and so forth, and when the information arrives, interpret it according to your needs and way of life.

Next, order a copy of each small town's newspaper so you can learn about food prices, real estate, cost of used farm equipment, and other matters. You can tell a lot about an area by reading editorials and want ads.

The final step is to write for copies of the local telephone directories. The yellow pages are packed with information about business opportunities, services available, restaurants, and so forth. If you need further information about people or organizations mentioned in other literature you've received, the telephone book will help you locate them.

Be Businesslike: When writing for information, type your queries neatly and enclose a stamped, self-addressed envelope. Psychologically, a reply envelope is almost as hard to ignore as a ringing phone, and a businesslike letter indicates that you're serious about your inquiry.

When requesting maps, telephone directories, and other materials, always arrange to pay any cost involved. Keep carbon copies of all correspondence.

At this point, begin making lists of things to look for in your "ideal" farm. Is there an adequate water supply? Drilling a well is expensive. Is the property on a mail and school bus route? If so, roads will probably be plowed promptly in winter. Will you have to install a septic tank, a bathroom, electricity? Take nothing for granted; many old farmhouses are appallingly primitive.

Realize that you probably won't find a dream house, and keep in mind that you may well wind up renovating an older home. You can repair a building, but you can't move a piece of acreage, so pay particular attention to the land's location.

When inquiring about a particular piece of property, you may find it's already been sold. Don't give up, though; write to several of the Realtors who advertise in the catalogs and ask what else is available. Some may not reply, but others will, and ultimately you'll find what you're looking for.

Learning the Lay of the Land

The best way of knowing that you are buying what you want when purchasing land is to examine the plot in person. This, however, often involves a great deal of legwork and expense, especially if you're looking at several pieces of property situated some distance from one another or well away from home. Maps can help cut the cost of hunting for acreage and let you evaluate land without ever setting foot on it.

Soil survey, geological, and topographical maps, available from state and local government offices, contain specific facts about an area: the kind of soil, the crops the earth is likely to support, the rock types and forma-tions, and the lay of the land. Other information such as average rainfall, sea-sonal temperature ranges, and first and last frost dates can be obtained inex-pensively or for free. With these types of data and whatever is learned from the technical maps, you can determine whether a piece of land warrants further consideration.

On a map, north is at the top and south at the bottom, east is to the right, and west to the left. The scale, which gives the relationship between distance on the map and actual distance, is usually found in the upper or lower mar-gin. There is also a legend, which contains an explanation of the various sym-bols, numbers, colors, and shades used on the map. Any map should carry the date that it was drawn or when the most recent revision was made. This last piece of information is valuable, because stream beds can shift, buildings are constantly being built or torn down, and roads change. Making use of a map involves translating the symbols, lines, and colors into an image of the actual land.

Topos: Topographical maps make an accurate and detailed one-dimen-sional representation of a section of the earth's surface. These maps indicate streams, lakes, rivers, wooded areas, roads, trails, railroads, buildings, mines, and other features. More important, they delineate the hills, valleys, ridges, and all the natural variations of the land itself.

Water is usually indicated by blue, wooded areas by green, roads and trails by black or red solid or dotted lines, railroads by crosshatched black lines, buildings by black rectangles, and mines and other features by other symbols. The ups and downs of the earth's surface are depicted by contour lines, each of which represents a certain elevation. Depending on the map, the vertical inter-val between the lines is either 10 or 20 feet. Knowing the elevation interval between two lines, the distance between them, and the scale of the map, a per-son can get an idea how steep or gentle a slope is. If the contour lines are some distance apart, the slope is gentle; if several lines are quite close to one anoth-er, they indicate a steep slope, possibly even a cliff. For example, suppose on a certain map the difference in elevation between contour lines is 10 feet, and the scale is 1:24,000, meaning one inch on the map equals 24,000 inches, or 2,000 feet, on the earth's surface. If the distance between two lines is 1/4 inch, the land rises only 10 feet over the 500 feet between the lines. If, however, there are 20 lines grouped in that 1/4-inch map distance, the land rises 200 feet in elevation over a distance of 500 horizontal feet, a much steeper slope.

In addition to showing the natural and man-made features of an area, a topographical map contains other useful information about the land. By indi-cating the steepness of grades, the direction a site faces, and erosion and drainage patterns, these maps can aid in selecting building sites, appropriate and feasible places to cut access roads, and good locations for planting crops.

Topographical maps are sold at local sporting goods stores. To investigate the land from afar, maps can usually be ordered from the department handling geological surveys in the state you're interested in. It may first be necessary to order an index so you can determine precisely which sectional maps you will need.

A Topographical Map

Geological Maps: Also available through state geological survey offices are maps that indicate the location of mineral deposits and rock formations, the planes and direction of strata, and other geological information. These maps are based on topographical drawings complete with contour lines, but also incorporate a system of dotted lines and letter symbols to represent formations and deposits. They are valuable during a property hunt for several reasons. Be fore selecting a well site, for instance, a geological map can be consulted to find the probable locations of porous rock formations such as limestone or sandstone that might hold water. Also indicated are the types of stone that could be used as a building material. The probable presence of mineral deposits on a piece of land should be reason enough for a prospective buyer to look into the ownership of mineral rights.

Soil Surveys: In addition to knowing something about the shape of the land and what lies below the surface, most people want information about the composition of the soil. This is provided by soil survey maps and accompanying literature that explains the symbols and describes the different types of soil. Similar to topographical maps in appearance, soil survey maps show the irregular outlines of each soil group, usually differentiating among them through the use of a system of color coding. By cross-referencing the map and the explanatory matter, you can find out how the soil was formed, what its physical characteristics are, the minerals and plant nutrients it contains, and the crops that will be most suitable. Soil surveys may also contain climatic data, and they list crops that have been grown on a plot of ground in the past.

Though it can take some time to obtain these maps and to study them in the detail needed to really familiarize oneself with an area, doing so can eliminate an expensive scouting expedition to property that might prove unsuitable. Technical maps will tell you a great deal about the acreage you're considering before you see it.

Buying Land Wisely

Buying your own parcel of land instead of sinking your money into rent year after year can be an attractive prospect, but there are pitfalls to be avoided.

Imagine spotting an ad that describes what sounds like an ideal piece of land: "Forty acres, year-round creek, partly wooded, some pasture, marketable timber, south-facing slopes, small down payment, easy terms. $26,000." It sounds like the deal of a lifetime.

However, before shelling out a large amount of cash that you may not be able to recover later, there are several matters to consider carefully.

Access: It's impossible to overemphasize how important access rights are. Be certain beyond the shadow of a doubt that permanent, legal, transferable access is specified in the deed.

Consider a couple who bought a secluded piece of land and built a house on it, acting on a neighbor's assurance that he had no objections to their using his road to get in and out. Later, they had a minor disagreement with the fellow, and he blocked the road. The couple started walking in and out across a bordering piece of government land but were informed by the agency in charge that they'd better cease and desist or they'd be hauled into court on trespassing charges.

Alarmed, they tried several other routes, each of which was eventually blocked when at least one landowner wouldn't let them through. Because the unfortunate couple couldn't afford an expensive legal battle, they were forced to abandon the place, and they lost the cash they'd invested, which amounted to all of their savings.

As you can see, it's imperative to make sure that no one can stop you from getting to your property. If it's possible to obtain access by paying for it annually, as is the case when dealing with some government agencies, make certain that the right is not revocable and will be transferable should you later decide to sell. You'll also need to find out who's responsible for the maintenance of the road.

Furthermore, don't assume that, because a piece of property is on a county state road, access is guaranteed. If the right wasn't granted to the previous owner or if no driveway has been put in yet, you may have to get a "curb cut" from the county or state. Such permits are not always automatic, and they may cost some money.

Water Rights: Water and soil drainage are also critical concerns. That creek running across your dream parcel may be lovely, but take the time to discover whether you have the right to use it. Wetlands restrictions can be imposed by federal, state, or local authorities. Your land could be part of a city watershed, in which case it's possible that you'd be unable legally to use a single drop. In addition, the law could require that all your livestock be kept several hundred feet from the creek or could prevent you from putting in a septic tank and drain field or an outhouse.

If a septic system is to be installed, law requires you to make several percolation tests before buying. This is necessary to assure that there are some places away from your water supply where the drainage is adequate. If land won't "perk" you may be able to install a composting toilet and leach pit for "gray water" from sinks. But, get the okay in writing.

Mineral Rights: Many buyers consider mineral rights to be of minor importance, but there are examples of what can happen to a farmstead when the owner doesn't hold them. One man bought property, built a beautiful home, and planted several hundred acres of orchards and gardens. In short, he invested a fortune in both time and money in his land. He knew he didn't own the mineral rights to the property, but the real estate agent had assured him that they weren't important.

Some 25 years later, however, after his orchards and gardens had matured and were supplying his entire income, he came home one day to find his house being bulldozed and one of his orchards already gone. Coal had been found on his land, and his deed stated plainly that the only compensation due him was the cost of the materials in his house and barns. The farmer had absolutely no legal recourse.

Just because no minerals of value have been found on a piece of property, there's no guarantee that one or more won't be discovered there sometime in the future or that a new use won't be found for a "worthless" mineral that's already known to be there.

Timber: Logging rights can create a similar problem. A property owner will usually receive them at least conditionally. However, be sure to find out whether there's a timber contract out on the place. If there is, extreme caution is in order. You'll want to learn when the contract expires, how many board feet and of what species the logging company is allowed to take, and how that

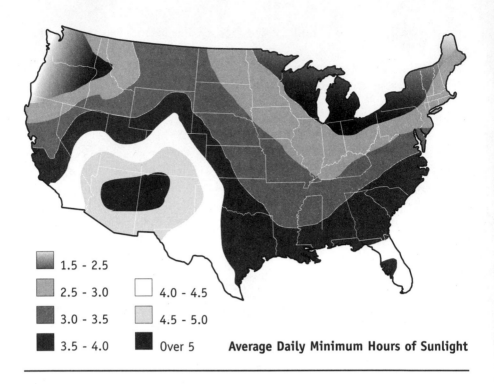

1.5 - 2.5		
2.5 - 3.0	4.0 - 4.5	
3.0 - 3.5	4.5 - 5.0	
3.5 - 4.0	Over 5	**Average Daily Minimum Hours of Sunlight**

cutting will affect the looks of the land. Also, be sure to find out what condition the loggers are required to leave the property in after the harvest.

Easements: It's also important to research easements: the rights and privileges that someone else may have to your land. First, find out what easements are available to you over other people's property. For example, if you're not on a county road, you'll want to know whether the easements all along your access road are wide enough to meet county specifications in case the local government is later willing to take over maintenance of the road. Take the case of a couple who lived on a fairly populated road that the county said it was willing to maintain if all 15 families along the route would grant a 60-foot-wide right-of-way. All but one landowner, a man whose house was almost at the beginning of the road, were eager to have that convenience, but that fellow refused to give up the 30-foot strip required—it was his front yard, after all.

In addition, you'll want to make certain that easements are available to you for power and telephone lines. Even if such trappings of civilization aren't important to you now, they might be later, and they almost certainly will be should you ever choose to sell your spread!

You'll also want to know what easements may apply to the land you're buying. That way, you won't plant your vegetable garden in the middle of someone else's right-of-way to the lake. Access can be stated as "walking" or

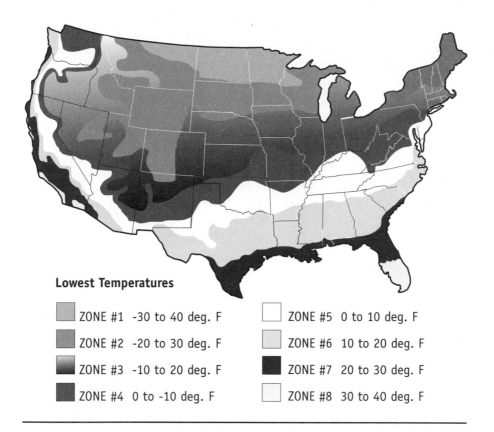

Lowest Temperatures

ZONE #1	-30 to 40 deg. F	ZONE #5	0 to 10 deg. F
ZONE #2	-20 to 30 deg. F	ZONE #6	10 to 20 deg. F
ZONE #3	-10 to 20 deg. F	ZONE #7	20 to 30 deg. F
ZONE #4	0 to -10 deg. F	ZONE #8	30 to 40 deg. F

"vehicular." Access rights can be contained in other's deeds, but not yours, which will have to be worked out in court. Public access can turn your lake into a noisy resort.

As far as utilities are concerned, you should know that if you live at a considerable distance from a power line, some companies have the right to refuse to put in an electric line on your private road even if you have the money and the desire to pay for the materials and installation—which can run into five figures for a mile of poles and line.

Pollution: We've all heard of Love Canal and other tragic stories associated with land contaminated by chemicals. Chemical poisoning from past industrial activity that may be hidden away under the soil can not only make your land useless but can also seriously affect your health and that of your children, your pets, and your livestock. You'll also want to know what common sprays are regularly applied in the area, such as those for roadside maintenance. Try to find out, too, what has been used on the ground in the past, what may have seeped into it, or what might come down the creek.

Permits: In most areas, permits are required to build a house, put in a sep-

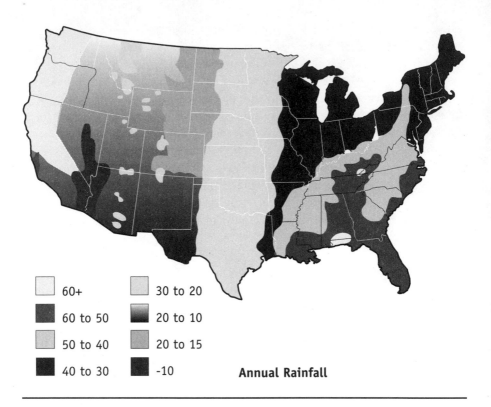

☐ 60+	☐ 30 to 20		
■ 60 to 50	▨ 20 to 10		
☐ 50 to 40	▨ 20 to 15		
■ 40 to 30	■ -10	**Annual Rainfall**	

tic system, and drill a well, so before buying find out how the property is zoned and whether you'll be able to get the permits you want. This isn't as routine as it may sound, because there are areas with very strict codes that, for instance, allow only so many structures to be built in any given time period. If you're serious about farming, be sure the property is zoned for agricultural use. Some zoning and deed restrictions can prevent you from keeping certain types of animals or engaging in a commercial venture, including the sale of surplus vegetables.

Before purchasing property, it pays to make sure the price is in keeping with the typical land costs in the area. Also, be certain that when you do put down earnest money, the final purchase remains conditional—dependent upon written contingencies. Just what these qualifications are will be up to you, but do be sure that your earnest money agreement covers legal access, mineral rights, timber, and water, and that it requires the seller to deliver to you a deed conveying clear title. Be certain to obtain a title search, which will tell you the legal history of the property, what, if any, encumbrances are on the land, and if the seller does, in fact, own the property.

Make sure that any advance money given to the seller goes into an escrow account and will be returned if the owner can't convey a clear title. Don't leave this up to chance; insist on such an agreement, since it's entirely possible to lose property and a good bit of money if this simple step isn't taken. If there's an underlying contract or mortgage on the property, get a statement in writing that it's being paid or that you're making provisions to assume it because if this isn't specified, the holder of the mortgage has a claim on the land.

You should also invest in title insurance. Read the policy carefully in order to understand exactly what it says. Also be sure to get the transaction recorded at the public registry, which is usually at the county courthouse.

Jargon: You will, of course, be faced with a lot of legalese when buying property. It'll be necessary, for example, to become familiar with such terms as: binders, mortgagor, mortgagee, graduated payment mortgage, variable rate mortgage, mortgage clause, loan origination fee, loan discount (or points), foreclosure, lien, quitclaim, and acceleration clause. An acceleration clause, for example, causes the entire debt to become due should one installment payment be late. It's something you definitely don't want in your mortgage.

Be sure, then, to consult a legal encyclopedia or dictionary whenever you come across a term that isn't absolutely familiar to you and to find out from a competent real estate lawyer exactly how that term is interpreted in your particular agreement.

Finally, study the area where you plan to live as thoroughly as possible. The time spent on this research can be critical to your future peace of mind. A few miles can sometimes mean a lot in terms of happiness and opportunity.

It's possible that the area's only industry can close down, leaving people with no money to pay for outside services. You could lose a job, real estate taxes could skyrocket, and more. People in some communities tend to be a bit hostile to newcomers. Make an effort to talk to new residents in the area where you're planning to buy and find out how they feel about living there. The answers you receive may be the deciding factors as to whether or not you purchase.

These, then, are some of the points you'll need to consider before investing your hard-earned savings in any land deal. You may decide, of course, to compromise on a few of the factors in order to make your homestead dream come true, but be sure you don't compromise so much that your dream becomes a nightmare.

Lease with an Option to Buy: Accumulating a down payment may delay your move to the country for years...or possibly forever if finances are tight. One of the best ways to moderate this impact on the pocketbook is to rent or lease the property with an option to buy.

Under such an agreement, part of the tenant's rent goes toward the purchase price of the property if the buyer decides to exercise the purchase option. There are financial advantages to buying land or a house under a lease-to-buy plan, but an often underestimated advantage is the time and opportunity to inspect the property more thoroughly than is usually possible before buying.

The prospective owner can live in the house before putting any money down. A renter-with-option has time to discover any quirks or problems in the plumbing, the electrical wiring, or the structure itself and can determine whether any major renovations are needed. The home is lived in under various weather conditions and during different seasons, insuring that there will be no unpleasant surprises later on.

There are usually some tradeoffs, however, that must be made when leasing with the option to buy. An unrefundable up-front option fee may be required. Or a slightly higher rent than normal might be required during the option period. All or part of this additional money will in most cases, be credited toward the down payment and will be lost only if the renter decides to forgo the purchase.

Depending upon the agreement, renters may be expected to pay for minor maintenance. Usually, however, the landlord foots the bill for major maintenance. Skill as a negotiator will help determine the arrangement in your particular case.

Where to Look: If you like where you live, begin searching for property in your own backyard—literally! The average rental landlord holds onto a house for only three years before selling it, so it stands to reason that if a tenant were to offer to buy the property for an acceptable price and terms, the owner might well be willing to listen to the proposal and to consider it. If the original offer doesn't spark a deal, an offer to pay a higher rent during the lease period might help capture the landlord's attention .

You can place an ad stating the kind of arrangement you might want. If there is a particular piece of property you're interested in that is not on the market, it's possible to find out from county or city records who owns the land and make that person a proposal. Be forthright. Remember, the worst response you can get is no.

Many sellers will not be interested in a lease-to-buy option, and some real estate agents will not want to handle this type of transaction. A refusal from the first few homeowners or agents contacted, however, is not a good reason to give up. Find out why your offers are not accepted, and perhaps it will be possible for you to make a more favorable proposal. Often the best prospects will be properties that are hard to sell due to being remote, run-down, or on bad roads—which may be just what you are looking for! Often, owners of such properties give up trying to sell after a while, de-list with a Realtor and either rent to non-buyers or just board the house up. If you see a place you like, inquire; it may be available for lease/sale—but the owner never considered that option.

Drawing Up the Agreement: There are two parts to the typical lease with option to buy: the lease and the sales contract. When preparing the former, it's necessary to reach an agreement concerning the length of the lease and the amount of rent. From the buyer's point of view it's advantageous to negotiate a fairly long term. Such an arrangement could allow a buyer to apply several years' rent, or a portion of it, toward the down payment and substantially reduce the amount of cash needed when the purchase option is exercised. Regardless of the length of the lease, however, make sure that the agreement allows you to buy the property at any time before the term of the lease is up.

The remainder of the lease portion should contain all of the items normally covered in a standard rental agreement. You'll want to include a description of the property and the addresses of the parties involved, an explanation of how the maintenance, utility, and insurance costs will be paid, an outline of the procedure to be used to return or not return the security deposit, remedies to be employed should either party default on the bargain, and any other information deemed pertinent.

Because a legally binding contract will go into effect when exercising an option to buy, it's generally best to include all the essential components of a formal sale contract in the original option agreement. As an alternative, a preliminary agreement to lease with the option to purchase can contain the written understanding that more complete final documents will be drawn up prior to the date of exercising the option and that the offer to buy is contingent upon mutual approval of those documents. Even such a shortened contract, however, should include the purchase price and the terms of sale, any conditions of and limitations to the title, the contingencies of the sale, and the apportionment of the closing costs between the parties.

Price: The purchase price and terms of sale detail how much the property will cost when the option to buy is exercised and where that money will come from. This information should include the amount of the down payment, the percentage of rent to be applied toward that cost, and an explanation of how the balance is to be paid. You might be able to convince the seller to carry the loan (so-called "owner-financing"), so that you don't have to arrange a mortgage through a lending institution. However the sale's financed, be sure to stipulate the type of loan, the amount, the payment plan, and the interest.

"Clearing the title" is a research project best done by a real estate lawyer or other expert. It gives assurance that the parcel is free of any outstanding debts, lens, taxes, and insurance premiums and that any limitations to the title such as land-use restrictions are clearly listed. Otherwise, you might well find yourself saddled with an unpaid bill after you've settled in. On states offering (but not requiring) it, be sure that the title is insured against unspecified claims.

All of the conditions that you'd like to have met prior to taking ownership of the property should be included, in writing, in the final contract. Contingencies for sale include such items as any inspections that need to be done before the sale is consummated. You might, for example, want to have the acreage surveyed and the dwelling appraised, require a termite and structural inspection, or request soil and water testing. Local or state agencies may require specific inspections before the sale can be completed.

Closing Costs: Final closing costs can include the fee for recording the sale, an attorney's charges for drawing up the final contract, the costs of clearing up any contingencies, and an escrow fee paid to a go-between who protects the interests of all parties involved in the deal. Some of the payments are typically shared by the buyer and the seller, while others are usually handled by just one of the parties. In any circumstance, it's very important to make sure that the amounts of, and responsibilities for, these costs are agreed to in writing.

Caretaking Seventy Wilderness Acres

Matt and Mary live on a wilderness ranch seven miles from the nearest road and neighbor. Their home is a huge log cabin that overlooks a cold, clear mountain stream. They swim and fish in deep green pools, surrounded by tall fir trees and giant granite boulders.

If you drop by at dinnertime, you may see Mary preparing fresh produce from the garden and orchard as Matt fires up the wood-burning cookstove. Dinner will proceed in peace and quiet: No phone will ring, and no television or radio will blare. Their thoughts and discussion will be of the day's chores and accomplishments. They'll be looking forward to the biweekly mail delivery, for they know it will contain no water bill, electric bill, or notice of rent, tax, or mortgage payment.

If what has been said isn't enough to convince you that the life they lead is a good one, you should know that they receive $200 a month for enjoying themselves in this fashion. How do they work this enviable deal? They're caretakers.

Out of the City: This wilderness life came about because Mary and Matt, like so many others, are forsaking the nerve-racking pace of city life and looking for more harmonious alternatives. Living close to the land and away from crowds was the direction in which their hopes pointed.

Still, gathering the energy to make such a transition is no easy task, and that energy must be used with forethought and economy. They admit it was difficult to decide what form their back-to-the-land movement should take. Did they want a subsistence-level farming venture like that of Scott and Helen Nearing, or perhaps a frontier experience patterned after the works of Bradford Angier? Would a planned community be the right choice, or did they need their own quiet Walden?

With no real experience to help them make a decision, they found themselves in a position that's all too common among people who are trying to make the move from the city to country.

They found that communes were too restrictive—many of them requiring adherence to a particular dogma or lifestyle. After checking out the possibility of renting a small farm, the couple agreed that the idea had merits, but they couldn't abide the thought of using their savings to pay off the loan on someone else's acreage.

Just as they were growing discouraged, Matt happened to spot a newspaper advertisement for a caretaking job that offered a chance to live in a rural setting for a trial period without the obligations of a lease or mortgage. The couple felt they could advantageously use that time to gain experience in gardening, animal husbandry, plumbing, carpentry, and other skills that they would need for an eventual place of their own. The caretaking deal offered the pleasant and practical prospect of being paid while they learned. It seemed to merit prompt investigation.

Getting Hired: Matt began by answering the ad, only to find the position filled. Undaunted, he began searching the papers for other openings. The positions generally fell into two categories. The first consisted of house-sitting jobs, mostly of short duration and located in the suburbs. They weren't particularly interested in these. The second, and largest, group of opportunities involved caring for summer homes, vacation cabins, and hunting clubs. Though a number of advertisers specified retired couples, some didn't mention age at all.

Finally, in the monthly newsletter of a local conservation organization, the couple spotted an offer that really appealed. The ad asked for a single man or couple to caretake a remote wilderness cabin in northern California.

Matt wrote to the prospective employer and told the man in glowing terms how interested he and Mary were and what eager and conscientious custodians they would be. The reply stated that there were several applicants and that a choice would be made shortly. Even after learning that it would be a seven-mile hike from the road to the front door of the cabin in question, they decided to pursue this particular caretaking job. After much correspondence, the husband and wife were notified that they'd been hired and were invited to their new boss's home to discuss the details of employment. Possibly their eagerness and enthusiasm had landed them the job.

The arrangement proved better than they'd hoped for. To begin with, the length of employment was up to them. They were required to be on the property from mid-May to September roughly, during trout season. The rest of the year was left open. They could stay all winter if they liked or could leave with the assurance that the job would still be theirs in the spring. They would receive $100 a month plus a charge account for all the hardware, tools, and supplies deemed necessary for the upkeep of the cabin. The owner used the place for two weeks at the end of the summer; the rest of the time Matt and Mary could consider it theirs. Their single official duty was to be there in order to discourage vandalism of the house and abuse of the property. The employer suggested several projects he'd be happy to have done, but only if the caretakers were so inclined.

Settling In: Since the cabin was seven miles from the road, the couple planned to hire a mule packer to carry in supplies. Unfortunately, they couldn't locate a driver with the proper permits (the property is bounded on four sides by national forest), and they were forced to trek in with the supplies on their backs. The undertaking made them doubly grateful that a sound, well-equipped cabin awaited them. It would have been impossible to backpack building materials, and the cost of transporting such a load by mule would have been prohibitive for anyone on a limited budget.

Before too long, they had hauled up most of their staples and went down for mail, beer, and diversion more than anything else. The 14-mile round-trip became a pleasant means of meditation and exercise. The couple found themselves looking forward to the hikes.

Chores: Once the caretakers were settled at the ranch, the first job they faced was gathering wood. Their equipment consisted of an ax, a 36-inch bow saw, two wedges, a sledgehammer, and a wheelbarrow. The steep terrain severely limited any search for fuel, but fortunately they were able to find plenty of wood on the ground within a short distance of the cabin.

For three reasons the couple chose to use the downed wood instead of cutting trees. First, by clearing away all the dead, dry branches that accumulate on the forest floor, they eliminated the fuel on which a forest fire burns, thereby lessening the danger that nature would accomplish this cleanup in her own way by kindling the dead material with lightning. Their second reason for preferring fallen timber was that it's already seasoned and burns better than green wood. And third, these folks liked their trees left vertical.

The cabin has both a fireplace and a cookstove, so the woodpile is divided accordingly. Into the fireplace supply side go all the less desirable pieces: knotty, twisted logs and stumps, and damp or green fuel. Wood for cooking is stored on the other side, and for this purpose, Douglas fir is unsurpassed in their part of the western United States. Matt and Mary were lucky enough to locate several trunks left over from a small logging operation. Big slices taken off the ends of logs measured about three feet thick and four to five feet in diameter, split easily, burned hot, left little ash, and were already dry.

Working off and on for about two weeks, the couple amassed a good supply of both types of fuel. However, this stock was only for the summer months when little heat was needed. If they had stayed through the winter in the cabin, every spare moment would have been spent gathering, splitting or chopping, and storing wood.

The next venture was the garden, and they picked an open spot in the orchard that received good, steady sun and had water via an irrigation ditch. They learned later, however, that alfalfa had been grown on that very patch as hay for mules, and the crop had never been turned under to replenish the soil. Since there had been no time to compost before planting, their garden on the run-down plot of earth was a little disappointing. A compost pile was started right away, but it wasn't of any use for the first year, of course. All the same, the gardeners kept building the soil with whatever organic material they could lay their hands on, and they were later rewarded for their efforts. They did grow enough fresh vegetables for meals, and fresh trout, wild berries, and foraged vegetables rounded out their diet.

The rest of the work consisted of mending fences, gates, the small barn and plumbing and whatever other maintenance jobs seemed necessary. Neither of the caretakers hesitated to take a break whenever they wanted to go fishing or swimming or just to sit and think.

Mary and Matt say that they learned, for the first time, the joy of labor. Like so many others, they had always equated manual labor with drudgery, but in this job they discovered the self-discipline needed to be one's own boss and soon became proud of their achievements. Work was no longer toil. Of all the lessons the experience taught them, they believe that self-mastery has been the most rewarding, because it's a tool that makes all other things possible.

Problems: And what about the job itself? Part of their only official task was to discourage camping on the property. Matt was given no real rules to enforce but was told to use his own discretion regarding the use of the land. He was willing at first to overlook the presence of passing hikers because he felt that the majority would have enough courtesy to treat the campsites with respect. Unfortunately, this was not true, and after finding equipment stolen or abused, sites left a mess, and litter strewn all along the trail, he closed the area to camping.

That was a sticky situation to handle, but one which everyone who owns or takes care of private property encounters sooner or later. It's unfortunate that for some people the attitude is "the land belongs to all of us, so I can do anything I want, but you're living here, so you clean it up." There may not be a fair solution to this problem, other than a caretaker's decision to prohibit all camping or trespassing.

If you don't believe that there is such a thing as private property (in other words, if you can't accept that an individual has a right to buy and control the land and thereby keep others off it—if you feel that the earth belongs equally and unconditionally to everyone...), you may not enjoy being a caretaker. You will be policing an area that belongs to someone else, and though you may have much latitude in your decisions, you will be obliged to carry out the owner's instructions concerning intruders. Find out exactly what your official position entails so that you'll have no misunderstandings with your employer, friends, and passersby. If you can't ethically consent to the conditions of the job, don't accept it.

Should you take the position, however, be ready to stand by your employer's requests even if your firmness makes you out to be a villain in the eyes of someone else. Responsible caretakers will agree that this is the best policy. As a custodian, you're a middleman and may be called to task both by your boss and by people who want to use the property. Be as honest as possible in your dealings, and ill feelings can be minimized.

A New Season: For Mary and Matt, time left over from caretaking and household duties was filled with swimming, reading, and relaxing. At the end of their first wilderness summer, they were sun-tanned, healthy, serene, and $800 richer. The freedom to leave after the vacation period was over was one of the greatest assets of their job. They were able to travel, work, plan, and play with the assurance that they'd be back at the cabin the next spring.

That was the first year. The second time around, the couple managed to engage a driver and pack mules to haul equipment and supplies to the cabin, and their employer offered to foot the bill this time.

As soon as the caretakers resettled themselves, they put in their garden, and because of the composting done the year before, it began to flourish. They anticipated a long, hot summer with a bumper crop of tomatoes and other fresh foods. Mary became increasingly skillful with the cookstove, and the variety and quality of food that came out of its oven constantly delighted the diners.

The Rewards of Caretaking: Mary and Matt consider their experience as caretakers to be one of the most rewarding adventures of their lives and believe that others would find such a situation equally exciting and educational.

Locating the right job is a mixed matter of stubbornness and serendipity. If you're industrious, you should be able to find enough openings to let you be choosy. Because of the low pay and occasional isolation, such jobs are not in great demand, and the market is definitely in the employee's favor.

These tips from longtime caretakers may help: Pick a region that interests you and check the help wanted sections of the local newspapers. Spend some time talking to the neighborhood realtors and postmasters. Read the bulletin boards in supermarkets, coin laundries, and churches, and then leave a card with your name, address, and phone number, stating that you would like a caretaking position. With conscientious footwork and a little faith, you may find a way of life as satisfying as that of the wilderness caretakers profiled here.

A Farm for Free

A husband and wife in Mourns, Michigan, are proudly homesteading 36.5 acres of land that they, quite cleverly, acquired for free. The property contains a spring-fed creek, 10 acres of bottom land, 15 acres of woods, and more than 10 acres of pastures and sandy hills. The farmstead abounds with hawks, owls, deer, muskrats, and other wildlife.

How They Did It: The couple's secret to winding up with a 36.5-acre farm for free was to buy it as part of a larger parcel containing a mix of level farmland and less desirable wooded hills and creek bottom. After saving their money for several years, the would-be homesteaders purchased 120 acres with $20,000 down and a land contract for the remaining $68,000, payable at $2,000 a year against the principal and 5% interest on the balance. The amount of their down payment was negotiable. They could have bought the original 120 acres with a much smaller investment.

The important part of their secret is the fact that the couple wanted only 36.5 of the 120 acres. They didn't want the 83.5 acres of flat land that was desirable for farming (or—sad to say—for potential real-estate development); they prized the "worthless" bottom land, buildings, and woods that would make an ideal homestead.

This, of course, gave them the advantage in their land dealing. Most people looked at the whole 120 acres and tried to balance the cost of "improving" the rough 36.5 acres against the profit that could be made farming the other 83.5 acres of field crops. Other potential purchasers would mentally calculate how long they'd have to farm the whole 120 acres to make enough money to be able to buy yet another piece of property and expand their holdings even further.

The homesteaders, on the other hand, had no intention of "improving" that rough 36.5-acre tract at all, because they liked it just the way it was and figured that 36.5 acres was a big enough "place in the country" for them. They had no desire to parlay it into "bigger and more efficient" landholdings of any kind.

So by "cash-renting" those 83.5 acres of fields to a local farmer, they made enough money to cover the land contract payments and real estate taxes for the entire 120 acres. This arrangement lasted for four years, during which the farm earned all the land and tax payments that were due, without the owners having to lift a finger.

When they checked out the local market, it was discovered that those 83.5 acres would sell for $1600 an acre. (That's a total of $133,600 for 36.5 fewer acres than they had paid $88,000 for, just four years earlier!)

And so the couple sold their "good" land, but not through a real estate agent. They knew the property was worth $1600 an acre, so they offered it for that amount to a neighboring farmer, who accepted.

It cost about $2,000 to have the 83.5 acres surveyed and a legal description drawn up. Another $200 went to a local lawyer for handling the contract. The owners accepted $12,000 as a down payment from their neighbor and allowed him one full year in which to come with the rest of the sale price. (Their lawyer drew up a land contract that stated no interest would be charged on the principal if it were paid within 90 days. After that, 10% interest retroactive to the signing of the contract would be due, and the entire amount would be due one year from the contract's closing.)

While they could have made more money by taking out a 30-year contract with the buyer at a higher interest rate than the 5% they were paying, they chose not to do that. Thirty years of making payments and receiving payments seemed complicated, so they elected to "take the money and run." After all, the real purpose of the transaction was to acquire a place in the country, and that was being accomplished.

The Bottom Line: As it turned out, the buyer took nearly a year to arrange his financing, and that year cost him $12,160 in interest. It also cost the sellers the loss of one year's rent on the 83.5 acres and one year's interest on their own debt (a total of $9,000)—but they came out ahead by about $3,000.

The settlement, then, looked like this: The homesteaders received a final lump-sum payment of $132,686.70 from the buyer. From this, they had to pay $100.00 for title insurance, $50.00 for document preparation, $8.00 for recording fees, $147.40 for state tax stamps, $1,194.80 for real estate taxes, and $61,000.00 to close out the balance on the original land contract. This left them with $70,186.50! Even when the capital gains tax that they paid was subtracted, they still got back more than their original investment, plus 36.5 acres with buildings free and clear. Their homestead, in short, was free!

You Can Do the Same: If you'd like to work the same economic miracle for yourself, just remember the facts of life in today's real estate market. Two kinds of property are in great demand: 1.) the minifarm of a few acres and 2.) the big farm made up almost entirely of tillable fields, and both types of property can be overpriced.

There are, however, countless small farms and family holdings of 60, 80, and 120 or more acres scattered throughout the United States and Canada. A great many of these places are mixed properties: various amounts of cleared and tillable land combined with some rough acres and a few old farm buildings. Big farmers who look at such acreage are usually put off by the rough land and old farm buildings. Back-to-the-landers generally don't consider these properties at all, because they are looking for only 20 or 40 acres, instead of 80 or 100 or more.

And this is where you come in. Save up a nest egg, and then use it to buy a larger piece of mixed property than you need. Next, cash-rent the good fields to someone while local land prices rise. Eventually, survey and sell the tillable farm acreage for more than you paid for the entire original parcel. This move will leave you free and clear with a picturesque little homestead and some money in your pocket.

Play the mixed-property game skillfully the way this husband-and-wife team did, and you shouldn't have any trouble duplicating their success. Just don't get greedy. Don't insist on buying at the absolute bottom dollar and then lying awake nights scheming to sell at the maximum top dollar. Instead, buy at a fair price, wait for the market to go up, split your property, and sell at a fair price.

Homesteading Michigan's Upper Peninsula

A young Michigan couple named Francie and Jeff decided to flee their city situation, and they laid elaborate and detailed plans. They were going to combine savings with some friends, buy land together, and leave Grand Rapids in the fall. Their would-be partners backed out at the last minute, however, and Francie and Jeff hadn't enough money of their own to swing a farm purchase. The thought of spending another dreary winter in their apartment seemed more than they could bear. Just when their spirits were at an all-time low, they met a sympathetic farmer at an outdoor market. "As far as I can see," he said, "the only way to get to the country is to go there." His frank and persuasive observation was the impetus they needed.

Escape: Francie and Jeff loaded everything they owned into the back of their old pickup truck, put their 2-year-old son, Aaron, in his kiddie seat, drove to the bank and put their life's savings into travelers checks, and with a road atlas propped on the dash, headed north to Michigan's Upper Peninsula.

They hoped to settle in the Upper Peninsula because they had camped there many times and had become enamored of its unspoiled countryside. Furthermore, land in the rugged region was still inexpensive. For example, real estate listings at the time included: a three-bedroom home on 39 acres with drilled well and a barn for $18,500, a 120-acre spread at $320 an acre, and some property as low as $200 an acre. Of course, prime farm land or plots with lake frontage commanded higher prices, but compared with most parts of the United States, land there was a real bargain.

Travels and Troubles: The adventurers were only about a half day's travel beyond Grand Rapids when it started to snow, which was enough to slow them down a bit but not enough to dampen their spirits. Without mishap, they reached Houghton/Hancock, twin cities with a combined population of about 14,000 on the Keweenaw Peninsula, where their migration came to a halt. Providentially, a little farm located just a quarter-mile from the Lake Superior shore was available for rent at only $280 a month. They snapped it up and had barely unloaded the truck when the snow began to fall in earnest, piling up more than a foot overnight!

Although the adventurers were grateful to have a roof over their heads, their adjustment to the new environment wasn't automatic. They had arrived in the north country just in time for the first real snows of winter without the slightest idea of where they could find work before their savings ran out, and Christmas time was upon them. Much of the holiday season was spent in the woods gathering wet wood to dry out on top of the the woodstove before it went in for fuel. Family outings during this time consisted of driving the 15 miles into town through a blizzard to call their folks from a pay phone on Christmas morning and feeble attempts to explore the terrain despite regularly harsh winter conditions.

Gradually, though, things began to improve. Neighbors dropped by with loads of dry wood and gifts of food, a local co-op extended membership to the newcomers, and both Francie and Jeff managed to find work that paid well enough to keep them from having to live entirely on lentil soup and boiled macaroni dinners.

Best of all, they discovered that they weren't alone. The family met many kindred souls who had been drawn to the Upper Peninsula by an honest appreciation of nature and who, like themselves, were willing to take any kind of job in order to stay. Some were survival role models for Francie and Jeff.

Getting By and Getting Better: Determining ways to make a living can be an exercise in creativity: One couple, Dennis and Janet, worked as substitute teachers. To supplement their meager salaries, Dennis sold drawings and photographs at local markets, while Janet peddled her craft items. Jay, another new acquaintance, had a degree in forestry, but he was washing dishes to make ends meet while he got started in his own firewood business. A neighboring family, Jerry and Christine and their four youngsters, had taken on a log home franchise.

Then there's Bill, who had worked part time at the Keweenaw Co-op for several years. He spent his winters as a tax accountant in California to help subsidize his summers in "(Lake) Superior country." Bob and Becky, on the other hand, put in a couple of months each winter planting trees "down south" in lower Michigan, but they returned to Bob's grandmother's blueberry farm for the rest of the year to trade room and board for help with the crop.

Although Francie and Jeff didn't find what they consider ideal employment right away, one thing is certain: their lifestyle in the north country was far more healthful than their prior city existence. Jeff's stress-related stomach condition disappeared, and the fresh air put color in their cheeks. Both husband and wife accepted having to change their career goals in order to live in an environment that contributes so positively to their physical, mental, and emotional well-being.

Despite their adaptability and cheerful outlook, the two had their doubts and did a lot of soul-searching that first cold winter, especially during the snowbound weeks that passed without their seeing another person. But spring finally came, and at last they could see how promising the surrounding territory looked without a blanket of snow to mask it.

And what a spectacular sight it is! There are hills (of up to 2,000 feet) and trees everywhere, and there is eye-filling Lake Superior. The world's largest inland sea is an amazing expanse of fresh water that measures some 31,800 square miles and has depths as great as 1,333 feet! The lake and its winds can cause unpredictable storms and snow measuring in yards, but Superior also can be dazzling with exquisite sunrises across the water's surface and a generous scattering of agates along the shore.

Some Facts and Figures: The Upper Peninsula of Michigan has a land area of well over 16,000 square miles, around 90 percent of which is forested, and 1,700 miles of shoreline. It offers 17 state parks and two national forests, and boasts 4,000 inland lakes and some 12,000 miles of streams. No mention of the wilderness area would be complete without a word about fishing: In good weather, anglers come from all over just to try out the trout-filled waterways, and the deep, dry snow during the cold months is perfect for winter sports.

Home Is Where the Heart Is: There are, of course, a few thorns in any paradise. Because of lengthy and severe winters, large undeveloped areas, and a declining job market, population on the Keweenaw Peninsula has decreased in the last few decades. Homesteading in this rugged part of the country is clearly not for everyone. The main challenge is earning enough money to live on. The best opportunities for employment are in the fields of forestry and tourism.

Jeff and Francie may yet have to shift their base of operations long enough to acquire the skills and training that will make them more marketable as workers in such an isolated area. Francie, for instance, would like to become a midwife and practice on the Keweenaw Peninsula. Though the couple may have to move south for a time to accomplish such a goal, they know where their home and hearts really are. The sight of their son, Aaron, bolting out the back door and grinning from ear to ear at the prospect of unlimited space in which to frolic proves to them that they did the right thing by leaving the inner city to make their way in the north country. Even severe winters and financial problems can't dissuade them from their plans for the future.

Suburban Homesteading

Dig up the side yard for a vegetable garden, plant fruit trees on the south property line, build a chicken coop on the back of the garage, and heat and cook with a wood stove. That's how most small-town dwellers lived a century ago.

Today called "suburban homesteading," it is a practical lifestyle for most any suburban couple with the urge for independence, moderate self-reliance, knowledge, and skills...even if they do have to manage full-time jobs and growing children. However, there are pitfalls that should be taken into account before anyone embarks on such an ambitious project.

Setting up what is really a minifarm in the suburbs or the city takes more than skill in gardening and log-splitting. Even though saving money in the long run is a valid reason to attempt such a venture, people also need a philosophical justification to fall back on during those inevitable occasions when things don't work out as smoothly as they'd hoped.

Essentially, a person has to believe that the individual can make a difference in the state of the world today. After all, saving energy and reusing resources won't always bring immediate and direct cash savings, but both will contribute to a global resource saving, which is just as important or more so, depending on the globalism of your outlook.

Other personal-value questions will have to be addressed and resolved in developing the homestead operation: Will gardening be done organically or with chemical fertilizers and pesticides? Should building be done with power tools or by hand?

Cash Outlay: Before starting a homesteading venture, read as much as possible about all the money that can be saved with a vegetable garden, a solar water heater, or other money savers, no matter how small. Most publications don't stress how much money you have to spend before you begin to save, but capital investment in a sophisticated suburban homestead can be significant. Space, for one thing, is limited and thus more expensive with higher taxes than in a rural area. There are minimum square-footage requirements in some suburbs, as well as neighborhood aesthetic standards. And because in many suburban households both the husband and wife have full-time jobs outside the home, time-saving equipment is needed. All of these factors will add to the cost of outfitting a homestead.

One way to help reduce these capital investment costs is cooperative ownership. If handled sensibly, this can save a great deal of money. For example, a shredder purchased in partnership with a neighbor, or the ownership of an old pickup truck shared with another friend, can reduce the individual cost considerably.

Time: No one ever seems to have enough time, and this is especially true in suburban homesteading. Managing gardens, green houses, chickens, and woodstoves takes time—a lot of it—and that soon exerts a painful pressure.

A small vegetable garden might demand only two to four hours of care a week during the growing season, but as the garden gets larger, and canning and freezing the edibles begins, the time factor may increase to as much as eight hours per week. Add to that the labors of tending livestock and manag-

ing energy devices, and you'll soon find yourself working 20 hours a week on things you never had to do before you got into homesteading.

Of course, a lot of pressure can be eased if all members of a family pitch in and help with the work load. There are also ways of saving time that will come with experience. It's likely that a task that at first took two hours a week to complete might take only 20 minutes a week when experience is gained in handling it.

The lesson to learn, then, is not to take on anything new unless there's time to continue the activity. If it takes five years to get a homestead all together, then let it take the five years. Taking on, all at once, more than can be maintained can lead to frustration and possibly to giving up on the whole idea.

Family Support: This issue is a critical one. True, one member of a family can manage suburban homesteading all alone, but it's difficult at best. If you are an ardent conservationist and the rest of the family wastes energy, water, and food, your frustration level will most assuredly rise. If your brood won't eat the bounties from your organic garden, then those beautiful vegetables are almost a waste of time and energy. If you don't mind turning down the thermostat to 63°F while wearing more clothing and using the woodstove to compensate, but everyone else gripes constantly about the chill, then family tensions will undoubtedly build.

Adopting a suburban homesteading lifestyle will affect the lives of the entire family in significant ways. Negotiations and compromises can often provide workable solutions, but cooperation and support of the entire group, even without actual labor from everyone, is essential. Otherwise, the homesteading attempt can be a negative, potentially destructive family experience.

Skills and Knowledge: Discouragement comes quickly to those who don't respect the amount of skill and learning required to pursue such activities as managing a large garden, processing a year's supply of food, tending chickens, and operating a solar greenhouse. So think of it as a long-term project. The necessary knowledge and skills must be developed slowly for the project to be successful.

The primary sources of this knowledge are magazines and books. Periodicals are motivational and informative, and they cover many subjects briefly. Books are most helpful when you need greater depth or truly technical information on one particular subject.

The next best sources are friends, acquaintances, and the local USDA Extension Service—the "county agent." Friends who have been gardening a long time will be extremely helpful, but keep in mind that they may pass along bad as well as good information. Since county agents work mostly with commercial farmers, they may emphasize chemical agriculture, but they can help with certain problems.

Finally, look into adult education courses at local high schools and community colleges. Full courses (for credit or not) as well as short seminars on small engine repair, gardening and horticulture, welding, woodworking, plumbing, and electrical work are extremely helpful and provide lots of hands on experience. Master Gardeners, associated with the Cooperative Extension Service, offers excellent courses and personal guidance.

Neighbors, Zones, and Laws: Most towns have zoning ordinances restricting what you can do with or on your property. Many were originated for reasons of health and safety: for example, the standards set for woodstove installation and operation. Others, such as the laws prohibiting or restricting the raising of farm animals, may have wound up on the books because someone complained about an odor or animal-trespass problem decades ago. The secret to suburban homesteading is to avoid creating new problems, and therefore more restrictions, by keeping your neighbors happy. And two ways to keep neighbors on your good side are to inform them of your plans, activities, and sincere intentions and to share your bounty.

The Outlook: In most cases, there are few limits on how a suburban homestead can develop. A large organic garden, berry patches, and fruit trees might grace the landscape and can be supported by a composting system that will provide much of the nourishment the plants need. Solar greenhouses and cold frames can enable a family to grow fresh food year round, and a root cellar used in conjunction with a canning and freezing program can store the surplus harvest. A woodstove supplementing an attached solar green house can drastically reduce fuel bills during the heating season. Raising bees, chickens, and fish is not out of the realm of possibility.

With planning and time to develop a working system, it is possible for a family to produce better than three quarters of its food supply and reduce its fossil-energy needs by even more on a quarter-acre suburban lot.

Paying Rent with Work, Not Cash

Richard, a married graduate student with two small children, paid rent for three years on a tiny apartment near the Midwestern university where he was earning his master's degree in horticulture. He and his wife, Amy, really wanted their own place in the country, and although they read books on the subject, made lists, and planned, the dream always seemed to stay well ahead of the small amount of cash they could save from Richard's salary as a graduate assistant. Amy contributed what she could, given two small children, typing manuscripts. But rent and bills pretty well used most of their income.

Deciding to capitalize on Richard's high school and college summer jobs with his uncle's home and garden supply firm and Amy's degree in interior design, they placed a classified ad in the county newspaper in the area where they'd been house hunting: "WANTED TO RENT. Country home w/in 15 miles of University. Two-three bedrooms, garden, yard. Christian student/family. Rental preferred, purchase possible. Will trade repairs for rent."

They mailed the ad, waited, and prayed. The first response offered a rental for cash plus labor, but even then, the amount was more than their budget could afford. A second reply said they sounded like "nice people," but the woman's house didn't need much work and was far too expensive for them to lease. The idea was to pay as much of their rent as they possibly could with labor, not cash.

Offer number three was the charm. A man called, saying he and his wife had just purchased a farm as an investment. The former owner had begun to do some remodeling but hadn't completed the job. The owners wanted the remodeling completed and felt that the house should be lived in and the property maintained.

The couple visited the place and fell in love with it. The homestead was better than any they had ever dreamed of owning. There were grapevines, apple trees, a huge yard, garden space, two creeks, a barn, and a pasture. The two-story farmhouse featured five bedrooms and a wood-burning stove. There was even a timber lot for fuel.

The main drawback was the daily 60-mile round-trip to school. The couple decided that the trade-off was worthwhile, however, and worked up a rental agreement with the landlords: At least half of the rent each month would be paid with labor. They initially gave the owners one month's payment in cash. After that, any work they did would be deducted from the following month's rent at an agreed-upon hourly rate.

Naturally, it would have been in their best interest to work all the rent off, but Richard's studies didn't allow him that much time to spend on the remodeling jobs. Each month's payment included 34 hours of labor, which kept him busy for about three Saturdays every month. The landlords provided all the necessary building supplies, and when the tenants needed to buy additional materials, they deducted the costs from the cash portion of the next month's rent. Such a setup works very well as long as accurate records of time and materials are maintained.

Projects in lieu of rent money included ripping out an old porch and using the wood to make compost bins, painting and electrical work, and clearing away fallen limbs and chopping the wood for fuel. A nearby farmer volunteered to plow their quarter-acre garden space "just to be a good neighbor," and for the same reason, the couple gave him a considerable portion of their winter squash at the end of the season.

Shortly after Richard moved his family to the farm, a friend of the landlords began to board her horse with them. In return for their keeping an eye on the animal and feeding it, the owner let the family purchase goods at cost from the in-town department store he managed.

When Richard learned that another of the owners' friends needed a place to pasture his small herd of cattle, he jumped at the chance to practice livestock tending without having the financial responsibility. Not only did the man bring five beef steers, but he also brought a cow and calf, 24 bantam chickens, and eight cats! The horse and cattle owners paid for hay and feed grain, so all the homesteaders supplied was care and cleanup (of soiled bedding manure that goes into the garden or compost).

Both husband and wife learned to milk cows, give vaccinations, and doctor sick animals. They can claim what is called "a farmer's eye," which enables them to spot and head off certain livestock problems. A resident Holstein is the source of the family's milk, butter, and cottage cheese. Richard delivers a gallon of milk to the landlord on his drive to school each Monday, Wednesday and Friday, and the price of it is deducted from the rent. The bantam hens that are boarded on the farm provide enough small but fresh eggs for the family of four.

These work-for-rent homesteaders have engineered an impressive series of swaps, to say the least.

Besides getting a farmer's education for free, they are enjoying homestead life without either the mortgage or much of the cash outlay that too many people believe is unavoidable.

૱

CHAPTER 3

Hands-On Housing

An Earth-Sheltered Solar Dream House

A high school art teacher, looking around her rented quarters and shivering from the chilly air that crept unchecked through the uninsulated walls, began taking stock of what she had to show for eight years on the job. Nancy had job satisfaction to be sure, and she could claim a car and a small savings account among her assets. But she also had huge utility bills, dreary living quarters, and a pervasive feeling of discontent. What she didn't have was a sense of home. Recognizing that a change was in order, she decided to buy a house.

It took very little house hunting for her to become discouraged by what was available and affordable. Being disenchanted with conventional, fuel-thirsty structures anyway, she was searching for an option when she happened on a little, one-bedroom underground house being featured at an alternative energy fair.

It was an idea whose time had come, and she determined to build an energy-efficient, earth-sheltered home just big enough for herself and her cat, add a greenhouse for heat and garden space, and put an end to her housing crisis. She obtained a set of small "dream" plans and some books on alternative house design, and with most of her savings, purchased two acres of wooded land with a perfect south facing slope.

Little did she realize that her problems had just begun. As the first person in her community (and a single woman at that) to apply for a bank loan to build an earth-sheltered home, she was in for some special, but not exactly privileged, treatment.

Floor Plan: The first step (designing the house) proved to be easy in comparison with the trials that were to come. With her background in art, and many hours of research, discussion with experts (including the town engineer who had to approve all plans) and work at the drawing board, she came up with an acceptable design for her new home.

This bit of half-buried/glass-fronted solar ingenuity was to contain 750 square feet of open living space, including one bedroom and a bath, with exposed, reinforced-concrete flooring and walls to serve as thermal mass to absorb and hold heat. It would have a conventional shed roof (which proved to be cheaper than a dirt berm), plus a solar greenhouse along the southern wall for capturing heat and cultivating plants.

Once the plans were completed, Nancy took them for approval to her engineer friend, who volunteered to estimate construction costs for no fee. He came up with a total of $66,800. At that point, it was time to apply for a loan…but interest rates were too high.

Hard Times: After waiting more than a year until interest rates dropped to 12%, Nancy took the next step. She chose the largest savings and loan institution in the area, because all the other lenders required roll-over terms that she couldn't afford on her rarely raised salary. In hopeful anticipation, Nancy submitted house plans—and was shattered to be informed by the vice-president, "We don't make loans on underground houses."

A determined idealism can work wonders sometimes. After Nancy pleaded with him to call the town engineer who'd been so helpful (and he did then and there), the loan officer agreed to present Nancy's proposal to the executive loan committee when they met next. Short of building the dream house a little at a time as expenses would allow, there was little to do but to accept his offer and wait.

Nancy called the loan office daily to ask about the status of her application, and her persistence finally paid off. Two weeks after Nancy was initiated into the world of home financing, the lender agreed to the company's first loan on an earth-sheltered home. Nancy's parents had financed their home with the bank, and apparently, the bank president had called the town engineer's office who confirmed that the area was conducive to subsurface housing.

Catching a bit of the "alternative-housing fever," he wanted his lending institution to be the first to get involved in this new trend in building. Since Nancy's home-drawn plans for the home displayed "reasonably good construction techniques," the lenders were willing to take a chance. The long hours of research and planning had paid off after all.

Patience: This breakthrough hadn't changed the fact that "conventional" was still the key word in home financing, however, and another six weeks of frustration ensued before final approval of the loan. (The usual time for lending assessment is two weeks.) Receiving any money was contingent upon several changes that needed to be made in the floor plan, including the addition of another bedroom and central heating. (Although the original plans included a greenhouse against the south wall for heating, the three-month time limit for construction eliminated it.) Exposed-concrete floors and walls wouldn't be permitted either.

There were compromises: Nancy was required to alter the bedroom floor plan to allow another wall to be built later, and she had to include a hallway from the bedroom along the back wall of the living area. This addition turned out well, as she later found that it provided needed privacy and also served well as a "mini-gallery" for her paintings.

Heating was the next issue. Although sunlight, supplemented by a wood-stove, would have been sufficient for Nancy, the loan officers, who were concerned with resale value, recommended the installation of three small electric-baseboard heaters. (As anticipated, solar gain and the woodstove keep the house sufficiently warm. The heaters have never been used.)

The most difficult problem was how to cover the concrete walls and floors in a way that satisfied the convention-bound bankers. The plan relied on using masonry for heat storage, and the usual applications, such as plasterboard, paneling, or carpet would block air-circulation across the the masonry surface. An exhibitor Nancy met at the alternative-housing fair, who had some experience in covering walls in underground houses, suggested a waterproofing/texturing compound called Thoroseal. The lender agreed, and a search for a satisfactory floor covering began.

Ceramic tiles for the floors proved to be too costly. As an alternative, odd-shaped, random-sized marble scraps were used to surface the largest areas. The shards, which were inexpensively obtained from a local stone-contractor, turned out to be a very wise choice. They were not only decorative but heat absorbent as well! And rugs in the bedroom and living room would protect bare feet in winter.

Once all of the changes were approved by the loan office, Nancy was asked to submit her plans, specifications, and color sketches to an independent appraiser. It took an entire week instead of the customary three days to get a preappraisal, and the news was once again discouraging. Because the design resembled a finished basement more than a conventional house, the loan amount was limited to only $59,600 (instead of the $66,800 originally requested). With the help of the only area contractor interested in undertaking the project, some recalculating was done and adjustments made to manage this lower figure. Nancy agreed to reduce costs further by having her friends and brothers join her in assuming a greater share of the labor.

Time to Build: After months of paperwork, construction of the dream house began, but problems continued to develop. The builder was acceptable to the loan office but was a self-acknowledged newcomer to underground construction. His initial enthusiasm for learning all he could about energy-efficient housing techniques proved fleeting. Once the loan was approved, his attitude changed, and he refused to consider anything markedly different from the traditional construction methods he had always used. He did, however, agree to "subcontract" unconventional jobs such as the thermal walls to Nancy and her crew of family and friends.

Unfortunately for Nancy, the school term started soon after construction on the house began, and she was unable to oversee all of the work. Yet, despite teaching obligations, she was careful to be on hand to direct the waterproofing and insulating processes, both of which are vital to the success of an earth-sheltered house. She personally applied the two coats of tar emulsion (water-proofing) to the exterior walls—a messy but money-saving experience.

Nancy continued to involve herself as much as possible in the construction. She was at the site to make sure that the specified perimeter insulation of extruded polystyrene was properly placed on the exterior walls, and during the backfilling, she and a brother grabbed roots, limbs, and rocks before they could puncture the plastic around the polystyrene or destroy the insulation itself. When she had taken all the time off that her teaching job permitted, she had to trust the remainder of the hired construction to be completed without her watchful eye.

Check Every Detail: She soon learned that it wouldn't be wise to take anything for granted. Getting the house built the way she wanted meant besieging the builder with nightly phone calls and countless notes left at the site. Disagreements over details became a daily routine because the builder ignored her and, more often than not, did things the way he was accustomed to doing them. The worst of the arguments concerned the covering of the inside concrete walls. Although drawings made it clear that the north wall (the thermal storage wall) was not to be overlayed with plasterboard, the contractor ignored the plans, feeling certain there was some mistake: "Every one knows that concrete is always cold!"

The moral support and helping hands of family and friends made those difficult days easier. Volunteer laborers spent innumerable hours in selected construction projects reclaimed from the builder plus all of the "finish work" of painting walls, staining woodwork, installing carpeting, and putting up wall coverings. This help, lovingly given, made the house uniquely Nancy's own.

In fact, the most extraordinary features of Nancy's house were created by the town engineer—the fellow she had badgered early on in the project. He not only suggested, designed, and built the 8' diameter round window that's the focal point of her home, but he's the one who found the marble for the floors and built a custom marble woodstove (along with the black marble platform on which it rests). What's more, he laid the interior stone for the 10' X 34' south wall of the living area, and planned and constructed the steel frame for the 11' X 31' pit green house that was added a year later.

Since, for structural reasons, the interior stone and exterior brick for the south wall had to go up at the same time, her friend guided her in laying the brick as he worked on the stone. It was back-breaking work that took three months of working after school and weekends, but their hard labor paid off: The total cost of Nancy's little house was $12,600 less than the final loan commitment. She relishes every penny she saved, especially when the monthly payment comes due.

Keeping a solar dwelling warm does require an occupant's participation. When Nancy leaves for work, she must make a guess about the day's weather: If she opens the living area to the greenhouse and the day turns out to be cold and cloudy, heat is lost; if she keeps the door to the greenhouse closed and it turns out to be a sunny day, solar gain is considerably reduced.

The Greenhouse: As well as energy savings, homegrown vegetables and flowers can be enjoyed all year long. There are few things finer than the taste of fresh spinach in the winter or more cheerful than the sight of yellow zinnias in the midst of a February snowfall. These pleasures, plus the satisfaction of turning her dream of an energy-efficient home into a reality, have made the struggles involved worthwhile. Nancy's overall feeling is a gentle triumph: "Hey, I did it! I really did it!"

"With a little help from my friends," she's sure to add with a smile—especially when her town engineer is listening.

A Hexagonal Oak-Log Cabin for Next to Nothing

Constructing your own home can mean substantial savings, and if the dwelling is built simply of logs from your own property, the cost can be almost nothing. Plus, you may be able to use attractive, long-lived natural materials that are not available commercially, such as the whole, round, white oak logs that went into the cabin described here.

Beginnings: The trees for the cabin were felled in the spring to take advantage of the sap flow, which makes the logs easier to peel. Some cabins are built with the bark left on the logs, but peeled trees are much less vulnerable to insect attack and season more rapidly than those with the bark left intact.

Once felled and trimmed, the logs can either be peeled on the spot or hauled to the building site before being stripped. In either case, it's best to support the logs so less bending and stooping is needed to remove the bark.

Everyone seems to have a favorite peeling tool, and you'll have to experiment until you find the implement that suits you best. Some folks like to sit astraddle a log and debark it with a drawknife. Others prefer to use a poleax with a broad blade, partly because the added weight of the ax can break through those stubborn places where the bark wants to stick. Most appropriate is a bark spud, a large, almost shovel-sized scoop-bladed chisel. All these tools—once forgotten in time—are being made again and sold by home-steading-goods and forestry-tool suppliers.

If you intend to let your logs dry for several months, you need not debark each tree trunk entirely. Peel a few large strips down the length of the logs and set them aside. As the wood dries, it'll pull away from the remaining bark, which can be easily shucked off.

Piers, Floor, Walls, and Center-Pole

The Design: By midsummer, the cabin's design had begun to take shape, though the owners had not yet put anything on paper. Two things were certain: They wanted to build a several-sided structure, something a little more aesthetic than the standard four-square Abe Lincoln log cabin; and the dwelling would have to be constructed from the relatively small logs that their mule could maneuver through the woods (which they did not want to clear cut, but harvested selected straight, same-sized logs selected from many acres of trees). This meant timbers no more than 12' to 15' long and 12" in diameter. With these factors in mind, a hexagonal shape with 13' long sides was selected.

With the design set and the trees felled and peeled, the logs were skidded to the construction site where they were stacked in layers, with the logs in each layer perpendicular to those in the layers above and below. The timbers were left to dry until the foundation could be built and a building party arranged to raise the walls.

Foundation: The area where the cabin was to be built had an abundance of stone, and this was used for the foundation. Large, flat rocks were mortared together to form seven piers: one measuring a yard-across at each point of the hexagon, and a giant version in the center. Since the 13' long logs, when notched and stacked, would overlap 6" at each end, the piers were set 12' apart.

The bases of the columns were set below frost line, and their above-ground heights were checked with a string level. The fact that the six outer columns were equidistant from each other and from the center pier made the hexagonal foundation very easy to lay out by scribing a circle with spokes radiating out every 1/6th of a circle—or every 30°.

Next, the builders constructed twelve smaller columns around the circle at points halfway between each of the original seven. These were first built up to ground level and then completed after setting the sill logs, which rest directly upon the stone foundation. Since, in log cabin construction, the alternate sides of the building rise in half log increments, the supporting columns must be of different heights. Besides, all logs have taper, humps, and bumps, so it's a great deal easier to set the sill logs or floor joists on their main supports first, then raise the other columns to meet those sill logs.

Floors, Walls, Windows, and Doors: About 25 people of all ages and descriptions showed up to help raise about two-thirds of the cabin's logs in two days.

The building team decided that the best way to join the logs in the dwelling was to cut tenons in the ends of the timbers with a bucksaw, a wedge, and a sledgehammer, and then stack the logs. The tenons were made by removing the upper and lower surfaces of the log ends, leaving a rectangle half as thick as the log itself. The tenons of one row of logs would rest upon the tenons in the row of logs beneath, and the tenons of the row above would rest on it. This way, the weight of the logs would hold the cabin together. (With oak, adequate weight is no problem. For safety's sake, however, 8" oak pins were used to tie the bottom sill logs together; all other joints were joined with 40-penny spikes.)

Floor Before Walls: Before the walls began rising, floor-support timbers or joists, one 24'-long log and four 12' timbers, were secured to the sill logs with mortise and tenon joints. The mortises were quite easily made with a one-inch chisel and provided very clean-looking joints.

Doors and windows were framed with 2 X 6 oak boards set on the sill logs. The wall-logs were cut to fit between angles and door frames. Window frames were placed on their mounts four or five log-tiers later. Then, between window frames and up to the ceiling plate, wall sections went up using logs cut to the appropriate length. As each cut-to-length timber was butted against a frame, a 40-penny spike was driven through the frame and into the log end, securing the butt in place until small sticks could be hammered into the cracks between the logs to give permanent support.

At the level of the twelfth plate log, a few inches less than 8' above the floor joists, the loft joists went into place. These members extend from the 6 corners of the building to a 15' tall cedar pole in the center of the dwelling. As with the main floor joists, the loft joists were tied to walls and central pillar with mortise and tenon joints. The resulting spoke and wheel arrangement makes for an exceptionally rigid structure.

To complete the main and loft floors the builders [1] nailed 2 X 6 oak boards on two-foot centers between the spoke-like main floor joists, [2] spiked rough-flattened log sections between the loft joists, [3] used chisels and adzes to chip the logs into a level platform, [4] overlaid the oak beams with one-inch rough-milled oak barn-floor planks, and [5] covered the oak subflooring with a layer of particle board.

Last of all, the crew evened up the cabin's walls at the top (or sixteenth) log layer by adding half logs to the three low walls.

The Roof: A low tipi of 12 oak saplings, each approximately four inches in diameter, comes together with the center-pole at the apex of the building to form the roof frame, giving the loft a ceiling height of 7' in the center and 2-1/2 feet at the walls. These rafters are bolstered with 2 X 4 oak stringers spaced two feet apart on center. The roof was finished by attaching custom-cut triangles of 5/8" plywood to the rafter poles with wire wound thorough holes drilled in the plywood, plugging thin spaces between the sheeting with thin strips, coating seams with roofing cement and covering it all with overlapping strips of 30-pound rolled roofing felt. At this writing, the next order of business was to hand split and install cedar shake-shingles over the felt and fabricate a sheet-lead or copper cap for the peak.

Chinking: Once the floors and roof were finished, the time-consuming task of filling the numerous gaps between the wall logs began.

The traditional method used involves splitting sections of log into wedge-shaped pieces between one foot and two feet long, hammering those pieces into the cracks in the wall, tacking them in place with six-penny nails, and then daubing the area with mud or special chinking mortar. The resulting barrier has much better insulating properties than mud or mortar alone.

The semi-mortar mud mix used in this rustic chinking job consisted of two-thirds of a wheel barrow full of hardpan clay, two shovelfuls of wood ashes, one shovelful of salt (the kind at the feed store), and sufficient water to yield a mud pie consistency. To pack the mix into the cavities, the mud was troweled off of a hand-held board.

Costs: Because this cabin was built largely from materials cut and prepared by the owner and a crew of like-minded friends, the cash cost was minimal. The only expenses were for mortar used in the stone foundation, particleboard sheathing, felt roofing, recycled mill lumber, fire-proofing solution for the roof, and assorted nails and spikes, as well as food and lubrication for the jolly crew.

Yearly maintenance costs are virtually nonexistent, and so long as the roof's fire-proofed oak shakes are installed before snowfall, and roof and chinking are well- maintained, there's no reason why the logs and the structure won't last a century or more.

Shingle Your Roof by Recycling Aluminum Printing Plates

Aluminum shingles are such an excellent roofing material they are used on commercial buildings. They can last a lifetime, are fire- and rustproof, and reflect sun and heat energy, so they can reduce heating and cooling costs.

To cover an 1,800 square-foot roof with aluminum shingles, a roofing contractor would have to charge thousands of dollars. However, by using salvaged aluminum from inexpensive, used printing plates to create shingles and by installing them without professional help, an enterprising do-it-yourselfer can roof a house for less than 5% of a contractor's fee. And such shingles are lightweight, an important consideration for the lone roofer who must carry hundreds of them up a ladder.

Shop Around: The best print-shop leftovers for shingle use are .009" thick and measure 24-5/8" X 36". Telephone calls to local newspapers, job-shop printers, and book presses will reveal that such plates vary quite a bit in availability and in price. But many small-job printers have quantities of the used plates that they are more than willing to unload at a bargain rate. Locate

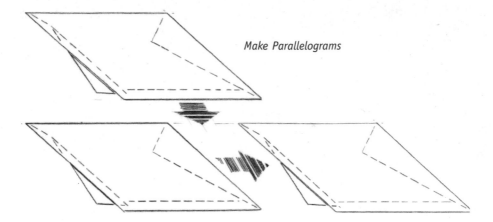

Make Parallelograms

the printer with the greatest number of usable plates for the lowest cost (sometimes as little as 10 cents apiece).

Carefully select undamaged plates that have a sturdy, 1/8" doubled over edge (created when the aluminum was locked in the press). When loading the plates into your car trunk or truck, you'll find that printer's ink blackens everything it touches, so always don gloves and old, stained garments when working with this type of recycled aluminum.

Cut Them Up: Cutting the 2' X 3' plates into fourths will produce shingles that are attractive, easy to put on and strong enough to resist high winds. Place a single aluminum sheet—printed side up—on a work surface, measure carefully to determine the midpoint of each side, lay a yardstick across the marks, and scratch in a "cross hair." Use scissors to divide the plate into four equal sections. These rectangles become the patterns for the rest of the plates.

The sheets are not difficult to cut if stout scissors are used. While it's possible to quarter 10 sheets in about 25 minutes, the job could be done much more quickly with a paper cutter. An even faster method would be to pay the print shop to cut the plates with a power knife.

Template and Folding Tool: Fashioning each shingle into a parallelogram works best for a number of reasons. They require only one thickness of aluminum, require few fabricating steps, allow overlapping of each shingle on all four edges, produce slanted vertical tiles (to shed water well), are easy to mount, and make it possible to secure three of each shingle's corners with only two nails. Plus, the shingles not only overlap, they interlock and will stay on in a hurricane.

In order to produce the finished metal shakes, however, one must first make a template 17-1/2" long and 10" wide from a piece of 1/8" plywood or other sturdy sheet goods. Mark two points 4-1/2" horizontally from the upper right and lower left corners. Next, scribe lines connecting these dots to, respectively: the lower right and upper left angles. Saw off the two indicated triangles to create the parallelogram form shown in the diagram.

After locating a table knife, a 16" scrap of steel strap, and a 6" piece of 2 X 4, you can set to work fabricating shingles.

How to Fold: To fold the shingles, place one of the minisheets, shiny side down, on the work surface. The 1/8" press-folded edge should be closest to you (turned under), and the sheet must protrude about one inch over the table's edge. Next, put the template on it so that the top edges line up, and the acute angles of the template are even with the sides of the printing plate. The 1" aluminum "tongue" that sticks out toward you is then folded up and over the bottom edge of the template to form a small pocket.

At this point, use the scissors to make two small cuts just through the 1/8" fold at the top of the pocket, positioning them four inches from the left side of the sheet and six inches from its right edge. After making these snips, begin the next step, which is to wrap the exposed triangles of metal up and over the sides of the template. A wooden block is used to press each fold almost but not quite flat.

Place the piece of strap iron along the slanting fold at the right side, and bend the triangle of metal back over itself. (When the strap is removed, it will leave a small trough or pocket.) A table knife is then used to lift the 1/8" tab between the two bottom-fold cuts.

This may sound complicated, but after a little practice, the steps flow smoothly in a "line up, fold bottom, make cuts, fold sides, remove template, squash folds, make right-side pocket, and open 1/8" edge" sequence that makes production a rapid process.

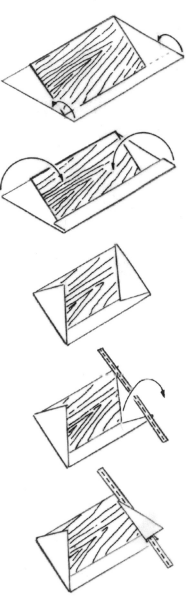

Folding Shingles

At a rate of 40 shingles every 20 minutes (not an improbable pace), in an easy-going week an adult can make about 2,000 shingles—the amount needed for an 1,800-square-foot roof—while tending the kids, listening to a ball game on the radio, or reading (once the work becomes automatic).

You can also hire the work out. You can make a contribution by training workers at a sheltered workshop or a boys' club—or have a gang of neighborhood teens to do the work for a nickel a shingle. Even if you pay a dime for each original plate, you'll get a permanent roof for less than $400. Compare that with the cost of tiles or shingles to make a conventional 1,800 square foot roof!

To mount the finished shingles in overlapping vertical strips follow the arrows in the illustration on p. 60. Lay horizontal rows with the right hand edge of each shingle fitting into the pocket on the left edge of the shingle to its right, the flap at each shingle's lower left-hand corner laying atop the next shingle to the left. Set nails through the overlap — one at the top corner and the other through the pointed end of the angled flap at the lower left. Lay succeeding rows so the upper-tier shingles cover seams in the row below, and the bent lower edge of uppers cover the upper edge of the lower row by the width of the flap bent into upper shingle's lower edge.

In this way, all sides of all shingles are overlapped to keep out water. Self-sealing rubber-fitted roofing nails are best for this job. If you can't get them, cover all exposed rail heads with roofing compound.

These homemade, interlocking shingles can not only weather 80 mph winds and heavy snows, but they can also provide insulation effective enough to lower heating and cooling bills. Even after they oxydise to an attractive roof-colored dull grey, aluminum shingles reflect the sun's glow in a particularly nice way, and the attractive diamond like pattern of the roof belies the low cost of the covering.

A Stacked-Haybale Structure for a Temporary Haven

Living in an inexpensive temporary structure while working on that dream home can make the difference between having the permanent dwelling paid for when it's finished or facing mortgage payments for years. As the bitter Minnesota winter approached, one couple that were just starting to build a stone house, realized they couldn't continue living in the screened-in hunting shack they had found on their property. Rather than pay to rent an apartment in town or buy a mobile home to put on their land—and then have to obtain a loan to cover construction costs—they chose to spend a few hundred dollars

Permanent Straw Bale Homes

History: Homes have been constructed of straw since one of the Three Little Pigs built his (though he failed to fireproof it against the Big Bad Wolf). One hundred year old examples of more permanent bale homes exist—many in the American Midwest, and the idea is being revived around the world; in the USA, largely among self-reliant folk in the Southwest.

Acceptance by local building code authorities is slow to come, but it's coming. Many straw-bale homes are bank-financed, insured and indistinguishable from conventional stick-builts but for their low, low cost: as little as $10/sq.ft., and at most less than half the cost of conventional frame construction.

Bales must be made of air-dried straw or hay—tied tight. If baled wet or allowed to soak moisture deep inside, the house can compost, heat up and combust spontaneously like a barn full of wet hay. Keeping straw dry is one r eason that the dry Southwest is an ideal location...however, there is one home in rainy Washington state that has gone unplastered for a generation. Another in humid Alabama has resisted decay since construction in the 1930s. So has one in Nova Scotia. It's all in how the home is built to match its environment.

During construction, bales must be kept high and dry off the soil, and be kept covered and ventilated. Foundations must rise (at least 6") above any possible surface water, or above a concrete floor where water could pool.

To let walls breathe enough to keep the straw from composting, they must be air-permeable. Moisture tends to move toward cool surfaces, which means that the outer sheathing must be more air-permeable than the interior walls in cool climates and vice versa in warm, humid climates where air conditioning is common. Local vapor-barrier rules will determine venting protocols.

Bales: Conventional bales can be had for as little as a half-dollar apiece—you pick them up in the field. But you may want to have yours custom-cut, dried, and bound.

Bales have length, height, and width dimensions that vary regionally, though most heft at about 60 pounds. The best configuration is a "flat" bale shaped like a brick, but not as long. Blocked and trimmed square, laid flat side up/down, placed in the wall one-over-two, two-over-one like bricks or a stone wall and connected with long stakes, bales are remarkably stable. For a thin wall, bales may be laid on edge, but should be tied and staked extra well.

Bales are made by reaping dry hay or straw, and packing it in box-shaped bales

(continued on page 64)

with the length of the stems running the length of the bale. Then, binding twine or wire is wrapped very tightly around the short dimension of the bales, which are cut or packed to length as they exit the baler. Hemp baling twine, still used in the Northeast, is subject to rot. Wire will rust. Best is packing-strap or "poly" twine. Most any string-baler can be adapted to use it. The more and closer the ties on the bale the better.

Often, bales must be notched and cut to size. A hay needle to thread twine through bales to tie off a short end and a fine-toothed hay saw are essential tools. A hay hook with a short "T" handle is a big help in lifting bales.

One construction method (there are several) uses straw as fill inside of bays in a timber-frame design. These designs can be multiple-story as the straw does not support the roof.

A more appealing and appropriate construction method (limited to single-story designs) is to build the hay walls strong enough to be "'load-bearing" and support a standard (or a hay-thatched) roof. Steel pins every foot or so are formed into the concrete foundation. A first course of strong, tight bales is impaled on the stakes. Further courses are laid in running bond (like bricks) and pinned with 5' steel rebar or bamboo; two to a bale. The roof rests on a 2 x 6 or larger beam called a "plate" laid atop the straw. The plate must be connected direct to the foundation with threaded rod or poly cord strapping; the connectors are cinched or screw-tightened to

(continued on page 65)

building a stacked-haybale house that would shelter them more or less comfortably for a year or two while they completed their permanent dwelling. This allowed the major portion of their savings and income to be spent on materials for their new stone house.

To maximize internal space, the hay-house builders selected an open, six-sided design. The structure was framed with poles, enclosed with stacked bales of hay and heated by a woodstove located in the center of the building, the greatest possible distance from walls that remained flammable despite being treated with flameproofing.

Frame and Roof: The homesteaders cut the poles for the framework and roof supports from spruce trees that grew plentifully on the property. But in their race against the threat of cold weather, postponed stripping the bark from the poles or coating them with preservative.

On a cleared, flat site with good drainage, the builders laid out a hexagon on a 30' diameter circle, and using a posthole digger, sank 2-1/2'-deep holes at

compress the straw from 1.5 to 3.5 inches or more. The plate runs across boxed door and window openings as well, and the roof is framed on top of it.

Most roofs are conventional fireproof shingles over frame and plywood sheathing. However, some adventuresome souls are roofing with old-fashioned straw thatch.

Stuccoing: The outside and inside of the walls are typically stuccoed—coated with mortar over wire-mesh—soaking up at least 50% more "mud" than conventional stuccoed walls. The "mud" can be conventional Portland-cement-based plaster, a clay/straw/ glue mix or other earth plaster—applied over 17-gauge or heavier stucco wire (heavy chicken fence). Giant hairpin-like "U" pins or (better) sewing-in with polycord is used to hold wire to bales. Some old bale-built homes, however, are sheathed inside and out with clapboard, wallboard, or plywood...attached to furring strips pinned to the bales.

Walls of stuccoed straw give a home an insulation value of up to R-60. If fireproofed (with common Borax), bales in the attic can give you the most heat-efficient dwelling in the county. And, yes—if stuccoed, fireproofed, and solidly framed, your low-cost hay-bale home can be heated safely and economically with wood.

Editors Note: For current (c. 1997) information about this old/new way to build a home for (a whole lot) less, contact: The Canelo Project, Athena and Bill Steen, HC 1 Box 324, Elgin, AZ 85611. ■

each of the corners and midway between each of these points. Six additional holes were sunk in the center area to form another hexagon with a six-foot diameter. Poles were placed vertically in all the holes, with the posts in the center of the building slightly taller than those located around the periphery so there would be some pitch to the roof. The tops of the uprights were notched with a chain saw, and crossbeams and tie-in supports were spiked in place.

With the walls framed in, work began on the roof. The support for the composite plastic, hay, and sod covering consisted of a nearly solid umbrella-like arrangement of poles that projected far enough over the hay bale walls to protect them from rain or snow. The tops of these poles were peeled to prevent bark and rough spots from wearing holes in the plastic that made up the next layer of the roof. Then the builders broke about 45 bales of hay into 8"-thick "books" and spread these over the plastic, locating the hay squares as close to one another as possible. Another layer of plastic was laid over the straw– insulation, and sod was cut and placed over this. Because freezing weather moved in, placement of the sod was left unfinished until the following spring. By that time exposed areas of the second layer of plastic had deteriorated and needed to be replaced.

The center section of the roof where the stovepipe went through was the most complex part of the construction. A small mitered hexagon supported by 2 X 4s radiating in and up from the center poles comprised the frame. This was covered with boards, which, in turn, were covered with plastic. Glass-covered square holes cut in this section served as small skylights. In the interest of safety and fire prevention, no hay was used on this area of the roof.

Walls, Windows, and Door: First, plastic was laid under the bottom (foundation) row of hay bales and was folded up around them to protect them from dampness. As each bale was set in place, it was stitched to those next to it with loops of baling twine tied tightly. Where possible, bales were attached to posts or to diagonal braces nailed between the uprights.

The walls went up quickly, with the bales laid in a 1-over-2, 2-over-1 staggered pattern like brickwork. At corners and window and door frames where only a portion of a bale was needed, the builders took a bale apart, retied as much as was needed, and saved the remaining hay for stuffing cracks later.

The couple had already obtained windows inexpensively at sales and auctions, but knew they would have to build additional frames that would be wide enough to sit on the hay bales and strong enough to support the tier of hay between the frames and the roof eave. For extra insulation they decided to sandwich windows for each opening. Deep frames of 1 X 6s were toenailed together at the corners, and strips made of 2 X 4s joined two matching frames to create a double-glazed unit with a dead-air space between. The window units were wedged in place on top of the third row of bales.

A frame was built in a similar manner to surround a door constructed of two inches of foam insulation sandwiched between 1/4" plywood faces.

Additional Touches: The final touches in constructing the hay house consisted of stuffing as much loose hay as possible into the spaces under the eaves and any other crevices, laying a plastic vapor barrier on the ground and covering it with rugs throughout most of the building but with linoleum in the kitchen area, and bedding two layers of bricks in a layer of sand in the center section to serve as a base for the woodstove. (A fire extinguisher was installed in a handy location near the stove.)

Several later additions were made to the house, some to gain protection from the elements, others to provide more space. Below-zero winds forced the hay-house dwellers to line both the inside and the outside of the porous hay walls with plastic. While this helped a great deal, they also found that too much heat was being lost through the building's cap, so they installed fiberglass-insulation batts against the inside surface of the roof by supporting them with wires strung from the center-pole of the house to the outside walls.

A doghouse of hay bales and old lumber provided shelter for the family's pair of Russian wolfhounds and took only about an hour to build as a lean-to against the down-wind rear wall of the main structure.

With the arrival of spring, a greenhouse constructed along the south wall provided a spot to begin seedlings early and to continue growing some warm-weather vegetables late into the fall. This was built using old railroad ties for a base, recycled lumber for the framework, and salvaged storm windows for glazing.

The following fall, the family built a 9' X 12' shop of poles and hay, adjoining the house so they could move their stained glass business out of the main living area. Access to this addition was gained by replacing one window with a door, and the shop was given its own heat source—a small gas stove to be used only when someone was working there.

Living in their temporary dwelling provided enough comfort so that this enterprising couple was able to complete their permanent home without being rushed. They were able to pursue their stained glass business, enabling them to to pay for construction costs without taking out a mortgage. Once the stone house was completed, they continued to use the hay house as their shop till a proper studio was built into the stone house.

Their stone-house christening party was a full work day; they and guests tore down the hay home...with some sentimental feelings, but no financial regret. The raggedy, old plastic sheeting was bagged for recycling, poles were cut into kindling, and the loose bales of half-composted hay were divided up among all in attendance for use as garden mulch.

Move a House and Move In

Coming up with the down payment on a house is problem enough for most people today, and 30 years of mortgage payments only drag out the difficulty of affording a home. However, by purchasing a house that is about to be torn down, moving it to a new foundation in another location, then patching a little cracked plaster, you can have yourself a home that costs in total about as much as the down payment on a new home—but that will have an appraised value several times the amount spent. Move the house to your country acreage, or spend some time and money remodeling or building a few additions. Then sell, and you can end up with the experience and funds to buy a farm.

The Early Steps: If you look, you'll find newspaper ads reading: "House for sale: $1"—all you have to do is move it.

Older in-town homes are available to be moved more often than most of us realize: land is purchased for plant expansion, to widen roads, and when anyone with the power wants to pave the house lot and put in a parking lot. Most are in perfectly good and livable condition. Some are mansions or antiques. But few will cost you much, if anything, as moving them is a major undertaking.

If you don't see an ad, call a house-mover (in the Yellow Pages). They know where their next potential job will be.

Selecting a house to move must be done carefully, with consideration for the soundness of the structure and the amount of work and expense of materials involved in bringing the heating, electrical, and other systems up to the standards of the new location's building codes. (Less-than "code" utilities are "grandfathered" in a home's original location. But, when moved, all systems must be brought up to current standards. This can mean all new siding, plumbing, insulation, roofing, and more.

Some subdivisions have prohibitions against bringing in houses built elsewhere, and some areas restrict size, cost, or type of structure that can be placed on a lot.

Distance from the old lot to the new one also must be taken into account, since most house movers charge not only for lifting the building off its original foundation, but also for the number of miles a dwelling must be moved.

There will be excavating and foundation expenses at the new lot, as well as fees for water, sewer, and electrical hookups. The building departments in some places will issue "homeowner's permits," which allow individuals to perform much of the work themselves rather than hiring professional contractors to bring the house up to standard.

When the site is ready, it is time to bring in the mover.

Making the Move: Relocating a house is heavy hauling for sure, but those in the business can usually get a residential structure from one place to another in a short time. For a frame structure, holes are knocked in the foundation, long I-beams placed under the house, and the entire building raised off its base with jacks. Then, either the house and the long beams are both lifted on shorter I-beams and are pulled away from the foundation, or the foundation is removed so the building and its temporary base can be towed away. Sets of wheels attached to the ends of the long I-beams allow the building to be pulled to the new location by a heavy truck tractor.

Electrical and telephone cables, stop lights—sometimes porticos and entries of buildings—must all be unhooked to let the house pass, then restored to service. All utility changes must be scheduled with the relevant authorities and utility firms, and fees must often be paid in advance. For a long moving route in an urban setting, these costs can be prohibitive. Be sure that the moving route is established and all clearances approved and costs contracted before you sink a cent into the move itself.

Setting It in Place: When the movers have brought the house to the new

Rammed Earth Building

Like straw-bale construction, rammed-earth building is an ancient technique that enjoyed brief popularity early in the 20th century—and is gaining renewed attention today in our search for environmentally acceptable and economical ways to construct homes. Ancient African palaces, Mayan pyramids, and Pueblo Indian Cliff Dwellings were all made of mud brick—adobe—a mixture of earth, water, and a binder such as straw that is packed into forms and dried in the sun. All around the earth's equatorial desert areas, mud brick was (and still is) laid up into walls like baked-ceramic bricks. The modern version is shaped inside slip-forms like those employed to form poured-concrete foundations and buildings. The resulting wall is massive, forming a heat sink for energy-storage and insulation, requires no curing time as does concrete, and it is cheap. Dirt cheap.

To answer the most common questions about this all-natural wall material:

How big can/must it be? Single-story buildings with standard 8' high ceilings and walls from 18" to 24" thick.

How does it hold up to rain? Fine...so long as the roof overhang is sufficient and the foundation high enough to prevent rain or flood from constantly washing at the wall.

How long will it last? Soil, design, and weather will all have an effect, but adobe cliff dwellings in the American Southwest are still standing after more than 500 years—the last hundred without any maintenance at all. With time, the packed soil actually becomes harder and more rock-like.

How well does it insulate? Like brick or stone, rammed earth has an R-value of only .25 per inch of thickness. So, a 12" wall has only an R-4 value—whereas walls in conventional new construction rate R-11 at minimum. But, the earth acts as a heat-sink, absorbing warmth and radiating it out gently much like a wood stove.

Foundations: The simplest foundation, one that is in use today around the globe in arid regions with well-compacted soil, is to build the wall around rocks or posts embedded in the soil. For more substantial dwellings, a trench a little wider than the wall and dug below frost level is filled with rocks and rubble. In arid regions the wall can be started in the upper foot of trench. In wetter climates where flowing water might undermine the wall, the rubble trench is topped by concrete with tie rods embedded in it, and the earth wall is built around the ties. The concrete cap can be limited to a grade beam or

(continued on page 70)

extended in wooden forms to well above soil level to escape even the deepest flash floods. For fully modern homes, a conventional reinforced concrete foundation on a wide footing is poured using the same type of wooden slip-forms used to build the walls. For a code-approved dwelling, foundation materials, sizes, and depths are determined by the load-bearing capacity of the soil and specified in engineering studies and/or in the building codes. In earthquake zones such as Southern California where many rammed-earth homes are being constructed, special reinforcements must be incorporated—again, specified by code.

Formbuilding: In traditional societies, rammed-earth walls are made like oversized adobe bricks. A wooden form shaped like a giant cheese box is placed on the spiky foundation and packed with about a 2" thickness of damp, straw-reinforced earth. Succeeding horizontal segments are made by removing one end panel, clamping the open-end sides to one finished wall-end, and building on around. When the base course is finished, the form is reinstalled on top of it. Extended skirts on the side panels are clamped to the lower courses, and successive courses laid. Where doors and windows are to be, floor sills, frames, and headers along the top are made of wall-thick lumber and built around.

Modern front-end loaders and hydraulic tampers permit much larger forms to be raised and walls built quickly. Typically, forms are made of 4' x 8' high-density plywood framed and reinforced with steel, set on end, and connected with clamps. Entire room-height sections of wall can be erected in a single pour.

The Soil: Ancient earth buildings that have best stood the test of time are made of 70% sand and 30% clay. The less loam the better, so you must dig down well below the dark topsoil for building-soil. Few soils are naturally composed in a 70:30 ratio. Typically, sand must be added—most easily by dry-mixing with a rototiller. In the old days, straw was mixed in—sometimes with burned lime—to form a binder. Today, about 10% dry Portland cement is added according to engineering data or local usage for the given soil type. Water (according to local usage and slump rates) is added to make a "dry" mix that is quickly transferred to the form.

The secret of wall-stability is tamping. A 4" to 6" layer of mud is poured into the form. Then it is compacted with a conventional wood-handled, iron-footed tamper or a home-made version: a 4' x 4" steel plate welded to 1" steel rod or plumbing pipe.

Stand inside the form, lift the ram a foot or more and ram it home till all air is driven out and the sound changes

(continued on page 71)

from a dull thud to a ringing sound. Figure that a worker can tamp from one to one and a half cubic yards an hour. Pneumatic tampers can speed the job considerably, of course.

In seismic areas the code may require a poured reinforced-concrete bond beam all around the top of the wall (and may also require poured concrete panels at strategic points around the wall.) But in most areas you can level the wall top, spike a stout 6"-thick header beam into the still-moist mud and build your roof.

In traditional construction, horizontal log rafters were embedded in the top layers of mud, then angled roof beams or a flat roof built. In wide homes, an interior wall was made along with the outer walls and used to support the interior ends of roof beams.

But anyway you design and build it, a traditional rammed-earth dwelling made from properly-mixed and well-tamped mud will be here long after most ticky-tacky tract houses and concrete and steel skyscrapers are ancient history.

Editor's Note: For current (c. 1997) information about this old/new way to build a home for (a whole lot) less, get a copy of the most modern book on rammed-earth construction: The Rammed Earth House *by David Easton (Chelsea Green, 1996)* ■

---

location and have positioned it over the excavation, the four ends of the I-beams are set on pillars made by stacking heavy timbers crosswise into piers. The wheels are detached and taken away, leaving the building on the pillars until the footings are dug and poured and the foundation or basement walls are laid to their proper level. By using jacks and removing the timbers, the structure is then lowered onto its new base and the I-beams are removed.

Electrical, water, and sewer lines can then be connected to the residence, and with backfill placed around the foundation or basement walls, the new owners are ready to undertake any renovations, improvements, and alterations. These might include anything from such cosmetic and protective measures as caulking and painting the dwelling to structural renovations such as changing the positions of windows and doors, adding a porch or a wing, and moving partitions to alter the floor plan.

Tips for Would-Be House Movers: Anyone deliberating the purchase of an unwanted house for the purpose of moving it to a new location should consider the following advice from those experienced in the process.

First, it's best to have the building official from the new area inspect the structure to determine whether it meets the codes, needs minor repairs to do so, or requires major renovations. In an older house, for example, it's entirely possible that the wiring and plumbing will all need to be completely redone.

Second, remember that there's always more than one house on the market and that there's no need to settle for one that needs a great deal of work or too much in moving costs.

Third, since the charges for trundling the house from one location to another can vary considerably from one mover to another, obtain several bids.

Fourth, it's a good idea to make your purchase offer on a lot contingent on being able to obtain all the necessary permits for relocating a house.

Finally, a tight schedule should be avoided. Many small problems can delay the move itself, as well as the building official's finally issuing an occupancy permit. Rainy weather can create mud, which might make it impossible for the mover to get the building off the old site or onto the new one until the ground is drier. Small electrical, plumbing, or structural problems can delay approval by inspectors until "just one more detail" is taken care of.

The Bottom Line: Even with delays of a week here and a week there, and the time taken for several renovations and alterations, it's possible to move a home and have it ready to occupy in much less time than it takes to build a comparable dwelling. And when it's done, the home can be free and clear of debt.

Buying and Restoring an Older Fixer-Upper

Purchasing old dwellings and restoring them for residence or resale can, for folks who are willing to invest a bit of initiative and effort, be a highly profitable enterprise or a way to own a home for much less than its real value. But buyers who don't know exactly how to choose a home to rehabilitate can easily take on a loser and end up parting unnecessarily with a lot of hard-earned money.

How Not to Get Started: One man, for example, found what he thought was an incredible bargain for only $47,000. The house needed repairs, but it seemed like a steal at the price. Unfortunately, as soon as work began on the dwelling, he discovered that the more things he fixed, the more he found to fix.

The wiring had been added to the house after it was built in 1910. It was all exposed and had to be hidden in walls and ceilings to satisfy the building code. He wound up replacing the plumbing, too, and these two jobs increased his cash outlay by $24,000. A new roof cost him $4,000, and installing a foundation after finding out that there wasn't one set him back another $9,000.

The disheartened owner next found that much of the first-floor wooden framing had been chewed to lace by an infestation of termites. Fumigation and wood replacement cost him $4,000 more.

And in addition to the surprises, there were the expected repairs to be made. The would-be home broker had anticipated putting in a new floor and insulating it, for example. That ran him $12,000, while painting, wall papering, and kitchen remodeling consumed another $17,000.

All in all, the man poured an extra $69,000 into his $47,000 bargain, making a total investment of $116,000 in a dwelling that was finally appraised at just $90,000. If he had only known what to look for and had made a few strategic phone calls, the unfortunate buyer could have avoided the heartbreak and budget-break of getting in over his head.

How to Get Started: However, all this can be avoided by using the following checklist as a guide to avoid pitfalls in purchasing a fixer-upper.

[1] With a specific house to consider, examine its structural condition carefully. What kind of foundation does it have? Are there shingles missing? Do water stains on the walls and ceilings indicate a leaky roof that requires a termite inspection be made? Ask the seller to pay for this and for any repairs necessitated by an infestation.

[2] Make sure that all the building's utilities are serviceable or fixable at an accepted cost. Is the plumbing functional? Is the wiring safe? Is the furnace efficient?

[3] Price the cost of repairs before making the purchase. It's best to call electricians, plumbers, carpenters, and masons to get rough estimates of typical jobs or the approximate price of work per square foot before you even start shopping. Find out how much it costs to insulate an attic, for instance, or to replace rotted floors, or to rewire a house. With average figures in mind, you can add the cost of repairs to the price of any given house.

[4] Find out about zoning. Should the house you're looking at be in a commercial zone, you might be able to sell it as business property, a classification that generally has greater value than comparable residential property. However, if you're looking at a lot with two houses or a duplex on it and find the zoning to be R-1 (single-family dwelling), you must realize that the site is zoned for one house, not two. The law may have changed since the previous owner acquired the property, but as the new owner, you could be forced to obtain a zoning variance, which is permission to use a piece of property for something not covered by its current zoning classification. And, you may not get it!

[5] Don't be put off by looks alone. Because a house with chipped paint and unkept grounds will tend to discourage buyers who see only appearances and not potential, the price of such property is often low. A shrewd person, though, can see that by some paint and elbow grease, the eyesore can become very livable. The same principle holds true for homes with superficial damage to floors, wallpaper, and old or abused appliances and utilities. Compared with the cost of structural damage, most cosmetic problems are easily and inexpensively repaired.

[6] Know the market. Before you make a purchase, have a good idea of

how much people will pay to rent or buy the house. If you plan to resell, either immediately or after living there yourself for a while, subtract the purchase price and the probable repair costs from the potential market price, and the difference will represent the profit or loss. If you plan to retain ownership and rent to others, figure out your mortgage payments, estimated yearly repairs and maintenance, and any tax advantages and weigh these computations against a reasonable expected rent. Consider, too, the consequences of those times when the house could stand unoccupied.

Hedging Your Bets: If everything checks out favorably, it's time to make an offer. On the other hand, few houses will be all you're looking for. When you find one that you think you'd like to buy but that doesn't measure up in every respect, consider making an offer anyway, but with contingencies that will relieve you of any obligation should the house turn out to be a nightmare. For example, you might make your offer contingent upon the building's meeting current building codes. Then, if upon inspection it proves to be not up to snuff, you'll have the option of backing out of the purchase or possibly of acquiring the property for a lower price.

Adding too many contingencies to a bid, however, could leave little room for bargaining, so if your offer depends upon a number of factors, be prepared to pay nearly the full asking price.

There's a lot of work involved in fixing up a run-down dwelling either for resale or to call home, but for anyone willing to put in the time it takes to find an old house that is worth repairing, there are financial rewards and much personal satisfaction to be reaped.

Stack Two Miles Of 2 x 4s and Move In

An innovative way of reducing the expense of building a home is to use inexpensive standard materials in an unconventional manner. This house was designed to be built entirely by a lone worker at a remote location without electricity. Its walls are made entirely of stacked 2 x 4 studs—at a cost of under $2,000. The timber and gravel foundation, roof and floor beams, 60 sheets of plywood, a little pine planking, and a tin roof added another $4,000.

The result is a 24'-square cabin with 3-1/2" thick solid wood walls, a cathedral ceiling lined with knotty pine, exposed rafters and beams, and wooden floors and walls. Inside there is a 9' X 12' bedroom, a full bath, a 12' X 24' living/dining area, and a spacious loft. Outside is an 8' X 12' screened porch.

It took only about two months to complete and cost far less than a similar structure built using conventional methods.

This house is built largely from stacks of 2 X 4 lumber laid broad face down; in fact, it took nearly two miles of them to construct the house.

Nailing down 10,000 linear feet of 2 X 4s may sound like a job for a covey of carpenters, but anyone willing to tackle such a task can do it using conventional hand tools.

Plan to Save: If such an innovative structure is to be finished within a minimal budget, more time and effort must be spent planning than will be needed for the actual construction work. Before buying any materials, the builder needs to visualize every step of the process, all the way down to mentally counting the nails in the molding around the front door. Allowances must also be made for plumbing, fixtures, and a metal chimney.

The first design for this house measured 16' X 20', but splitting up the space to obtain the rooms needed couldn't be done. The owner/designer/builder considered all possible layouts before settling on the final 24' X 24' plan.

Paying careful attention to actual building material sizes is also important. To give an idea of what a lack of such planning can mean, imagine what could happen to a builder who planned a house expecting a 2 X 4 to actually measure two inches by four inches. Since dimension lumber 2 X 4 boards are actually 1-1/2" X 3-1/2", the walls would come up two feet short in height, or in the case of the 24' X 24' bungalow featured here, 1,536 linear feet short of having enough lumber to give standing room inside.

On the positive side, planning a design around standard material lengths can save both time and money. The 24'-square layout allowed the use of combinations of 2 X 4s ranging from 8' to 16' long in 2' increments and full sheets of 4' X 8' plywood. Because of the wall construction, this home required only 60 sheets of plywood for the subfloor, the loft floor, the roof, and the skirting. It was much faster and easier just to plop down a full sheet and nail it in place than it would have been to cut each piece to size with a handsaw. Furthermore, the roof pitch (when combined with the floor plan) allowed the use of 16'-long 4 X 6 rafter beams and combinations of full sheets of plywood.

Stacklumber: Why choose to construct a house of stacked 2 X 4s that many people assume is excessively expensive? Contrary to the builder's own expectations, preliminary figures showed that a 2 X 4 house would give a conventional stick-built home, sheathed with imitation board-and-batten plywood and finished with inexpensive paneling, a real run for the money.

The builder felt that walls made with 2 X 4s would have the solidity and beauty of those constructed with logs, but would be easy for a lone worker to build. Then, too, the beams and the pine boards used for the floors and ceiling would complement solid wooden walls, adding to the attractiveness and warmth of the home. In the end, the only nonwood material used was 15-pound roofing felt and 28-gauge metal roofing.

Buying at the Best Price: Nearly all of the materials needed had to come from a lumberyard, yet the "local" yards ranged from 60 to 180 miles from the building site. Since cost was a major concern, suppliers were chosen by comparing bids on a fixed list of materials. After receiving preliminary prices from a dozen different lumberyards, the three lowest were selected for detailed bidding.

The three final bidders received detailed lists describing each item as specifically as possible. At the same time, each bidder was asked to include the delivery cost and give the expiration date on the prices quoted.

When the bids came back, their totals differed only slightly, and though the closest yard to the site bid a little higher for the materials, its offer of free delivery tipped the scales. In any building project, no matter how carefully planned, there will be some returns, exchanges, and unforeseen purchases, and it's a lot easier to drive 120 miles than it is to travel 360 miles to do these errands.

Final Obstacles: One problem with all three of the materials' bids was that they exceeded the budget. Consequently, something had to go. One sizable expense was windows and doors.

Since too little natural lighting can turn even the best space into a cell, the builder was unwilling to compromise on the window area. Consideration was given to using a lower grade lumber than planned and to using roll roofing instead of sheet metal on the roof, but both ideas were rejected as being false savings. The builder reasoned that a lower grade of lumber would contain more culls and result in more scrap and that the toll taken by the sun, hail, and snow would bring on the need to repair or replace the roofing if the rolled material was used instead of metal.

Instead, windows that had been ripped out of a doctor's house during remodeling and doors from an old telephone company office were found for a reasonable cost at a salvage yard.

Auctions also helped keep the budget intact by providing a 4-1/2'-long cast-iron bathtub for $20, along with a toilet, a cast-iron sink, faucets, and another old tub for a total of $60. (One bathtub ended up as a watering trough for horses.) The kitchen counter tiles came from another auction, where more than 100 of the 6" X 6" pieces cost a mere $22.

Tools: The building site had no electricity, so the only power tool available was a chain saw. The list of essential tools for a project like this is quite short: two well-sharpened crosscut saws, a well-balanced construction hammer, framing and T-squares, a 25' measuring tape, 4' and line levels, a combination plumb bob and chalk line, a combination wrecking bar and nail puller, a keyhole saw, a brace and bits, wood chisels, a spade, a 6' stepladder, and a 28-foot extension ladder.

Foundation and Floor: The unconventional foundation consists of three 24'-long pressure-treated 4 X 12s set on 4" of gravel in trenches deep enough to keep the tops of the wood flush with the ground. The beams were set parallel, 12' apart, and a 16"-high wall of pressure-treated 2 X 4s and 2 X 6s was nailed along the full length of each.

The 2 X 8 joists were laid across these foundations, and 1/2" CDX plywood was nailed on top of them with the nails 4" apart along the joists. After lapping a layer of 15-pound felt over the subfloor, the builder set 1 X 6 tongue-and-groove pine flooring at right angles to the 2 X 8s. As is often the case with long pieces of tongue-and-groove material, minor twisting of the boards required that they be forced to fit. A long 2 X 4 set alongside a reluctant floorboard and nailed to the floor at one end, combined with a 6" piece of tongue-and-groove between it and the board to be set, makes a wonderful lever. Once the floor was in place, it was mopped with a clear sealer and preservative.

Two Miles of 2 x 4s: Preparing to build the walls called for laying the door frames out on the floor and carefully marking the necessary clearances. The first layer of 2 X 4s was set painstakingly on the marks, much as the sill would be in a stud-frame house. This made raising the walls a matter of proceeding upward while keeping the stack plumb.

To keep the joints staggered, every other row of 2 X 4s was laid down in an opposite direction from the one below it all the way around the perimeter. Crib construction requires only careful measurements, square cuts, attention to plumb, and a lot of nailing. Admittedly, this is a laborious process, but it can be sped up by laying out the materials in neat stacks according to length. That way, the longest possible pieces can be used in combination while still staggering the joints. It's also important to position the nails so that they don't hit the ones in previous tiers.

On reaching the bottoms of the window openings, a note was tacked to the lintel, listing the number of tiers and the height of the opening in inches. This provided a direct reference to show how far up to carry each window opening.

As the walls began to rise above the lower edges of the windows, it became necessary to brace some of the sections until the boards once again spanned an entire side. This involved constructing an upright triangle of 2 X 4s, setting one side against the section, and then temporarily nailing the brace to the 2 X 4 stack to keep the wall plumb.

Since the interior partitions with the exception of the plumbing wall between the kitchen and bath were also built of stacked 2 X 4s, some board-end-sized openings were left in the outside tiers to help anchor the inner walls. Interlocking such right-angled stacks stiffened the whole structure substantially.

Once the walls were up far enough for the ceiling beams to go into place, the 4 X 10s were slipped through a window from the outside and then dragged onto the floor from the inside. Working alone and using 2 X 8 planks on sawhorses as a scaffold, the builder lifted first one end of each beam and then the other. This procedure was a bit tricky. Since the beams are as long as the house is wide, getting them up required turning them sideways a bit. And then one hard jerk could pull a poorly lodged beam off the narrow ledge and send it crashing onto the floor.

Filling in between the beam ends with 2 X 4 wall sections required five rows, or nearly 500 linear feet of lumber. This quickly exhausted the supply of boards planned on for building the front porch. Fortunately, there was still some leeway left in the budget.

With the beams set and leveled, 1 X 6 tongue-and-groove pine was laid to form the ceiling for the rooms below, and plywood was added atop that to form the loft floor. This produced a solid platform from which to work on the gables and the ridge beam of the roof.

Two 2 X 4 X 16s nailed together at right angles, set against the outside of the existing wall, pushed up until the top ends reached the expected height of the roof peak, and spiked solidly in place insured that each gable continued as a straight extension of the wall below. Sixteen-foot boards extended from the peak to the walls as temporary guides to establish the pitch of the roof.

Raise the Ridge Beam: Putting the ridge beam in its place atop the gable ends was far too heavy a task to be accomplished by lifting the 26' long 4 X 10, as was done with the ceiling beams. The beam was hoisted onto the floor of the loft to lie with one end against the finished gable and the other projecting beyond the wall of the house where the gable had not yet been begun. By lifting the timber by hand and with a hydraulic jack, the builder raised the end overhanging the wall and supported it by building up the wall with 2 X 4s underneath it. When the angle of the timber became too steep to continue this, the end at the finished gable was raised and supported on wood scraps.

Eventually, something sturdier was needed to support the 4 X 10, so vertical 2 X 4 tracks were built at each end of the loft. The beam slid snugly between the boards, and each time it was jacked up about six more inches a 2 X 4 block was nailed to the tracks beneath it to support the weight. Working upward in such steps, it was finally possible to finish the second gable. Then, using a wrecking bar, the beam was jimmied until it rested firmly and squarely across the roof peak.

Roofing: The peak angles and wall-top notch to be cut into the 4 X 6 rafters were carefully measured, remeasured, calculated, checked, and rechecked before any cutting took place. To be completely certain that it was right, the builder cut a pattern from a long piece of scrap and after checking it, transferred the guide to each rafter board. The care proved worthwhile when that first roof-holder fit perfectly into position.

The next task, trimming the stepped 2 X 4 ends off the gables to form smooth angled edges, turned out to be quite a chore when the chainsaw failed to get a firm bite on the wood and left a jagged, unsatisfactory cut. The only alternative was cutting by hand at an angle through almost 70 running feet of wood.

The plywood sheathing for the roof was hoisted piece by piece up from the rack on the builder's pickup truck and installed from the gutters upward so that each new sheet would have a lip to hold it in place until it was nailed down. Then came 15-pound felt, which was tacked over the sheathing, and then metal roofing went on with a minimum of fuss.

Housewarming: It was two more days before the windows were in, and another four more passed before the screened porch was ready for the determinedly solitary builder to invite friends over to enjoy the cool of the evening and thumb their noses at the mosquitoes.

A Stackwood Barn

Homestead livestock can often be allowed to roam in a fenced pasture or be tethered in a field so the animals can graze, but when the air grows chilly or it becomes too hot in the open, a shelter becomes a necessity. In a limited operation, a barn that serves only to house animals calls for too much of an investment in a single-purpose building, and the combination post-and beam and stackwood structure here is a good example of an economically built multipurpose farm building.

From the very beginnings of this do-it-all outbuilding, it was apparent to the builders that the entire structure would probably never be devoted to housing only one kind of animal and that not only would space be needed to house several different breeds of animals at a time, but storage would be required for a variety of feeds and equipment. This projection proved true, as the building has housed beasts ranging from horses to rabbits and has even served as a milk-processing center. At one time, hay, wheat, buckwheat, and straw were all stored in the loft.

Given the construction techniques used in this building, it's a small matter to alter the layout to suit the needs of a particular homestead.

The Structure: At 32' X 45', the barn is larger than the average outbuilding but considerably smaller than a full-scale dairy barn. Furthermore, the structure's 10"-deep, 24"-wide footings offer the possibility of dividing the ground floor into stalls as small as 10' X 10'. The interior could easily be left more open, though the posts, which are an integral part of the load bearing structure, must be positioned as shown.

The 45' back wall and one 32' end wall are earth-bermed and made of 12" concrete block, mortared, and laid to a height of 10". To withstand the pressure of backfilling, one core of every second block was reinforced with two lengths of No. 4 rebar and filled with concrete. Before the backhoe pushed the earth against the walls, the builders tarred the exterior of the block surface and laid on 15-pound felt and 4-mil polyethylene. In addition, they placed 4-inch-diameter plastic drain tile over a 4"-thick bed of gravel against the footers, and poured another eight inches of rock over the ABS pipe to prevent it from becoming plugged with mud.

Both 3" X 6" and 6" X 6" rough-sawed oak, hemlock pine, and white pine posts make up the second-story support framework, and angle braces are used to connect the posts to concrete block stands built up from the footers. The connecting beams are also 6" X 6" rough-sawed timbers, and are supported by both the 6"X 6" posts and the 3" X 6" boards that brace the gates.

The beams are tied to the posts with 1/4" X 6' X 18" steel plates and 1/2" bolts as well as by bolted 3" X 6" diagonal beams. Longer 3" X 6" diagonals also span the boxed-in sections at the open end of the building to add strength.

Sills were built on the 6" X 6" beams by nailing two 2" X 8"s together, and then toenailing the double boards on edge on top of the timbers. A pressure-treated 2" X 8" sill was then tied to the crest of the block wall to level things up for the addition of 2" X 8" floor joists on 16" centers.

Laying down the rough-cut 1" flooring on the framework presented quite a challenge since few of the boards were of the same width. To insure that the

spacing would work out correctly, the crew started laying the lumber in the center of the floor and worked to the edges across the 32' dimension. After every two feet of outward progress, the builders snapped a chalk line along the 45' dimension and ripped along the entire length to correct irregularities in width.

In order to get the greatest possible use from the loft, the roof was built as a free span, eliminating the need for interior roof-support posts. The 2" X 6" rafters were tied into the flooring and sills with spikes, and plates were wedged between them to provide additional support. The span itself is a self-supporting angled arch that consists of a 12-in-10 pitch proceeding up from the loft floor, and a 3-in-12 pitch finishing to the roof peak. A vent runs the length of the peak to help keep the loft from overheating or retaining too much moisture. The roofing material is galvanized metal, laid over 1" X 4" nailers running perpendicular to the rafters. The result is a truly spacious loft, 13' tall at its highest point.

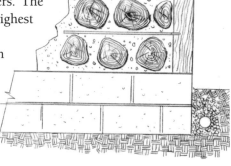

Finishing Touches: The construction crew closed in the ends of the loft with standard framing on 24" centers, using purlins 24" apart. Then the same 1" rough-cut lumber that made up the flooring was applied as siding. Generous double doors are centered in each end, but as a result of the earth berming, one loft door is at ground level to make

Foundation and Corner

bringing hay or other bulky, heavy material into the upper level easier. The other is at second-story height to facilitate loading material from the loft into a truck or wagon. A 16" X 72" tapered gable-end vent sits above each pair of doors and assures proper ventilation of the space.

To ease the job of getting feed downstairs to the barn's hungry clientele, a 29" X 30" trapdoor was cut into one corner of the loft floor. While bales of hay can be simply dropped through the opening, a ladder allows access from above to the feed room below.

The walls of the feed storage room and the milk room (as well as the partitions between stalls) are formed from stackwood set between the post-and-beam framing. The logs for the cordwood partitions were cut to 12" lengths at the site, and then carefully mortared into the spaces between the timbers. The stackwood walls enhance the building's appearance, and as they're constructed of firewood-length logs, there's no question that building them was inexpensive

A Bargain: About 5,000 board feet of lumber went into the barn, but

3,800 feet of it came from trees cut to make room for the structure. Thus, the bulk of the lumber was obtained for no more than the cutting fee charged by a local sawmill.

CHAPTER 4

჻

Growing Your Own Food

The Low-Labor Organic Garden

Raising vegetables can certainly help a family reduce its grocery costs, but planting and maintaining a natural, organic garden capable of providing food for several people calls for a heavy investment in time and labor. This demand can be held to a minimum and bountiful harvests can still be reaped by using proven labor reducing techniques including rotating the planting areas, mulching and tilling on a sensible schedule, choosing hardy and disease-resistant varieties, experimenting with companion planting, and encouraging natural controls for pest insects, disease, and weeds.

For Starters: You'll often find that as much time is spent preparing for a chore as completing it, so plan to have as large a garden as possible. The maximum size of a plot will be determined by the amount of sunny land available, the tools on hand, and the quantities of manure that can be obtained for fertilizer. A large garden allows room for nice, wide paths between a double-width row layout that provides built-in soil relief and easy crop rotation. Vegetables use lots of soil nutrients, and they grow especially vigorously in earth that has lain idle for a while. The paths between the crops should rest under a natural mulch one year and can be put into production the next.

A good-sized garden will also provide habitat for a variety of "good" insects, making it less likely that any one particular bug will become a problem. A diverse population of these small creatures in the garden will limit the chances of an infestation because the separate insect types will control each other. A productive and healthy organic garden is not insect-free but is a bal-

anced system in which the gardener works with, rather than against, the other creatures of the earth.

With plenty of space, more food than is needed will probably be grown, and there'll most likely be enough to feed you and your insect population, which means that you won't have to worry about their snacking.

Soil Nutrition: In order to produce a lot of food, the ground must receive a lot of food of its own—so feed the garden! In addition to the mulch and crop residues that should be worked into the earth, spread about an inch of chicken manure or four inches of cow manure on the soil every year and turn it under.

To get that plant food underground, the entire garden will need to be tilled-or turned by some other method at least twice in the spring and once in the fall. This may sound like a fair bit of heavy labor, but it's a fast way to kill weeds and to get organic matter into the soil. Also, by turning the soil this way, time-consuming composting won't even be necessary: spread vegetable wastes along with other mulch, and leave this until tilling time.

It's a good idea to grow a cover crop during the garden's fallow seasons. Buckwheat and annual rye both make good covers, because neither will develop a persistent root system or set seed before the first spring tilling. Such plants protect the soil from erosion in life and supply valuable green manure when tilled under.

When planning a low-labor, "minimum intervention" garden, it's important to concentrate on soil building. Plants grow faster and stronger, become more insect-resistant, and are better able to take care of themselves when they grow in healthy, humusy, fertile soil.

Choose and Plan Wisely: Taking into account which crops best suit the climate, choose disease resistant varieties whenever possible. Most seed catalogs note which varieties have a certain amount of built-in insect and disease resistance. With good soil and strong seed, the battle will be half won.

During each winter, draw up a garden chart for the following spring, and in this plan make certain that the crops are rotated from year to year. Even if a garden is quite small, the annual rotation of crops to new locations is very important, because diseases build up in soil and many insect eggs remain in the soil over the winter. Shifting the vegetables' positions at least keeps the diseases and varmints from multiplying to feast on their preferred host plants year after year.

Mixed Vegetables: Companion planting, another technique for warding off insect pests, should be kept in mind when drawing up a garden plan. The scents of some plants mask the insect-attracting odors of a neighboring cultivar; other plants actually repel insects. Rather than planting related vegetables such as cabbage, cauliflower, kale, and broccoli together, separate them with patches of onions, tomatoes, potatoes, and beets, which are unattractive to the bugs that consider the plants of the genus Brassica a delicacy.

Keeping Seeds

Nature endows seeds with varying degrees of viability—from two to six years for most common garden vegetable seeds. The following list gives the years you can keep home-raised seed and be sure it will grow.

Gather seed when fully field-dry. Separate from pods, leaves, and other chaff. Store in paper (not plastic) bags in a cool, dry place. A refrigerator is ideal.

Note that purchased seed packets read "Packed for (year)." This doesn't mean that they are fresh this year, but that they are young enough to sprout at acceptable rates. Brand-name seed will be freshest; off-brand and bargain-priced seed is generally at the end of its "shelf-life."

To save, be sure seeds bought are dry, and store in their packets in a cool dry place.

Subtract one year from the following to determine best storage periods for purchased seeds. ■

Years to Keep	Varieties (in families)
6	Beets
	Cucumbers
	Tomatoes
5	Sweet Corn
4	Broccoli, Brussels Sprouts, Cabbage, Cauliflower, Eggplant
	Squash and Pumpkins
3	Beans
	Spinach
	Peas
2	Carrots
	Onions

Marigolds are particularly beneficial throughout the garden both as general soil conditioners and because of their strong insect-repelling odor. Nasturtiums, basil, parsley, summer savory, and sweet marjoram act in the same manner.

Planting Time: Sowing the garden as late in the season as possible increases the number of times that weed seed can sprout and be tilled under before the seeds are in the ground. This will reduce the amount of painstaking hoeing around each young vegetable plant later in the year. While it might take only about two hours to till an entire half-acre, it can take about two days to hand-cultivate around the plants in a plot that size.

Plan to turn the soil once as soon as it becomes workable in the spring. Then wait about two weeks for a good flush of weeds to appear and till the plot again. If it's possible to wait a week or more before planting the seeds, till the soil a third time. The delay will pay off in the long run and save hours of hand weeding and hoeing. The repeated tillings will also expose most of the cutworms that have wintered over in the soil so your songbird allies can get them.

A relatively late planting could make it difficult to grow such cool weather crops as lettuce unless plenty of mulch is applied. A good organic ground covering will keep the soil cool and moist, build fertility and humus as it's turned under from year to year, and shade out most of the weeds that survive the spring tilling.

Cool-weather crops and root vegetables should be mulched to within a few inches of the seeds as soon as they're planted. Squash, corn, tomatoes, beans, and other hot-weather crops should not be mulched until the soil has warmed up considerably. It's also a good idea to mulch the garden's paths even more thickly than the rows. Heap the organic matter on the paths to a good foot deep.

Even after these many preparations, which will insure that your vegetables have all the growing advantages you can give them, there's still going to be the problem of dealing with the weeds and bugs that remain. Also, the newer a garden is to organic culture, the more uninvited plants and insects you should expect.

However, much of the remaining control work can be done by wild animal "helpers." To keep the problems in hand, just call on toads, birds, and, if possible, chickens. It won't take much to attract the assistants to the garden, and by harvest time your efforts will have been paid back many times over. A single toad will eat up to ten pounds of insects during one season, and snails, slugs, and cutworms are among this amphibian's favorite treats.

It's easy to get a few toads to take up residence in the garden: sink a small water-filled tub in the ground, and near its rim place a few upside-down flowerpot caves with entrances chipped in their bottom rims. A sticky-tongued midnight pest patrol will move right in.

Wild birds will help control insects during the day. They'll eat just about any bug that moves. To attract them, provide nesting sites and water. A stream is best, but a small birdbath will do if it's kept really clean. Birdhouses can be put up when there's not much natural shelter nearby. The backyard songsters will also need high places to perch near the vegetable patch. Garden fenceposts make great lookout towers for insect-hunting birds, and a few tall poles set among the rows will provide similar vantage points.

Poultry: Chickens are birds of a different feather. They're great weeders and cultivators and will eat grubs, ants, and worms. However, they can be too thorough at scratching and cultivating if they're not controlled. If let into the garden early in the season, hens may well wipe out all the newly sprouted seedlings.

When the crops are well along, chickens can be a real asset. Their soil scratching will control weeds. They are efficient and methodical insect hunters. Plus, they'll eat your household food scraps and provide wholesome fresh eggs in return for the privilege of sharing your garden. The biddies will even supply fertilizer while they work.

Even city dwellers may be able to keep some chickens if local ordinances permit. If a small flock is allowed, city ordinances usually specify that premises must be maintained in clean and sanitary condition. A call to the local health department can determine whether raising these birds is permissible.

Savings: Even with these gardening methods, raising a successful vegetable crop will require hours outdoors spent spading the beds, tilling the soil, and sowing the seed. But cooperating with nature rather than spraying harsh chemicals everywhere will produce a more abundant yield and still save a great deal of time so you can pursue those other pleasant summertime activities.

Finding Garden Space in the City

Urban gardening is as old as city living itself, and now, more than ever, it's an essential practice for city dwellers who want to retain a link with nature and save money by growing some of their food.

By the year 2000, more than half of the planet's population could be concentrated in metropolitan centers. Much of the developing world is wisely turning to urban agriculture, aquaculture, and small-scale energy production as a way to recover the value of the cities' vast discards and to cope with burgeoning populations. Americans, especially, despite our "use it up, throw it away, and buy a new one" cultural conditioning are looking anew at urban detritus (organic wastes, recyclable building materials, and unused space) and discovering fresh ways to use it productively.

What city gardeners lack in the way of ready-to-use soil, panoramic landscapes, and unobstructed sunlight, they make up for in resourcefulness, persistence, humor, and the satisfaction of making the concrete desert bloom. The fact that plump cabbages and dazzling dahlias can be successfully nurtured amidst traffic and towering buildings is enough to make any city gardener believe that with a few basic horticultural techniques and a little specialized know-how, great things are indeed possible.

Site Selection: All gardens, no matter where they are, need sun, water, and fertile soil. The differences between a rural and an urban vegetable patch are, in fact, largely superficial. A "back 40" could be a row of old dresser drawers filled with soil, and the first spadeful of city soil could unearth only rusty nails, broken glass, and other archaeological evidence of your metropolitan forebears. Perhaps the backyard measures only 7' X 7' with trash cans on half of it and laundry flapping overhead. So what? City growers must seek new definitions of the word "garden." Look around. Does your building have south-, east-, or west-facing walls? A flat roof? Sunny windowsills? An exposed porch? Does a neighbor have such spaces to share in exchange for fresh produce? Is there a vacant lot nearby or an unused corner of a local park that united efforts could turn into a community garden?

Finding a site that gives you everything you want may be impossible, but you can begin with what you have. You'll be amazed at what you can do with a less than perfect location.

Sunlight: At least some solar exposure is essential for growing food. In examining a potential garden, keep in mind that the sun shines from the south, that it is highest and casts fewest shadows in the summer, and that most herbs, flowers, and fruiting crops such as squash, cucumbers, and tomatoes do best with a minimum of eight hours of daily direct sunlight throughout the growing season. Anything tall (such as a tree) on the south side of a garden will cast a shadow all day long, and anything on the east or west will do so in the morning and afternoon respectively.

Be ruthless in making an evaluation. You can adjust your garden's design to the path of the sun, but the sun and the buildings that may block its rays aren't equally flexible. Wishful thinking will not convince tomatoes to grow without adequate sunlight. While vegetables such as lettuce, chard, and spinach can grow in partial shade, a garden must get some sun.

Adequate Water: Generally, city gardeners are close to a source of piped-in water. Those who aren't, like many farmers, must rely on rainwater, which can be collected in barrels or steel drums located beneath downspouts. Rainwater can also be conserved in the soil by mulching heavily (don't use an impervious material such as matted leaves, however). Another possibility is to use plastic jugs to bring water from some other site to the garden patch.

With access to an outside faucet, you can save labor and money by using a drip irrigation system, either a commercial sort (such as a perforated "trickle hose") or something along the lines of a system invented in Boston, which uses plastic jugs with pinholes burned into their bottoms. The containers are set, bottom down, among the plants at two-foot intervals and filled with water and liquid fertilizer or manure tea once a week or so.

Unfortunately for urban gardens, city water has usually been treated with "purifying" chemicals that kill virtually all bacteria, including the kinds that break down organic material into plant nutrients. Letting such water stand before using it gives volatile chemicals a chance to evaporate. Take care to empty the containers often, however, because mosquitoes breed in stagnant water.

An Indoor Garden

For small-scale hydroponics, conventional indoor gardening or starting seedlings in the spring, you'll need a way to suspend a light source over your growing trays. The light fixture must be height-adjustable to illuminate different sized plants and be easily raised as seedlings grow.

You can buy multi-tiered "starting batteries" with lights built-in, but the frames are rickety and the plastic growing trays are flimsy. They are expensive too—really expensive—and better suited to hold a few African violets in some suburban entry way than to start a big garden supply of broccoli and tomato plants on a self-sufficient farmstead. Plus, fiddling with the hidden hold-on bolts to adjust the lights takes teenie-tiny fingers, and its all too easy drop the heavy lights on your seedlings.

Here's a plan for a seed-starter/ indoor-garden that is straight-forward, usable by any sized hands, and is built as strong as a house. Indeed, it is made from 2 x 4s and plywood—the same materials used to frame a new home.

Build yours of thinner, stronger, and more elegant hardwood if you like—say, 5/4" x 6" maple instead of 2 x 4s. Or, make verticals of 6" strips of 3/4" A/B exterior-grade plywood, or bang the whole thing together from coarse framing lumber. What's important is that it fits the area available for indoor gardening.

While brand-name grow-lights provide the full spectrum and theoretically perform better than standard fluorescent, they cost three times as much (and don't grow three times better seedlings). Plain bulbs will do the job, and a secondhand lamp such as a 48",

(continued on page 91)

Once you begin gardening, you'll probably notice a gradual change in your perspective on weather. On rainy days, when non-gardeners stomp around under their umbrellas and mutter to each other about how awful and wet it is, you'll find yourself feeling grateful for the raindrops trickling down to your plants' thirsty roots.

Soil Considerations: Before doing anything about the soil (or lack thereof), you should consider the possibility of lead contamination. Lead, a toxic heavy metal that even in small quantities can cause serious and irreparable damage, especially to young children, has contaminated soils throughout residential areas of the United States. It's particularly concen-

twin-element ceiling unit can often be found at surplus or purchased inexpensively.

The lamp should be kept two or three inches above the soil-filled flats or tops of just-emerging seedlings, and operated for 12 hours a day. Seedlings should be in full dark the rest of the day to adjust to the day's growth. As the plants grow, the lights should be raised to maintain a 3" to 4" distance above the growing foliage.

Heating cable units can be put on the base for starting and growing tomatoes and other plants that like warm feet.

If seedlings grow at different heights, put blocks under the shorter flats lest they get "leggy" from straining too hard at a light too far away.

A plant-healthful addition is a conventional incandescent lamp or a gro-lamp that can be moved around the plants, adding full-spectrum light. If you have a photographer's light meter, use it to place the gro-lamp so that its light is about the same level as the flourescent's. ■

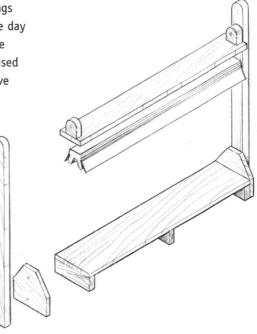

trated in older neighborhoods where lead-based paint has been routinely scraped off the exteriors of houses prior to the application of a new coat and then left on the ground.

The local Environmental Protection Agency office, the extension service in your area, or a local laboratory may be able to test your soil for toxic minerals. In any case, keep in mind a few basic facts: any wooden house built before lead was banned in exterior house paints is likely to have some lead-contaminated soil around it out to about 10 feet from the edges of the structure with the greatest concentration nearest the building. The older the home, the higher the level of lead is likely to be. And remember, too, that the poison will be primarily in the top three inches of soil, because lead tends not to leach deeply into the earth.

Therefore, if the only available space for planting vegetables is close to an older house and, especially if you have children under the age of six, remove the top three inches of soil from around the building and treat the material as a hazardous waste. Keep in mind that fuel-lead contamination can also occur near heavy traffic, particularly within 100 feet of a street, and in rubble containing the paint from the walls (exterior and interior) of demolished buildings. Heartbreaking as it is (especially if your soil is otherwise ideal), heavily tainted earth should be thrown out or used only for growing ornamentals. If necessary, you can purchase topsoil in bulk from a supplier (look in the Yellow Pages) and have it trucked in.

Soil Improvement and the Mud-Pie Factor: Assuming that you've found poor to average soil among the buried treasures in your backyard, your next step is to improve its quality. This you will do by adding "soil amendments." The amending process varies from individual to individual and is largely dependent on how that person went about making mud pies as a child.

If, say, you're neither squeamish nor broke and never much cared for mud-pie making, chances are you'll go to a garden store and buy fancy bagged amendments labeled "composted cow manure" and "bone meal," for example. If you're squeamish but somewhat less well off, you can compost leaves and organic kitchen wastes such as vegetable trimmings, coffee grounds, and egg shells (avoid meat and fish, though, because they attract rodents). If, regardless of your income, you're not squeamish and loved concocting exotic mud pies in your youth, you may develop an outright fervor for composting and building up soil.

Enthusiastic urban composters and soil amenders have been known to ferret out such obscure sources of organic wastes as spoiled bean sprouts, hair clippings from barber shops, and leather dust from shoe factories. Those individuals view their urban surroundings as a veritable treasure trove of organic riches. Truly passionate urban composters can be observed shuttling back and forth between their gardens and the local police stables or the municipal zoo on weekends, and they can also be seen tirelessly toting bulging plastic bags of leaves and grass clippings from suburban lawns, pine needles from the woods, and dripping seaweed from the beach. These people don't take trips out of the city…they make hunting forays. There are many methods for making and using compost, and you'll find an explanation of most of them in any good gardening book. If you don't have room for the usual compost piles, however, try this technique: First, dig a knee-deep hole the size of a standard door. Then fill it halfway with well-mixed compostables and put the soil back in the cavity on top of the material. If you have any finished compost or a bagged soil amendment, combine it with several inches of dried grass clippings, hay, straw, or shredded leaves. To plant seeds or seedlings, just make a hole or furrow in the mulch.

Garden Design: Whether you like tidy, weedless rows of vegetables or a somewhat more overgrown and cluttered look, you'll need to do some planning in order to make the most of available space and solar exposure.

First, measure your chosen location and draw a map of it to scale. Note the locations of trees, fences, or adjacent buildings, and be sure to take into account the areas of the plot that do and do not receive direct sun.

Now, think about the kinds of things you'd like in your garden: Do you want benches to sit on...paths to stroll...a toolshed...compost bins...a cold frame? Whatever you decide, make and cut out scale drawings of the items, so that you can arrange them as you wish on your map and get a bird's-eye view of the various design possibilities.

For growing vegetables, intensive raised-bed gardening will give the biggest yields in the smallest space. A series of 3' X 6' plots positioned in the sunniest part of the garden makes a good arrangement. Use less-exposed areas for seating or sheds and for shade-tolerant plants. Try to position tall botanicals (corn, sunflowers, pole beans, dwarf fruit trees) on the north side of the garden where they won't shade other plants. If you can't find a suitable place for a particular crop, look for a reasonable substitute that you can grow. For example, your plot may not have enough exposed space to support fruit trees, which must have lots of sun, but you can almost certainly find enough room somewhere for a few raspberry or blueberry bushes.

Do take advantage of vertical growing space: sunny walls, fences, and even lampposts will support climbing vines such as beans, peas, or morning glories. A tree or post makes a fine place to hang baskets of strawberry plants, and you can espalier fruit trees and grow them flat against a trellised wall or fence.

Because city gardens may be the exception instead of the rule in your neighborhood, residents and other passersby will naturally want to see (and maybe even taste) its bounty. You can avoid unnecessary self-torment by resisting inbred territorial urges from the start and viewing your garden more communally: as a gift of sorts to the neighborhood. Be generous within reason, unless your conscientious work is being undone by the inconsiderate or destructive behavior of others, of course. Plant cherry tomatoes, grapes, or raspberries along the sidewalk edge of your garden and encourage people to sample the fruit in season. Or sow morning glories, which are strikingly beautiful (and bountiful), to twine along an exterior fence for everyone to enjoy. Help your neighbors up and down the street start their own gardens and flower beds, too. Gardening can be contagious.

Generally, vandalism and theft are not much of a problem. In fact, they're almost nonexistent in gardens (whether in front of private homes or in public housing developments) that have become a source of pride in the community. In town-bound agriculture, neighborliness plays a very important role!

The Bucket Garden

An apartment gardener, living many stories above the ground, can raise enough food on the edge of a 30' balcony to equal the produce from a 6' X 20' country garden. The setup costs little more than the price of the seeds, doesn't drip or damage the decking, and can be tended in the little time left at the end of a long work day. Hard to believe maybe, but it's been proven.

Container Gardening: The obvious alternative to hauling numerous loads of soil and lumber up to an apartment, perhaps many stories high, is to grow crops in containers. This option presents two notable problems: drainage and weight.

It's important to avoid using any kind of open drainage system at the base of balcony plant boxes because of the mess and the possible rotting of the deck floor, to say nothing of complaints from neighbors below! Also, hot-weather wilt is a major drawback to gardening in drained containers. At temperatures above 95°F, large plants in these vessels, though thoroughly watered in the morning, can be severely dehydrated by midafternoon. Vessels with no drainage, on the other hand, can hold water in reserve that will carry the plant over a two- or three-day period, which allows the owner to leave for a weekend and find the garden still thriving upon his or her return.

For containers without drain holes, a special planting medium is needed: something spongelike to hold water so that it doesn't pool in the bottom of the planter, drowning the roots. This problem occurs routinely in drainless containers filled with soil as the only medium. Even good soil is heavy, and in pots or planters it usually settles and hardens into a brick mass that discourages root growth. The perfect nutrient system (soft, lightweight, and inexpensive) is a mass of leaves. And as these naturally occurring premixed packages of trace minerals and plant residue decay, they support a variety of microorganisms essential to plant growth and health. The gardener needs only to add water, fertilizer, and seed. Nature does the rest! Besides, leaves are free for the raking from parks and lots all over the city. In many neighborhoods, they're bagged and sitting by the roadside, waiting to be carted away.

Leaves at Work: To set up a bucket garden that will be roughly equal to a 6' X 20' plot, you'll need a large load of fallen leaves, four gallons of potting soil mix, about 20 nonmetallic, light-colored, drainless containers (plastic paint cans, polystyrene foam coolers, trash cans, baby baths, or wooden boxes, buckets, or tubs), a water source, and a variety of seeds. Try one package each of tomatoes, carrots, squash, radishes, lettuce, pole beans, a cole such as cauliflower or broccoli, and two packages of snow peas. Climate and season may dictate starting seeds indoors and later transplanting the seedlings to outdoor planters. Egg cartons or shallow, plastic-lined cardboard boxes can serve nicely as seed flats. If indoor space and light are inadequate for such flats, consider purchasing nursery-started plants for some or all of the crops.

Select a sheltered space that receives at least three hours of direct sun each day. Then fill the assorted containers with well-packed leaves, water them (using 1/4 gallon of water per gallon of container volume), and repack with leaves as needed. Add a commercial fertilizer, fish emulsion, or packaged cow manure in amounts appropriate to the size of the container.

Cover the surface of the packed leaf layer in each container with three inches of potting soil or humus. Plant most of the buckets with a variety of vegetables and flowers, and make two other "quick crop" containers for fast-growing vegetables such as lettuce, radishes, and peas. Keep soil surfaces slightly damp until the young plants grow to be about five inches tall.

Tending the Bountiful Bucketfuls: To help determine moisture requirements as plants become established, insert a pointed wooden stick in each container and leave it there. When the stake is dark and wetly glistening from one to four inches above the soil, moisture conditions are perfect. If drippiness occurs along the stick as far as five inches above the soil's surface, excess water is present and must be poured out. Dried-out, whitish patches on the stake indicate a need for water. (A rule of thumb: Full-grown plants require about a gallon of water per container every other day.)

Because a bucket garden has a limited amount of soil from which to draw nutrients, fertilize vegetables and flowers as heavily as possible. If green leaves wilt or shrivel, the plant food is too concentrated. If older leaves turn pale or yellow and if growth slows down, more nitrogen is needed.

High-rise horticulturists seldom have serious garden infestation problems. Nematodes and cutworms are precluded because of the use of dried leaves and sterile potting mixtures, and any insects that do appear are usually predatory and pollinating types attracted by the fragrant flowers, dense cover, and colorful variety.

When bucket plants grow to four or five inches tall, thin a single container's contents to three of the healthiest bean plants, three of the best peas, and two of the most vigorous tomatoes. When tomatoes reach 10" in height, thin them to one per container. Most plants can be allowed to grow naturally; only those that intrude on a deck's or balcony's walking space need staking.

As quick-growing crops reach maturity and are harvested, replant the container. By successive planting, you can harvest fresh produce throughout the growing season and achieve high yields. From a five-gallon plastic paint bucket, you might expect, for example, several bowls of leaf lettuce, two heads of lettuce, 35 snow peas, 20 pole beans, four radishes, 25 tomatoes, and two carrots!

So, enjoy the success to be had with the foliage method for superb plant production in buckets or other containers. As the handsome leaves and flowering vines of beans and squash trail graceful along railings, and lovely white pea blossoms alternate with the bright green of ruffled lettuce and the red orange of decorative tomatoes, you can reap a bounty not only of food but of beauty.

Biodynamic/French-Intensive Gardening

Maximizing the crop yield for a given amount of space has long been a necessity in many countries in the world and is a desirable goal for many North Americans who must plant their gardens in limited areas or in places where poor soil makes cultivating large plots economically prohibitive. Biodynamic/French-intensive gardening is a method that combines the economic use of space characteristic of the gardening practices found in turn-of-the-century France with the Biodynamic theories developed by Rudolf Steiner in the early 1900s in Austria.

The techniques were demonstrated in 1966 in California by Alan Chadwick, an English horticulturist, and were later subjected to careful testing and modification by John Jeavons of Ecology Action of Mid-Peninsula in Stanford, California, in an effort to produce the optimum yield from the smallest possible space. Yields on a per-acre basis of between four and six times the national average have been obtained, and in rare cases, gardens have recorded yields of 31 times the national average for a given space. The system uses no fuel-requiring tools, no toxic pesticides, and no highly processed chemical fertilizers. It improves the soil with each crop grown and requires only a hundredth as much energy and an eighth as much water as does commercial agriculture.

How It Is Done: The goal of the Biodynamic/French-intensive method is to help the gardener produce as many healthy plants as possible on a given piece of land. The raised beds that are characteristic of such gardens serve several purposes. Since the growing areas are wider than are "normal" garden rows (approximately five feet, which still allows the gardener to reach plants in the middle without stepping on and compacting the soil in the bed), less space is needed for walkways. The rectangular beds are raised 4 to 10 inches above the original ground level, and their edges are angled at a 45° slope, which provides more surface area than if the same piece of ground were left flat.

Most important of all, the beds are double dug to a depth of two feet. Because of the resulting deep cushion of well-worked soil, plants have less trouble sending their tiny root hairs down to gather in the water and the nutrition supplied by compost, ashes, bonemeal, and other such organic plant foods that are necessary to grow healthy, insect-resistant, nutritious, delicious vegetables.

Double Digging

Remove top 12 inches of soil

1'

5'

Mix topsoil with compost

Loosen subsoil and mix with compost

2'

Add mix and form raised bed

The arrangement of the plants in the bed is also a bit unusual. The seeds or flat-started seedlings are placed in such a way that the foliage of each mature plant will just barely touch that of all its neighbors, creating a living mulch, which keeps weeds down, helps moderate the swings of soil temperature, and improves the bed's ability to retain water. Close-quarters planting is another reason for the gardening technique's incredible yields.

It's difficult to give a rule of thumb for plant placement in a Biodynamic/French-intensive bed. The spacings recommended on seed packets will often work out well, since the plants grown this way tend to spread farther than their conventionally raised cousins.

Of course, a technique that can enable an average homeowner to raise an abundant crop in a small backyard involves more than merely digging beds deeply and planting vegetables close together. Further preparation of the soil includes [1] the use of a specially prepared compost that has aged for at least three months and consists by weight of one-third dry vegetation, one-third wet vegetation or kitchen scraps including bones (but not meat), and one-third earth, [2] an organic fertilization program specifically designed to meet the needs of each crop, and [3] daily light waterings with special hose nozzles and cans that simulate the fall of rain.

Companion Planting: The way in which the growing space is used is at least as important to successful Biodynamic/French-intensive gardening as the preparation of the soil. Vegetable types are grouped together in single beds or, if the garden is a large one, in groups of adjoining beds according to compatibility.

Biodynamic/French-intensive gardeners believe that different plants grown in proximity affect each other in a number of ways. For example, the vegetables must be placed with a regard for physical compatibility: A slow-growing variety shouldn't be planted where it will soon be overshadowed by a rapidly maturing plant.

But companion planting goes far beyond such common sense dictums. Certain vegetables, flowers, and herbs are actually mutually beneficial when grown together, helping eliminate each other's insect pests, and even influencing the quality of each other's produce. For example, when planted near beans, potatoes can be very helpful in controlling the Mexican bean beetle, and Bibb lettuce will taste better if it's grown in companionship with spinach.

In order to make the most efficient use of both garden space and growing season, gardeners using this method also practice succession planting, a kind of companion planting in time, or a short-term, small-scale form of crop rotation. This practice allows the grower's plot to yield the greatest possible amount of produce.

A significant aspect of succession planting as practiced by Biodynamic/French-intensive gardeners is the alternation of plants that are heavy feeders (such as corn, cucurbits, and tomatoes), which take large quantities of nutrients from the soil, with varieties that contribute to the soil (such as nitrogen-fixing legumes, including peas and beans). The contributors return to the soil some of the nutrients that have been removed by previous plantings.

Planning for any garden should start long before the first warm days of spring beckon one outdoors. With proper planning, a Biodynamic/French-intensive bed only 5' wide and 20" long can yield a full year's supply of vegetables for one person.

Magic in the Cole-Crop Patch

Most gardeners know how to trick broccoli into producing more than one crop. After the main head develops, don't pull the plant, but remove the green curds with only a little stem attached. Most strains will develop three to five side shoots that, bunched together, are as ample—and every bit as scrumptious and super-healthful—as the first cutting. But, if you get your seedlings going extra early, such strains as old-time Walt ham will even produce a third—and sometimes a fourth and fifth—cutting of little Brussels-sprouts-sized miniheads that grow tight to the stem.

What's less well-known is that you can have a second crop from your cabbage plants as well. It's easy. If you cut the whole stem, the stubble will wither quickly and die. So, when you harvest the main cabbage head, leave a rosette of big, spreading bottom leaves to constitute a viable plant.

To harvest the first head, pull down all the large, open leaves till you expose a nice, tightly wrapped cabbage. Then insert a sharp knife into the stem at the bottom of the head to be removed. Cut down at an angle and saw the blade around in a circle to make a cone-shaped cutout in the middle of the stem. Hold lower leaves tight with one hand and twist the head with the other to remove it. (Sometimes this takes two people.)

Now, make believe that the strange, empty-looking green dish that remains is a new plant. Treat it like one by cultivating shallowly, watering, and working some rich manure into the first inch of soil around the base (be careful not to injure the weak and very shallow roots).

Soon small sprouts will form around the rim of the main head stub. Continue to treat the plant with care, and in time these little offshoots will grow to the size of a fist. There may be as many as six second-crop cabbages per plant, and together they'll provide almost as much food value as the big main head did...but with a delightful difference. The interior is loose—more like leaf lettuce than hard cabbage—and the cores of these little cabbages will be pale green and deliciously tender. The outer leaves will be darker green, but the whole plant will be tender and tasty.

Green Tomatoes

In the fall of every year nearly every vegetable garden contains a long, sad row of tomato plants, still staked, but with once-lush foliage drooping and burned from frost and garlands of green tomatoes sagging on the vines. Some years, an early frost will catch a majority of the late crop.

Such waste of nature's provender and loss of juicy tang and Vitamin C-rich tomato goodness is needless. Every tomato grower should have a way to protect tomatoes from first frost until well into the fall. Long plastic tunnels on wire hoops or individual domes can be made or purchased at reasonable cost.

But even with the best of late-season care, many plants will sport sub-ripe fruit in varying stages of development when days become too short and sun too low to provide ripening-power. That's the time to harvest the green fruit...before frost has a chance to burn the skins of fruit, killing areas that will soften and admit rot organisms.

Harvest only fruit with mature seeds that have entered the ripening phase and show at least a tinge of yellow.

(continued on page 101)

The small size and fine quality of the mini-coles make them especially suitable for Chinese stir-frying, delicately steamed single-servings, or adding to soups and stews a few seconds before serving. (If you harvest in the late fall when the first chill winds are blowing, the leaves will sweeten, making them wonderful in soup.)

Some gardeners claim that harvesting cauliflower the same way as cabbage (not easy because of its short stem) will produce a ring of mini-cauli-heads. No harm in trying it yourself.

These feats of cole-crop magic aren't difficult to perform, and they can double your Brassica yield.

Dead-green fruit will never ripen. But pick all fruit that have grown large enough that they are not rock-hard if you are a green-tomato pickle relish fan.

Do not bruise the green fruit. The best technique is to snip the stems with pruners and place picked fruit one-layer-thick in a box filled with straw. Discard (or plan to use immediately) any that are discolored or evidence bug or mouse nibbles. Inspect for bug eggs.

Bring fruit in the house and place in a single layer on a fluffed straw bed in a bright, cool place. An enclosed back porch is ideal. The straw will let air circulate under the fruit, evaporating moisture that would encourage rot if trapped between fruit and a solid surface.

Turn fruit every few days.

The tomatoes will ripen gradually so long as the process was well underway to begin with. Use the ripest first—placing the two or three ripest on a bright windowsill to turn bright red. Don't let them overheat in the sun. Behind window glass, in still air and lacking the shade they had on the vine, they will heat enough to cook—killing ripening enzymes. From then on ripening becomes rot. Sugars will quickly turn to vinegar. Little black vinegar flies will arrive, and the fruit is ruined.

Some fruit will resist ripening. These should be placed along with an old apple in a clear plastic bag. Keep in the light. The apple will produce ethylene gas as it begins to decompose. This natural gas will encourage the tomatoes to ripen uniformly (it is the way commercial growers "ripen" the tomatoes they pick when mature but not soft or red.)

Some gardeners leave tomatoes in the gas treatment till they are used. Others find that the fruit can be transferred to a windowsill and will ripen fully. ■

A Desert-Town Patio Garden

Even if your garden space is limited to a little fenced-in plot behind an apartment, you can enjoy plenty of freshly grown produce for the table. A minimum of tillable ground did not deter a Tucson, Arizona, couple whose backyard was only 15' X 29 in area—about a quarter of that paved with concrete and much of the rest lost to a path leading to the electric meter.

The minuscule yard was flanked by a tall wooden privacy fence on three sides and a high building wall on the fourth. And, each day the enclosure received only a few hours of scorching desert sun, which seemed more likely to burn the plants than nourish them.

The native flora in the tiny patio's parched soil consisted of a few especially stubborn weeds, which the couple pulled up and stuffed into the open spaces under the fence to form a crude retaining wall. They hoped this dike would deter drying winds to help keep desperately needed water in the garden space. Once that was done, the path to the meter was outlined with discarded bricks, and the rest of the earth inside the fence was dug to a depth or 8" or 10".

The soil was rich, but it packed down quickly. In order to keep the sun-baked earth loose, the couple mixed in 10 cubic feet of peat moss. Where the patio sloped up to the far-back corner, they built terraces with small clay walls to help hold the precious, life-giving water.

From Plan to Plants: With everything ready for planting and with space allotted for various plants, six hybrid tomato seedlings were set out in the area between the path and the house, which received direct sunlight from 10 a.m. until noon. A few mint sprigs and some purple and blue violets went in as a border. The very back corner of the patio was sunny from noon until 3 p.m., so that part became the cornfield with hills 15 inches apart in three rows. Four mounds of yellow squash, two rows of beets, and a patch of lettuce and parsley rounded out the vegetable section. Near the end of the yard, they planted pansies and marigolds in a small plot surrounded by water-saving dikes. White clover provided ground cover over the remaining barren spots and served to replenish the nitrogen in the soil at the same time.

Waste Not, Want Not: The yard didn't provide sufficient space for a compost pile, but as the plants grew, they received a mulch of clippings from the apartment lawns, with vegetable and fruit peels, coffee grounds, tea leaves, and other kitchen scraps added. This waste soon crumbled in the desert sun and was mixed into the soil, preventing odor and pest problems in the process.

Pouring dishwater and wash water into the garden helped reduce the amount of irrigation necessary, and though the soil still needed to be soaked thoroughly three times a week, the series of little dikes and canals reduced the runoff and captured every possible drop of precious moisture during the rare Tucson rain showers.

Surprisingly, insects didn't prove to be a problem at all. Occasional aphids were washed off the plants with soapy dishwater, inchworms were squashed, and tomato worms snipped in two with shears. The bug control program was simplified, thanks to a large number of praying mantises and desert lizards that took up residence on the patio.

Sweet Rewards: Although the small garden didn't provide all the vegetables needed, the couple was more than happy with the results. They harvested over 75 juicy, red fruits from the tomato plants, and the parsley and mint were so profuse that some was dried for winter use. The corn yielded a couple of sweet ears per plant, after which the stalks were pulled up and zinnias planted in the space. The lettuce lasted until late June, when the blistering Arizona summer heat finally killed it. The squash produced abundantly throughout the hot weather, and the couple was eating beets well into the winter.

In addition to the fresh vegetables, the patio garden provided many lovely flowers. The violets bloomed early in the spring, the pansies from March to late June, and the marigolds and zinnias from early June until late fall. By the time the pansies had finished flowering, sunflower, millet, kafir, corn, and other seeds that birds had scattered from the bird feeder were already up and growing. The couple permitted these "weeds" to flourish for their moisture-conserving mulch value and also because Nature "plants" species that best aid the soil. As the native grains matured, they enjoyed the antics of migrating finches as they fed from the tops of swaying stalks.

When plants died or finished bearing, they were pulled up and returned to the soil. Organic matter from the kitchen, plus a little dried manure, was added throughout the winter, and the following spring more peat moss was dug in.

When the garden was begun, not a single earthworm could be found in the dry, hard ground, but just 12 months later every shovelful of soil was rich with the squirming, helpful little creatures.And thanks to these natural composters, the second year's garden was even more lush and productive than the first had been.

Gardening Without Soil

Growing plants without soil is known as hydroponics, a food production system in which plants live with roots suspended in a nutrient-rich water bath or an inert substance rather than soil. In view of the world's eroding crop soils, urban encroachment on open lands, diminishing natural resources, and increasing human population, hydroponics may be the gardening system of the future. And for the urban dweller or small-scale gardener with little space and time to maintain a conventional vegetable patch, this essentially soil-less method may be the key to raising a wider variety of plants and harvesting greater yields.

Hydroponics isn't a new concept, but because of its particular advantages, growers are continually experimenting with improved techniques. Most of the current systems, resulting from research in plant chemistry, use water or an inert medium (such as perlite, vermiculite, gravel, sand, pumice, peat, or even sawdust) to which a nutrient formula is added. The solution must provide all of the vital elements that would usually be provided by a well-prepared soil bed.

Exaggerated Claims: When hydroponics first came to the attention of the media, overzealous proponents of the idea including many garden writers and the distributors of commercially manufactured equipment claimed that such water-culture gardens could produce yields 15 times greater than those of "normal" plots, bring plants to maturity 30% faster, use only 10% of the water and fertilizer required by crops grown in soil, and allow a considerable saving of space without a comparable loss in produce. Because the claims were greatly exaggerated, and many hydroponic greenhouses subsequently failed, home gardeners became justifiably skeptical.

Despite exaggerated or poor press, however, hydroponics can offer several advantages to the home horticulturist: complete fertilization control, utilization of small areas, a yield approximately one and a half times greater than a comparable soil-based space/light/nutrient mix, and the elimination of guesswork regarding moisture requirements. Most important, hydroponics makes it possible to grow plants anywhere light and warmth are adequate, such as on rooftops, windowsills, or parking lots. Even basements can become impressively productive garden spots if supplemental lighting is provided.

Homemaid Beauties: There are quite a few hydroponic outfits on the market, but many people prefer to build a setup with their own hands. For these intrepid souls, there's a wide variety of simple do-it-yourself hydroponic designs and system-components to choose from. The development of lightweight plastics has made it possible to avoid the high construction cost associated with earlier concrete-bed systems, and newly available small pumps, time clocks, and solenoid valves allow today's units to be almost completely automated.

No matter what type of system you design or buy, though, it must: [1] provide support for your plants, [2] allow for the proper distribution of nutrients, and [3] give adequate aeration to the roots. Hydroponic systems fall into one of two broad categories: those in which the nutrient solution is stored "standing," below the growing medium, and those in which the solution flows constantly or at regular intervals through the medium.

Of the standing solution types, the wick systems are probably best for small-area, low-work setups. In this design, the nutrient solution stands in a container directly beneath the growing medium and is drawn up through wicks made of cotton, glass, wool, or the like. (This method is similar in operation to the familiar clay pot and gravel-filled saucer arrangement.) A simple unit could consist of little more than a trough of nutrient covered by a lid or shelf with several holes in it. The wicks are presoaked and run from the solution up through the lid holes. Then the wicks' ends are frayed open, and a seedling in its starter cube is set on top of each one. Every two weeks or so, the nutrient formula will need to be changed, but otherwise the system is virtually maintenance-free. This design is most suitable for small containers such as pots, hanging baskets, window boxes, or pans not exceeding 6' X 2' X 2' in size. Unfortunately, this method doesn't supply the nutrient fast enough to satisfy large plants or those with lush foliage.

Tabletop Hydroponic Systems

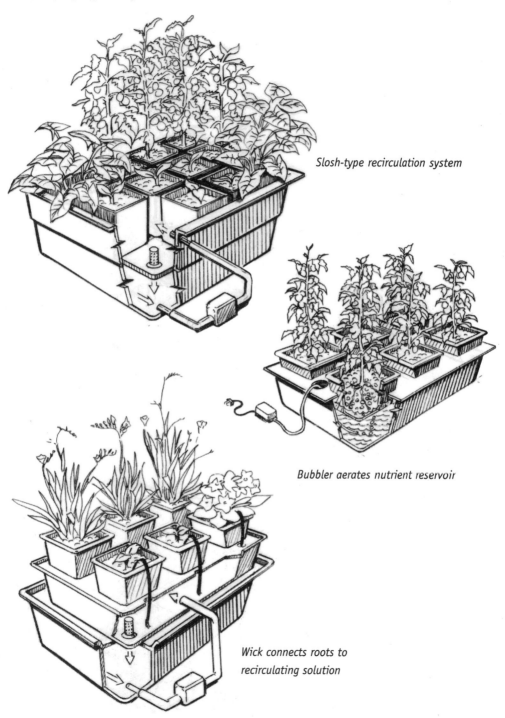

Slosh-type recirculation system

Bubbler aerates nutrient reservoir

Wick connects roots to
recirculating solution

The tank method is another example of a standing solution hydroponic design. In such a unit the plants are supported by plastic or nylon mesh. Their roots grow through the mesh and extend down into a container of solution below. The submerged roots are provided with oxygen by an aquarium pump that bubbles air into the nutrient.

The basic "slosh" method, the simplest of the flow systems, is very easy to set up but quite demanding to maintain. In this design, the plants are set in an inert growing medium, and the nutrient solution is placed in a bucket that's attached to the garden container by a tube. When the bucket is lifted, the solution floods into the growing medium. When the bucket is lowered, the solution drains back out. Of course, unless you use a growing medium that retains moisture adequately, some one will have to lift and lower that bucket at least twice every day. Many gardeners would find this method a bit confining.

The NFT Variations: Particularly appealing is a variation of the slosh method that's automated and involves the use of float valves, a recirculating pump, and a continuous flow of feed formula. The Nutrient Film Technique, called NFT, evolved from the work of Dr. Allen J. Cooper of the Glasshouse Crops Research Institute in Littlehampton, England. Dr. P.A. Schippers further developed the technique.

In the NFT system the nutrient solution flows from a container through a growing bed that's placed on a 3% to 4% slope and filled with a coarse grade of perlite. The solution runs into a receiving basin at the far end of the growing bed. A float switch in the nutrient container operates a recirculating pump located in the receiving basin. When the life-sustaining mixture falls below a certain level in the first tank, the float switch is activated and turns on the recirculating pump, and the solution is sent back into the first container. A second float valve, connected to an outside water source, is placed in the receiving basin and acts to compensate for loss of water through transpiration and evaporation. (The outside water source can be another tank, which must be filled periodically, or a domestic water line, which would further automate the system.)

The NFT system can accommodate several physical layouts, but the basic trough design is both inexpensive and versatile. The required troughs can be constructed out of 1" X 6" pine or plywood and then lined with black polyethylene. A screen (or screen-protected drainage tube) is placed at one end, and the container is filled with perlite. The nutrient tank must be placed higher than the bed to allow gravity flow. Moreover, it's important that all elements in this design: nutrient container, receiving basin, and refill tubes be both enclosed and opaque. Any light striking the rich solution will stimulate the growth of algae, which could eventually clog the system. The basic trough design can easily be enlarged into what's called a "flat bed." In such a system, a 4' X 8' sheet of plywood is fitted with 6" sides to make a large garden-growing area.

PVC pipes have also proved very useful in the construction of hydroponic systems. Large (8" or so in diameter) pipes, with a 2-1/2" to 3" channel cut in them, can be employed as single troughs, or 3" pipes can be channeled and suspended from an A-frame in what is called a "cascade" design.

Still another design utilizes PVC pipes suspended not horizontally, but vertically, with 2" holes drilled at strategic points along their lengths. Young plants are inserted in the holes, and the pipes are then filled with perlite. The nutrient-bearing liquid flows down through each pipe to its receiving basin and is recirculated.

The vertical design proves particularly useful in areas where space is at a premium, and it works well with such relatively small crops as herbs and strawberries. Large plants, such as tomatoes and cucumbers, are suited to the basic trough design, while the flatbed lends itself to leafy crops like spinach, chard, celery, and lettuce.

Feeding Facts and Fancies: There are a number of effective plant food mixes on the market, but it's also possible to mix your own. If you're just starting a hydroponic garden, it's probably a good idea to use a prepared mix, but eventually you may well find it less expensive and more satisfying to make your own.

Be aware, though, that hydroponics is more chemistry than art. It involves substituting controlled, artificial nutrients for natural systems found in organic garden soil. The more one attempts to supply substitutes for such natural elements as soil fertility, light, temperature, humidity, pollination, and pest control, the more complicated and prone to instability the artificial system becomes.

The major problem facing the small-scale hydroponics gardener is monitoring and correcting the pi and fertility levels in the nutrient solution. If you've ever operated an aquarium, you know how easily imbalances can occur in an artificial water-medium.

Too often these imbalances go undetected in a hydroponic system until the plants exhibit visible signs of distress. Continual testing is needed for any imbalances in pi, N (nitrogen), P (phosphorus), K (potassium), or the minor elements. You will need more than a little garden-soil test kit to ensure that an adequate fertility level is being maintained.

Organic or Inorganic: The question of whether organic or inorganic nutrients are best for a hydroponic system is principally a matter of cost, preparation time, availability, and personal conviction. The so-called chemical (inorganic) nutrients do fit more easily into an automated, strictly controlled system. Because they contain additional and variable elements, organic fertilizers such as fish emulsion, seaweed extracts, and manure tea generally need to be more carefully monitored and more frequently adjusted. On the other hand, the very presence of the additional trace elements can be seen as an advantage, since soil routinely provides many such nutrients which, though minute in quantity, contribute to the well-being of the plants. Chemical fertilizers warrant a few philosophical and economical considerations as well. After all, such intensively processed fertilizers are made from nonrenewable resources and consequently are becoming more and more expensive.

Continuing Research: Small-scale hydroponic gardening is evolving, and more experimentation and study will reveal its full potential. But even now, venturesome people who yearn for home-grown lettuce in February or have limited space for gardening can try this efficient, low-labor method that will challenge the scientist in us all.

Safe, Home-Grown Pest Repellents

Growing vegetables to supplement the home food supply can certainly help keep the cost of living down, but much of savings can be lost if four-legged and eight-legged produce-plundering creatures get to the crops first. Home grown pest repellents and pesticides can inexpensively and easily reduce the loss to insects and animals, deterring the bandits from taking their toll on valued crops.

While taking preventive measures at the beginning of the gardening season is undoubtedly the best course of action, there are also remedies that can be taken after the cherished plants are up and beginning to bear.

Protect Cucumbers, Squash, Corn, and Tomatoes: Maturing cucumbers and squash can be protected by using an always-handy kitchen discard: onion skins. Strew a big handful of these leftovers loosely across the top of each hill, and let the legendary pungency of the allium drive away the most stubborn of cucumber beetles. Further guard the mature plants by spraying a mix of equal parts of wood ashes and hydrated lime in water on the upper and lower surfaces of the spreading foliage. For advance protection, you might border next year's hilled areas with orange nasturtiums (*Tropaeolum majus*).

One of the high points of summer, the first fabulous feast of field-fresh roasting ears of corn dripping with butter, can quickly turn into one of the low points if raccoons, squirrels, or earthworms get to the dinner first. To prevent such a catastrophe, consider trying a few of the following plans of attack.

Surround this native American crop with soybeans, which will tempt any furry, four-footed invaders to fill their bellies with beans before they reach the succulent maize. It's best to choose a soybean variety that matures at the same time as the corn. In addition, the color and pungent aroma of nasturtiums (which also repel aphids and Mexican bean beetles), marigolds, and mustard rebuff numerous gnawing pests. Roasting ears can be further protected by putting a pinch of cayenne pepper on the silks.

Some folks also place crumpled newspapers between the rows, scatter sections of garden hose cut in one-to three-foot lengths to resemble snakes, hang pieces of a broken mirror about, string Christmas tree lights all through the rows, and even play Pat Boone recordings that are guaranteed to repel any living creature.

Sowing dill (*Anethum graveolens*) and borage (*Borago officinalis*) around the tomato patch in the early spring will help repel hornworms as the fruit matures and ripens. These two flavorful herbs are also useful in their own right for adding zest to both cooked and fresh foods.

Marigolds and Mole Plants: While both French and African marigolds (*Tagetes erecta*) help rid soil of nematodes, the Mexican marigold (*Tagetes minuta*) apparently exudes a substance from its roots that's actually toxic to certain invasive weeds. Try sowing the potent flowers as a cover crop in the autumn, and when the next year's planting time rolls around, the plants can be turned under for one of the finest, most soil cleansing green manure crops available. Mexican marigolds also repel rabbits and destroy innumerable soil borne pests. Be extravagant with the flowers; scatter them throughout the orchard, surround roses with them, and use some of the foliage to brew up a tea to spray localized areas.

If the garden plot comes under attack by moles, try planting a few mole plants (*Euphorbia lathyris*) around the edges of your garden next time around. The exotic looking biennials with their thick, milky sap have long been known as mole deterrents, and they'll reseed themselves for the second year, providing seedlings to place in other mole-ridden spots.

Two other plants that can be sown to help eliminate moles are the castor bean (*Ricinus communis*), which also tends off flies and mosquitoes, and the common dandelion (*Taraxacum officnale*). Castor bean seeds are poisonous, so take caution when growing this plant.

Slugs, Beetles, and Moths: Slugs, which are among the most damaging above-ground pests, can be discouraged with a preparation made from silicon rich horsetails (*Equisetum arvense*). Once dried, the plants produce a powder that slugs find highly unpleasant. A second method of deterring slugs involves placing discarded cabbage leaves, grapefruit rinds, or even old boards throughout the garden in the evening. When day breaks, check underneath, remove the occupants, and either add them to your ducks' breakfast menu or squash them.

If Japanese beetles appear to be your primary enemy, try planting castor beans, white-flowering geraniums, zinnias, and garlic throughout the garden.

For more general purpose garden protection, consider the roadside herb, yarrow (Achillea millefolium). It not only repels a number of pests, but is commonly believed to enhance the growth and flavor of plants growing nearby. Furthermore, yarrow's friendly qualities can be utilized throughout the year by brewing the foliage into a liquid fertilizer and watering periodically with the "tea."

When cole family vegetables face an invasion of cabbage moths and their larvae, which can mutilate plants in just a few days, rely upon an item from the kitchen. Pour soured milk over the young cabbages and other crops. It will keep the moths aloft and the worms away.

Indoor Repellents: Tender greenhouse tenants need protection too, so always allow a few shoo-fly plants (*Nicandra physalodes*) several places of honor in the solarium. The attractive, fast-growing annuals are toxic to all pests that chew them and rebuff the white flies that often plague enclosed gardens.

Homegrown repellents can also keep the kitchen and food storage areas free of unwanted guests. For example, a couple of bay leaves (*Laurus nobilis*) in the bottom of grain containers will keep them bug-free, and tiny cloth bags of ground black pepper will prevent weevils from infesting dried beans. If silverfish are setting up house keeping in cupboards, place fragrant leaves of costmary (*Chrysanthemum balsamita*) in each section of the cabinets to make the squatters move on.

Moderation in All Things: Resourceful gardeners have found innumerable common plants that have pest-chasing abilities. They can be mashed, ground, or brewed into sprays or dusts. The alkaloid exudates from nearly every type of tomato foliage will deter aphids; stinging nettle (*Urtica dioica*) spray encourages healthier plants. A turnip or anise mist will rid crops of spider mites and aphids; basil spray discourages flies; and onion, garlic, horseradish, mint, and chamomile-flower sprays all have bug-chasing qualities.

In putting organic pesticides and repellents to use, bear in mind that not every single insect poses a threat to the vegetable crop. A few of the invaders must be tolerated to provide food for such natural predators as swallows, each of which may consume 2,000 insects a day. Every concerned gardener should respect the natural balance and use even the suggested repellents only when pest populations threaten to become excessive.

No-Pamper Perennial Produce

Thanks to today's escalating food costs and shortages, as well as a growing concern over the chemical additives often found in supermarket produce, gardening is booming as never before. Perhaps you've joined the "home grown is better" movement yourself.

But are you still growing only annual vegetables—carrots, corn, radishes, beans, and so forth—that must be planted and laboriously tended every year? If so, it's time to move on to some perennial plants such as asparagus, rhubarb, dandelions, bamboo, Jerusalem artichokes, Egyptian onions, and other edible lilies (onions belong to the lily family).

Asparagus: To many people, asparagus is the "choicest of the choice" of

Production Rates: Vegetables

Variety	Pounds per 10 foot of Row Per Year	Variety	Pounds per 10 foot of Row Per Year
Asparagus	2 to 4	**Lettuce**	4 to 8
Beans (bush)	4-12	**Onions**	4 to 8
Beans (pole)	15 to 22	**Peas**	2 to 5
Beets	8-12: roots	**Peppers**	4 to 8
	3 to 5: greens	**Potatoes**	10-15
Broccoli	8 to 12	**Spinach**	3 to 5
Cabbage	12 to 22	**Squash**, Summer	10 to 15
Carrots	7 to 10	**Squash**, Winter	15 to 25
Cauliflower	8 to 10	**Corn**	10 to 15 (ears)
Cucumber	12 to 20	**Tomatoes**	10 to 25
Eggplant	5 to 10		

all the spring vegetables. In addition to the plant's palate-pleasing qualities, another attribute is that an established bed of asparagus will just keep on filling your plate with its early spring spears for 20 years or more.

This perennial thrives best when grown in areas where the winters are cold enough to freeze the ground to a depth of at least 5". This covers most of the continent north of upper Georgia.

Plant asparagus in sandy soil that receives six to eight hours of direct daily sunlight during the summer and that is located away from trees and shrubs.

Many asparagus growers prefer to plant roots rather than seeds in order to avoid waiting an extra year for their first harvest. Prepare the bed the fall before planting, if possible, by digging trenches at least 15" deep and about 10" wide. Tamp a 3" to 4" layer of well-rotted manure into the bottom of each trench and cover this with 4" to 6" inches of rich garden loam that has been mixed with sand, compost, bonemeal, and some lime. (Asparagus prefers a slightly acid soil with a pH between 6.4 and 6.8.)

The following spring, after giving the soil a good soaking, place 1-year-old asparagus plants or crowns in the trenches. Space them 18" apart with their roots widely spread and their crowns or buds pointed up. Firmly and carefully pack two inches of sandy soil around the plants without smothering their roots, and continue to water for two weeks.

This will leave an indentation in the soil along the length of each trench, but since the plants tend to rise as the season advances, cultivate the earth in and around the ditch frequently to remove all weeds and gradually fill it in until the trench's surface is leveled off with the surrounding ground.

The chief enemies of asparagus are little asparagus beetles and rust. Both can be avoided to some degree by cultivating only strains of the plant that are resistant to such problems.

If you really want your asparagus patch to bear bountifully year after year, take the time to bed it down each winter. Some gardeners advise cutting off all the plants' summer growth before spreading three inches of mulch over the bed. Others—most notably the "No-Work Gardener" Ruth Stout say, "Just leave the stalks where they are. Like everything else, they'll die when their time comes, so let them rest in peace. Besides, they add a certain amount of organic matter to the mulch you spread around the asparagus patch."

You can also take your choice when spring rolls around: Some gardeners prefer to pull the mulch back from their asparagus plants so the sun can warm the earth around them faster and encourage their early growth. Others, especially those who've seen late frosts ruin their early produce, leave the mulch where it is and let each year's new growth of asparagus find its way up through the covering.

Try (if you can resist the temptation) to avoid harvesting any of your succulent asparagus spears until the plants are 3 years old (if you originally put out 1-year-old sets, you can start to cut the second spring after they went into the ground). Don't make more than three cuttings the first season, but after that you should enjoy an extremely liberal six- to 10-weeklong harvest (the cooler the season, the longer the plants will bear) each and every spring for 20 or more years.

Gather asparagus spears when they're four to eight inches tall, just before the scales on their tips begin to open. Always harvest in the morning and, to avoid damaging other nearby sprouts, either cut each spear individually or snap the shoot by bending it across your index finger with your thumb.

Rhubarb: Rhubarb, like asparagus, prefers a rich, slightly sandy soil with a pH of 5.5 to 6.5. However, it prefers colder winters than asparagus and, as a result, grows well from the upper southern states all the way north to Alaska. Check nursery catalogs to find which varieties will do best in your area.

Although rhubarb can be propagated from seed, it's a longer and slower process than most gardeners want to tackle. For that reason, new beds of the plant are usually started from root cuttings. (A mature rhubarb crown is dug up and divided into several pieces, each of which contains one or two good "eyes" or buds.) Plant the cuttings in the spring as soon as the ground can be worked, usually four to six weeks before your area's last frost date.

Rhubarb sets are generally planted three feet apart in rows spaced four feet from each other. Dig a hole about 2' in diameter and 2' deep for each cutting and place a half bushel of manure in the bottom. Then fill the pit to ground level with a mixture of compost and topsoil. Plant the crown three or four inches deep in the center of the prepared soil and cover it with earth. The top of the root, where the buds are, should lie about 2" underground.

Five to ten good roots will supply enough "fruit" (this is the only vegetable that is truly used as a fruit) for a year-round supply of stewed rhubarb, pies, and preserves if the patch of plants is well fertilized each fall with a plentiful cover of compost, straw, and manure. Pull the mulch back or not, as you see fit, in the spring, and water the rhubarb regularly during dry weather. It's important, too, to remove the lower stalks as they develop during the growing season.

Rhubarb occasionally suffers from "foot rot," which causes its stalks to rot off at the base and fall over. The best cure for that infrequent ailment is to move the patch, but it can usually be prevented by choosing a well-drained location. Once in a while, rhubarb is attacked by the rhubarb curculio, but the beetle can be picked off the plants quite easily. This insect is attracted by wild dock, and gardeners who clear that plant away from their rhubarb beds are seldom bothered by the beetle.

Wait until the second year to begin harvesting stalks that are 10 inches long or more (not including the leaf) and an inch thick at the base. Cutting the rhubarb with a knife can cause root injury and disease, so just twist as you pull them from the ground, and they'll come up easily. Rhubarb is usually one of the very first plants that you can enjoy in the spring, and its stalks are tender enough to be edible for four to six weeks. CAUTION: Only the stems of the plants NOT ITS LEAVES OR ITS ROOTS should be eaten. A good rhubarb bed will bear for 10 years or more, but most gardeners like to divide plants and renew their patches every five years or so.

Dandelions: Why would anyone want to cultivate dandelions when wild ones grow so profusely? One reason is that far too many of the lawns and fields where wild dandelions grow have been chemically treated, and another is that cultivated dandelions (just like cultivated asparagus and cultivated rhubarb) can be tastier, more tender, and otherwise more palatable than their native or volunteer cousins. In addition, they will grow almost any place. Most of the larger seed companies now sell packets of dandelion seeds, so leaf through a few catalogs and try the varieties that especially appeal to you.

Dandelions prefer a soil pH of 6.0 to 8.0. Work manure, rock phosphate, and other natural fertilizers into the earth and then plant your seeds in rows 18 inches apart. Thin the sprouts so that they stand a foot from each other as they develop, and, at least in more frigid sections of the country, cover them during the winter with three or four inches of mulch. An annual mulching is about all the care that these hardy plants will ever need.

Dandelion leaves (greens), crowns, and young roots may all be eaten in a

Make An Economical Cold Frame

Even though the spring weather's too chilly to sow seeds in the garden, you can get a head start on the season with a cold frame. It will admit filtered sunlight to the plants within, supplying them with the heat and light they need to prosper and allowing inside-sprouted seedlings to be "hardened off" in the outside, but safe from bitter early spring winds and the worst cold.

This version requires little more than some 1"-thick rigid-foam (polystyrene) insulation board, some scrap wood, duct tape, and a section of fiberglass-reinforced plastic glazing. Old storm windows, or even heavy-duty sheet plastic can be used as a suitable, and much less expensive, substitute for the specified glazing.

To build the foam-board sides of your cold frame, cut the board to fit the

(continued on page 115)

1. Light-Admitting Lid
2. Inner Cover
3. Base
4. Handle Attachment

(continued from page 114)

area of your old storm sash or handmade sash frame. Attach at corners with duct tape. Make the ten holes for dowels.

Press a 3/4" X 24" dowel through the two center holes to make the spine that connects the front and back walls, and push the remaining pegs into the rest of the openings in such a way that they protrude past the inner surface to form shelves at strategic points around the frame. Keep the spine in place by fastening scavenged milk jug lids, plexiglass disks, or some other disc-shaped keeper to its exposed ends with No. 6 X 3/4" flathead wood screws. Complete the frame by attaching the two handles to the night cover, again employing plastic disks as stops.

The light-admitting lid is a rectangular wood framework with plastic glazing tacked to its upper surface. Easiest is to make the wood frame just big enough to fit around the top of the frame, and attach the reinforced plastic glazing to the frame with nails through small holes drilled in the plastic. To make the more complicated version illustrated, you need woodworking tools: miter ends of side and end rails with 45° cuts. Then cut a 3/8"-wide by 1"-deep rabbet (long notch) into the lower inside edge of each board, and fashion a 1/4" X 1" dado (shallow groove) centered in the upper surfaces of the two longest rails.

Fasten the casing together with three No. 3 X 1/2" oval-head wood

screws at each corner, then tack the 1/4" X 7/8" X 25-1/4" cross brace to the dadoed 1/4" rails. Finish the job by laying the glazing over the framework and driving brads or finishing nails through the lath-strip-molding-skirt to secure it.

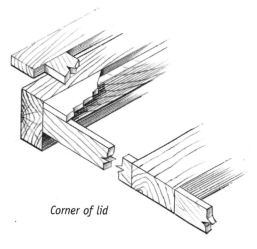

Corner of lid

Because polystyrene is apt to deteriorate after long exposure to direct sunlight, it's best to protect it and the wooden parts of the cold frame with acrylic latex exterior house paint.

To put your budget cold frame to use, sink it about half a foot into the earth or set it on top of some turned-up soil, making sure its sloped lid is facing in a southerly direction. If you choose not to bury the frame, secure it against gusty winds by driving a pair of stakes into the ground and fastening them to the ends of the spine with screws.

(continued on page 116)

To provide ventilation, you can remove the lid completely on sunny days or prop it open by placing some 2 X 4 scraps at the corners when the weather is overcast. Hold the propped lid in place with a restraining cord tied over it and behind the spine stops. The night cover should be installed in the evening and left in place until the sun rises the next day. On especially cold nights, or if you should want to use your cold frame as a hothouse, you can put a few strips of electric heat tape (the kind used to keep pipes from freezing) several inches beneath the soil or set up a light bulb inside the frame. ■

variety of ways, especially in the spring and fall. Surprisingly enough, dandelion greens from cultivated plants (unlike their wild relatives that turn bitter quickly) are generally also tender and flavorful right through the summer and the roots of the cultivated varieties can even be dug up and eaten in the winter. Use leaves raw or cooked like spinach; use roots like parsnips.

Bamboo: Although it's a mainstay of Chinese, Philippine, and other Asiatic schools of cooking, bamboo as a vegetable is hardly known on this continent. More's the pity. "Bambooor cane" as it's sometime called in our southern states does very well in almost any section of the country where there's rich, well-drained soil and plenty of water. If there's any complaint about cane, in fact, it's that the plant sometimes does too well. Once given a start, it's been known to take over whole gardens. The ideal site for a stand of bamboo is in rich loam adjacent to a brook that's partially shaded by a canopy of large trees.

About 70 species of cane can be raised on this continent and almost any issue of most gardening magazines will contain ads run by growers who have the plants for sale. Bamboo is best propagated in the spring by dividing starts from its thick, tangled network of roots. Shoots are also "layered" from the stems. Either method of propagation is better than attempting to start cane from seeds.

When allowed to grow to heights of 25' or more, the stalks of the bamboo plant have myriad uses: fishing poles, rafts, furniture, pole-vaulting poles, rug rollers, and so forth. If picked while still young and tender in the spring and summer, however, the shoots of the plant are delicious sautéed in butter, added to salads, and prepared in many other ways. Any good Chinese cookbook will have more serving suggestions than you'll be able to try in a year.

Jerusalem Artichokes: Despite their misleading name, Jerusalem artichokes are really a member of the sunflower family and are native to North America not the Holy Land. They seem to do best across the middle and northern United States, but their range extends far into Canada and south to all but the driest of states.

"Sunchokes," as they're sometimes called, will grow in almost any kind of soil though it's easier to dig their tubers from loose and sandy earth. Once established, they must be harvested regularly to keep them from getting out of hand.

Most of the larger nurseries sell the plant's tubers. Generally it's best to order the smooth, white "French" strain, instead of the smaller, red native variety. And don't go overboard! You'll probably get all you need by putting only three or four of the roots into the ground. Plant them three to four feet apart and 4" to 6" deep in a sunny, well-watered spot any time between mid-October and mid-December.

Jerusalem artichokes are harvested by digging up their tubers after the first frost. Additional tubers may then be dug right through the winter and well into the early spring. Dig them only as you need them, because they store better in the ground than in a root cellar, and don't worry about harvesting all you need, as you only have to leave a few tubers in the ground to ensure an even bigger crop the following year.

Jerusalem artichokes contain no starch (which makes them a prescribed food for diabetics) and are loaded with vitamins and minerals. Enjoy them pickled, oven fried, boiled and mashed, in soups and stews, even cooked and crushed and added to cakes and breads. One way or another, this prolific plant seems to have only one mission in life: to feed you year after year.

Egyptian Onions: Another perennial that too few gardeners know about is the Egyptian onion, also known as the tree or multiplier onion.

Like all onions, this variety prefers a continuous supply of moisture and does well when generous amounts of rotted manure, compost, and bone meal are worked into the soil until the entire onion bed is of a fine tilth.

The bulbs, which look like tiny acorns, are planted in the fall 12" apart in rows spaced 30" from each other. Some of these mother bulbs can then be left in the soil, where they'll grow larger year after year and produce a crop of new little bulbs on top of 3' stalks.

In late summer, after these baby bulbs have set and have started showing signs of drying, they can be harvested and dried thoroughly in the sun, then stored in a cool room in a mesh bag.

Southern gardeners are advised to remove the stalks from each mother bulb before winter sets in. Vegetable growers up north, on the other hand, find that the frozen stalks, plucked during the winter, thawed quickly, and used as scallions, taste as sweet as spring scallions.

Once started, this unusual onion just keeps on producing for your enjoyment. Just lift the parent bulbs every three or four years, separate them, and replant the divisions.

Day Lilies: Although they're cultivated in nearly every section of North

America, day lilies are grown almost entirely for the beauty of their blossoms, and very seldom for their four edible parts: spring shoots, flower buds, blooms, and tubers. All are so delicious, however, that it's little wonder the residents of many other countries of the world, especially China and Japan, look upon the day lily as an important food crop.

This hardy member of the lily family can be grown from seed, and once started, is perfectly capable of spreading underground until it forms dense clumps along roadsides and across whole abandoned fields. It is, in short, an extremely carefree perennial to raise.

When plucked in the spring and simmered in a little water and butter, the fresh shoots and outer leaves of the plant taste much like asparagus. Later, as buds develop, they can be gathered, dipped in a batter, and sautéed. During June and July, the flowers themselves (which, as the plant's name implies, each bloom for a single day) can be prepared the same way. The buds and blossoms can also be dried and added to fall and winter soups and stews.

Any time of the year when the ground isn't frozen, the crisp, nutty flavored little tubers of the day lily can be dug, cleaned, and eaten raw, either alone or in a salad. Or if you prefer, boil the miniature "potatoes" in salted water till they're tender and serve with butter.

There are many other perennial plants: horseradish, ground cherry, garlic, sea kale, comfrey, and chicory that can be added to the garden. While each has its strong points and defenders, all are easier to cultivate and all give a bigger return for the time, money, and energy invested than do the annual plants that most gardeners specialize in.

࿔

CHAPTER 5

Putting Up The Harvest

A Year-to-Year Food Plan

Long-range plans are fundamental to a rural way of thinking and living, and back-to-the-landers who lack the vision and determination necessary to put such plans into practice soon return to their cities and towns, where paychecks come on a regular basis instead of with the harvest.

The inflation fighting and conservation techniques described here will deal specifically with the family food supply, but the philosophy behind these methods can be applied to our personal management of all the earth's bounty.

Year-to-Year Shopping: Time and money-saving techniques should first be applied to shopping for the staples we cannot produce ourselves. Before considering bulk purchases, read the local newspaper to compare prices at supermarkets, keeping a special eye out for seasonal and house-brand sales. When the cost of a particular item is right, buy as large a quantity of the bargain goods as money and storage space will allow.

If inflation picks up again (as it surely will some time), stocking your cabinets with adequate supplies of staple necessities offers some protection against ever-rising prices.

Before soaring food costs can again attack everyone's budget, as happened in 1973-74, stock up on one to three years' supply—as determined by each item's perishability—of oils, syrups, coffee, tea, milk powder, dried beans, and sugar and salt for cooking and canning. Another strategy is to stockpile canned food that you can't satisfactorily process at home: evaporated milk, tuna, salmon, pineapple, tinned meats.

In addition to food, you might want to accumulate at sale prices a number of household staples. Paper products, detergents, cleansers, bleaches, and paper towels can be purchased by the case, and soaps, shampoos, and other personal hygiene articles by the dozen or even by the gross—a dozen of dozens. This means that on some necessities, inflated prices can be avoided for years. (Remember, at its peak, the 1973-74 inflation rate was 17% annually! Money spent at that time on these basic items wouldn't have earned nearly as much interest in a savings account as it would have on your own pantry shelves!)

It certainly takes no longer to buy a case than it does to purchase one item, so you also save a tremendous amount of time by buying in quantity. If you live a good distance from town, large-scale purchasing can eliminate many miles of travel and thus conserve gallons of gasoline.

Beating Price Increases: While hoarding items that are in short supply isn't right, it is only smart to listen to the news and pay attention to trends. If the government makes a price-raising deal with sugar cane growers, increase your stores of sweetener before the supermarkets increase the price. If disastrous weather destroys a major portion of the cacao bean crop in South America, replenish your supply of chocolate items. Should you run short of a particular product between sales or when prices are abnormally high, buy one or two of the needed items; then wait to restock your shelves until increased supplies or sales lower the cost again.

Some may consider this method of saving money to be too complicated or self-serving, but there is no simpler or more common-sense way to level out the wild swings (that seem to be mostly upward) in the marketplace. Volume buying encourages a shopper to purchase more carefully than would be necessary on a week-to-week or day-to-day plan, and a long-range food plan doesn't use up any more of the earth's resources than does ordinary grocery shopping. In fact, when transportation is taken into account, the toll exacted from these resources will be less. And, to the degree you are not buying when prices are high and supplies short, you help just a little to ease things for others.

Cold Storage for Staples: Most large-scale purchases can be stored on pantry, basement, or root cellar shelves. Any sale purchases that require low storage temperatures can be kept in a freezer. A spare refrigerator can be used to hold large quantities of such foods as crackers, flour, instant milk, margarine, corn meal, and cracked wheat. (Airtight jars would serve to keep weevils out of such items, but the food would become stale faster if stored on a pantry shelf, nullifying any savings.)

During the coldest months of winter, a garage or small (varmint-proof) shed makes a walk-in cold-storage facility in which to keep cases of apples, grapefruit, and oranges or sacks of locally grown potatoes, yams, onions, and carrots.

No Money for Planning Ahead?: Perhaps many of you on stringent budgets or small incomes are thinking: "Hey! You don't know what it's like out here! How can we buy a year's supply of anything when we don't have money even for next week's groceries?"

When money is a problem, start small…but start. Instead of buying a case on sale, buy two or three cans, boxes, or packages. When there's extra money (and there will be at some point), you can buy a sale priced case. You'll soon be well on your way to working within a full-scale year-to-year plan. Be patient. It's worth the time and effort.

Time/Money Saving Gardening: It's evident that the list of supermarket commodities mentioned so far is limited. A garden, even a small one, and fruit trees can supply much of the balance of a family's food needs. An important part of your food-supply planning should involve the home production of some fresh foods.

However, since growing food can demand an almost unlimited amount of time, plan very carefully to get the most from your gardening efforts. By planting late, perhaps two weeks to even a month later than other gardeners in your area, it's possible to avoid competition from early weed species and much violent spring weather (including hailstones, sandstorms, and deluges), permitting the plants to grow with less stress.

Buying bedding plants isn't a must. Cabbage, tomatoes, and peppers can be seed-sown in the same space they'll occupy during the entire growing season. You can also start seeds indoors and then transplant the seedlings. Thus, the gardener saves money and time and knows exactly what variety will appear, which often is not the case with purchased seedlings. Because the late planted vegetables encounter less damaging weather, they're generally healthier and produce longer and more prolifically.

Besides an annual cultivated garden, another source of fresh food would be perennial vegetables set out in protected, slightly shadowed spots around the edges of the lawn, or grown in containers on patios, decks, or balconies. A very limited amount of hand weeding will take care of beds of garlic, chives, onion, poke, asparagus, spearmint, and rhubarb, while New Zealand spinach, leaf lettuce, dill weed, and wild lamb's quarters will spring up voluntarily from unharvested seed in sheltered areas. Peaches, apricots, plums, cherries, apples, and a grapevine can be grown in most areas.

An Investment of Time: Any bounty harvested from the garden and orchard that isn't eaten fresh can be preserved for later use. The fruits may be juiced, canned for salads and desserts, or made into preserves and jellies, delicious pancake syrups, and fillings for fruit pies (to be frozen and baked later). Any vitamin-rich fresh fruits that are still around late in the season may be either dried or turned into delicious fruit leathers.

Tomatoes, which may be canned whole or as juice, will provide a base for pasta sauces. Homemade soup combinations such as tomato, zucchini, and onion or tomato, okra, and onion are wonderful ways to stock pantry shelves, too. Various relishes and sauces can be created by using tomatoes, ripe or green, as a base. Caliente sauce, a Tex-Mex distillation of liquid fire made with tomatoes, onions, and jalapeno peppers, is one example, and there are many variations on basic ketchups, barbecue sauces, and tomato sauces. Dried tomato slices can later be pulverized for instant additions to soups and casseroles.

If the value of home-processed food is measured in money only, there might be no way to justify the lavish amount of time one could spend on it. But there is another measurement: the quality of the finished products.

The excellence of stored homegrown food may be assured in a number of ways. For one thing, chemicals needn't be routinely applied to your soil or to the plants that produce your fruits and vegetables. Crops should be harvested at peak perfection and immediately processed to preserve as much of their natural nutrition as possible. Furthermore, the preservation processes will be according to your demanding requirements for sanitation, and unless you choose to, no artificial preservatives will be included. Balance that knowledge along with the cash and time invested, and you will probably consider your hours well-spent.

Economical Consumption: The ultimate test of a year-to-year food plan is using the goods in an economical manner. It's always possible, of course, to "throw more out the back door than can be brought in the front," unless you continue to plan carefully after you buy.

When you serve a roast, for instance, remember the proverbial hog butcher who uses everything but the squeal. Leftover meat and drippings can provide a headstart in creating a delicious, nutritious, stomach-filling casserole, and the leftover casserole can serve as a basis for a tasty, full-bodied soup. Even after that you can store the remaining soup in the freezer; then on a busy day, thaw and serve it up with hot corn bread. No one will notice that you've used, reused, and used again the original roast. As for the leftovers of the leftovers, use your imagination before adding them to the diets of your miscellaneous animals.

Only your vision and determination need limit your conservative use of food, which is one of the earth's scarcest resources.

From a personal perspective, commonsense planning means money in your pocket, food on the table, and abundance in the pantry, a reassuring buffer against whatever hard times may come.

Preserving Summer's Bounty

Getting late-summer's sudden abundance of ripe produce stowed away for off-season feasting can seem like a formidable task to a first-time gardener. As with any project, the beginning step is to get an overview of what's involved.

Some Like It Hot and Some Like It Cold: The first decision that a prospective food putter-upper faces is what method of preserving to use. The process or processes that you choose, whether freezing, canning, drying, salt/pickling, or root cellaring, will depend on the amount of time, space, and free cash you have available and on what types and quantities of foods you plan to preserve. Many homemakers weigh the pros and cons of each method and conclude that a combination of canning and freezing will best meet their particular needs.

Canning is a relatively inexpensive way to keep the backyard bounty, as long as you "put by" enough food to justify the initial outlay for processing equipment: canning jars and lids, a pressure canner, and a few specialized utensils. With this versatile method, you can preserve pickles, relishes, jams, jellies, and soups, as well as fruits and vegetables. But canning does take time.

Freezing requires less time and holds the garden-fresh flavor and fresh nutrients better than other (older) food-processing methods. However, the cost of a freezer makes a definite dent in the budget and may be prohibitive for folks just getting started in a self-sufficient lifestyle. Electrical use is surprisingly low once produce is frozen and the freezer is full.

Dehydration, a technique that's been around for millennia, is still a prime method of preserving foods, especially in areas of the world where other means aren't feasible. Limited drying doesn't require the initial investment needed for canning or freezing. (If you decide to dehydrate on a large scale, however, you may well want to purchase or build a solar or electric food dryer.) Dried foods can be stored in less space than frozen, canned, or fresh produce and, if kept dry, will remain edible for years. The drying process does, of course, change the texture of the food, so it's advisable to experiment some before dehydrating in quantity.

Root cellaring—storing food in a naturally chilly atmosphere for several months after harvest—was once a popular method of food preservation, being easy and energy-cost-free. Today, most homes have cozy, dry basements instead of cool, damp cellars, and root cellaring has become less common. However, if you do have access to a root cellar or to the labor and materials required to build one, this can be an excellent way to squirrel away root crops, cabbages, apples, and other "winter-tough" orchard and garden gleanings. The foods that can be stored in this manner will be preserved without being processed at all!

Canning: The whole canning process can appear overwhelming to a novice preserver, and if enough stories of food poisoning have made the rounds, canning may even seem a questionable practice altogether. Actually, it is a simple and safe method of handling surplus harvest, but following instructions is a must.

How It Works: Canning stops the natural decomposition process of perishables by heating, and thereby sterilizing, them. At the same time sealing the food containers protects the edibles from outside contamination during storage. This heating and sealing technique destroys potentially harmful microorganisms such as bacteria, molds, and yeasts, and it denatures the enzymes in plant tissues that could otherwise cause toxic substances to form in the canned goods.

As you might expect, different foods promote the growth of different types of microorganisms that cause spoilage; therefore, processing times and temperatures must vary accordingly. In general, though, canned foods are divided into two groups: low-acid and high-acid types. High-acid foods (all fruits, including tomatoes, are in this category) either contain plenty of natural acid or are acidified by the addition of vinegar, as in the case of relishes and pickles or by fermentation as with sauerkraut.

Low-acid comestibles are what their name implies: foodstuffs with little or no acidity. Vegetables, meats, poultry, seafood, and soups are grouped in this category.

What It Means to You: This distinction is of concern to the canner-to-be because the natural "sourness" of a food determines how it's to be processed. In tomatoes and other fruits, the high-acid content protects against harmful bacteria, while molds, yeasts, and enzyme toxins can be easily destroyed by heating jars of these foods in a briskly boiling water bath.

Low-acid foods such as snap beans, on the other hand, allow the growth of heat-resistant bacteria (notably *Clostridium botulinum*, which causes fatal botulism poisoning). These eatables, therefore, must be specially treated by being heated to 240°F in a pressure canner in order to destroy any and all bacteria. (To be on the safe side, it's also a good practice to boil all low-acid home canned produce for 20 minutes before eating.) Consult a canning manual to find the appropriate method and the prescribed amount of processing time for each food you harvest. Properly adhering to these guidelines is the key to successful canning.

The Equipment You'll Need: Once you've determined what sort of canning process you'll be using, your next step will be to gather all the proper preserving accouterments. If you plan to put up only an occasional batch of pickles and relishes or to make a few pints of Aunt Sally's conserves, common kitchen utensils will be adequate. A big pot (20- to 21-quart capacity) with a tight-fitting lid will serve nicely as a boiling-water bath container. All you'll have to do is find or fashion a canning rack to keep the jars from touching each other as they are processed.

If, on the other hand, you have visions of packing the pantry clear to the ceiling, you'll require some specialized canning equipment. A pressure canner is a must for putting up all those low-acid carrots, beets, and beans basking out back in the sun. However, if you can't afford to part with the $60 to $160 required to purchase a canner (and if you plan to process only pint jars), a pressure cooker will suffice if it has an accurate gauge and will hold 10 pounds of pressure. Because pressure cookers heat and cool more quickly than the larger canners do, you should add 20 minutes to the recommended processing times if you use this "make-do" method.

You'll need to buy canning jars and lids. Most people who can are partial to the newer two-piece, self-sealing lid that has a non reusable rubber-rimmed top and reusable outer band, but the older-style lids (such as the "Lightning" glass tops with rubber rings and the zinc caps with porcelain liners) work perfectly well but only if rims of the old jars and lids are chip-free and if new rubber rings are used.

Be certain to buy an ample supply of pint- and half-pint canning jars and lids early in the season, so you won't be left containerless just when the produce is at its prime. Never use anything but the regular canning jars in a pressure canner. Mayonnaise-type jars are too thin and not tempered to withstand the heat and pressure involved in low-acid canning.

Employing ordinary ketchup, pickle, or mayonnaise jars to put up high-acid produce in a boiling-water bath is a common practice in some canners' kitchens, but it is cautioned against by experts. There is always a risk of cracked jars with the ensuing loss of both produce and time.

You'll find that a jar lifter or wide tongs especially made for grasping con-

tainers of boiling foods will prove itself well worth the small purchase cost. A canning funnel that helps guide hot vegetables and fruits into the jars is equally helpful.

The remainder of the necessary equipment: tongs, saucepans, knives, chopping boards, spoons, a timer, hot mitts, and dish towels or a cooling rack may already be right on your kitchen shelf.

Readying Yourself and Readying the Kitchen: Once you've bought up a supply of jars and lids, located a pressure canner, and rounded up the rest of the necessary canning gear, you'll no doubt be eager to begin packing food away. Before rushing out to gather armloads of your garden's offerings, however, take the time to make sure you really are properly prepared.

For one thing, you should be sure you know precisely how you'll preserve the harvest. For example, you must determine whether the folks who'll be enjoying your canned tomatoes would like them better whole, in juice, or as a sauce, or whether you might want to can them in a combination of ways.

In addition, you need to decide whether to use the hot- or cold-pack canning technique with each item of produce you're about to put up. (In general, hot packing—precooking the food and adding the heated product to the jars—is used when the victuals need to be softened to fill their containers solidly.

Cold packing—putting raw food into the jars—is used for low-density eatables, such as tomatoes, to allow the food to better retain its shape.)

Next, you're ready to read through the recipe and assemble all of the ingredients. Frantically rushing from store to store in search of spices while vats of cucumbers are waiting at home, awash in pickling brine, is not a recommended procedure, so be sure that you have everything that you'll need! Gather the canning equipment and examine the jars for hairline cracks or nicks. Then wash and rinse the unblemished jars and leave them immersed in hot water. Put the jars lids in a saucepan, so you'll be ready to sterilize them in a boiling-water rinse.

Perhaps most important, allow yourself plenty of time to complete the entire canning process. Rushing the operation will only increase the chances that you'll make mistakes, and you can't afford mishaps in canning. The wise worker will schedule a solid block of time for the canning operation and put off cleaning the barn or basement until another day.

Once you've determined that everything inside is set to your satisfaction, you can head out to gather the harvest. It's best to get the goods from garden to jar in under two hours to retain the maximum nutrients in the final product. Reap only enough for one canning run. Trays of cut, but not yet processed, food will quickly discolor and lose quality. You should pluck only ripe, unblemished food, since the quality that comes out of the jar will be no better than what originally went into it. One piece of overripe produce can spoil an entire batch.

Making a Run: Although an in-depth canning guide will include more details on the step-by-step process, here are the basic steps. First, sterilize jars, lids and rubber rings by boiling for 20 minutes. Leave in the sterile water. Then: [1] Pack the food into the sterilized jars, wipe the rims of the containers clean, and screw on the sterilized lids—but leave them loose enough for steam to escape. Then [2] carefully load the jars into the water-filled canner. (A pressure canner is required for low-acid foods, and the instructions for using the particular canner should be read carefully before processing is begun.) [3] Fasten the processor's lid and heat for the recommended time.

Once the jars have been processed in the prescribed manner, remove from heat [4] let everything cool down just enough to safely remove the lid of the canner and then the jars. [5] Tighten lids, then place the canned foods where they can finish cooling slowly. Before long, you'll be treated to an unusual sound that is one of the delights of canning: as each lid seals tight, it will bend inward with a clearly audible PING or POP! After the jars have "rested" undisturbed for a day, you can store your produce in a dark closet, and look forward to some good eating this winter!

Keep in mind one last bit of canning advice: Have fun. The return to a self-sufficient food supply can be a budget booster and an enjoyable experience.

Canning won't seem like drudgery if you allow enough time for the job and do no more work than you can comfortably handle. Another idea is to make canning a group effort. (It takes longer than you may think to cut up all the ingredients for soups, pickles, and relishes!)

Putting It on Ice: The main "utensil" required for freezing is, of course, the freezer itself. You'll have to decide what size and shape will be best for your situation. A low, chest freezer is most economical to buy and operate; an upright is easiest to load and unload; a combination freezer-refrigerator is most flexible for a small family. Providing 6 to 10 cubic feet of freezing space per person is a good guideline if you intend to freeze a lot. (If you're not yet ready to purchase your own appliance, you might want to rent a freezer locker in a nearby cold storage warehouse for the first year to help determine how much food-stashing space you'll actually need.)

Whatever cooling plan you decide on, don't consider the small freezer section of your refrigerator to be adequate for long-term storage unless that unit has a separate door, an independent temperature control, and a good bit of room. Food should be kept at 0° F, and no 'fridge-freezer' can hold that temperature throughout.

Wrapping: After storage space has been determined, the next consideration is what type of packaging to use. The freezer container has three purposes: It keeps the victuals from drying out (known as freezer burn), preserves flavor, texture, and color, and it helps to retain valuable nutrients. Therefore, you'll want packaging materials that are moisture-vapor resistant. Zip-top plastic bags are one option. Nesting plastic box-containers with snap-on lids in half-pint, pint, and quart sizes are more expensive, but will last for decades…but, buy the better quality containers with clear tops in preference to the cheaper kind—even if they do offer color-coded lids.

From Soil to Storage: Preparing your garden's produce for freezing is quick and easy after you assemble your equipment and gather up the edibles. As with canning, it's best to preserve the food within two hours after picking, if possible. Therefore, you should pluck small quantities of your best homegrown harvest. Then trim the vegetables as if for table use, blanch them by boiling briefly for a minute (or according to a freezing schedule) to kill natural decay enzymes, and pack them in freezer containers.

Freezing Fruit: You'll need to make one preliminary decision when freezing fruit: whether to "drypack" or "wet pack" the edibles before you put them in bags (best for loose, dry produce) or rigid containers (best for foods packed in liquid). When you wet pack, you add sugar or a sugar syrup to the fruit, but when you dry pack, you freeze the fruit in its natural, firm, fresh state. (If you choose to use syrup, be sure to allow 20% head space in the container for the liquid to expand, and be certain that the container has no holes and is sealed tightly to prevent leakage.)

If you plan to freeze apples, apricots, pears, peaches, or any other fruit that discolors in storage, another factor to consider is whether or not to add ascorbic acid (vitamin C) to prevent the food from darkening. You could also use plain lemon juice to achieve the same effect, but ascorbic acid won't change the taste of the fruit as much as the lemon juice will.

Chilling the Vegetables: The method for freezing vegetables is slightly different from that for fruit. Such low-acid foods as beans and peas require blanching to arrest enzymes in the plant tissues that can cause the foods to become tough and lose their flavor. (This pre-heating is necessary for all vegetables except sweet green peppers.) To illustrate this technique, let's consider the snap bean.

On the day that you decide to freeze some "snaps," go out to the garden and pluck the young, tender beans. After washing the green beans in several rinses of cold water, remove the "strings" and tips and either snap or cut them into bite-size pieces or slice them lengthwise (French style). Next, put the prepared vegetables in a wire basket, lower them into a pan of boiling water (or place them in a steamer), and blanch the beans for the time specified in your freezing guide. (Don't overcook, or you'll end up with a bag of "mush" when the food is thawed.)

Immediately after blanching, dunk the heated beans in ice-cold water and then rinse until they're cool to the touch. (In midsummer, be sure the water is ice-cold by adding ice to the cooling bath.)

For "flash-freezing" and best quality, chill metal cookie sheets in the freezer. Working fast, lay cooled and drained produce on the sheets in single layers, not touching, and pop in to the freezer. It's best to freeze one sheet at a time. For faster freezing, stack sheets, separating them with two-inch-high wooden blocks at the corners. When produce is rock solid, remove, package quickly and return to the freezer.

Name and Date: Before packing and freezing the harvest, you'll want to label each food container. A felt-tipped pen with waterproof ink works best on plastic or on freezer labels to record the name of the food and the date it was preserved.

It's also a good idea to write down the food type and the amount frozen on a chart, so that you'll have a running list of your iced inventory. By taping the list to the freezer door, you can conveniently cross off each parcel that is removed from storage. Also, a rough map of where a given food is located in the freezer will help you "keep your own cool" later on, as you try to locate something like that last pouch of spring peas!

Keeping It Cold: Freezing works by allowing the extreme cold to retard the growth of microorganisms and slow down the enzyme activity in the food. Because freezing does not sterilize the produce, you'll have to make sure that the edibles stay sufficiently cold and that they are used within a reasonable period (not more than a year). There will be a gradual but inevitable loss of quality as the food ages.

The Rewards: There are few things more satisfying than walking into a pantry holding shelves packed with a rainbow of brightly colored jars, or peeking into a well-stocked freezer.

And remember, it's not just nostalgia for the "olden days" that's sending more and more folks back into the kitchen to make their own pickles, relishes, jellies, and canned or frozen goods. By turning back to gardening and preserving, it's possible to control the quality of your food and to pare down that ever-rising grocery bill.

Dry Fruits and Vegetables at Home

Dehydration as a method of food preservation has been around a long time. Primitive man dried victuals by the heat of the sun or with the aid of fire, and then ground the stores into a long-lasting powder. Now, thousands of years later, dehydration is still one of the most widely used methods of food preservation in the world, and there are good reasons:

[1] Drying retains the vitamin, mineral, protein, and fiber content of foods more successfully than can-preservation techniques that expose them to great changes in temperature.

[2] Dehydrated foodstuffs often are more flavorful than the original, undried food. Frozen and canned edibles, on the other hand, are usually less tasty than their fresh or dried equivalents.

[3] It costs little or nothing to dry foods, whereas both freezing and canning require a potentially large initial investment in equipment.

[4] Dried goods can be stored in a smaller space than either frozen, canned, or fresh foods. (For instance, 20 pounds of tomatoes, when canned, will fill 11 one-quart jars. When dried, the same quantity of tomatoes weighs a little more than a pound and occupies a single No. 10 can.)

[5] Dried foods that are kept dry remain edible almost indefinitely.

By buying fruits and vegetables in bulk at low, in season prices, you can enjoy your favorites year-round, in season or out, for a fraction of what you'd pay by buying them throughout the year whenever the mood strikes .

How to Get Started: If you want to dehydrate foods quickly and if you don't mind warming up the kitchen, you can dry your fruits and vegetables in the oven. This method, however, can cause a greater change in the color, flavor, and vitamin content of foods than open-air drying.

A better, though more time-consuming, way to dehydrate foods is to use a cabinet-type food dryer or to rely on the sun alone to do the job. Sun-drying requires little in the way of equipment: a couple of tables that can be set up outside, some cookie sheets, aluminum foil, or butcher paper on which to dry the edibles, and a protective netting to keep insects off the food.

There's nothing complicated about preparing victuals for drying. The key things to remember are: [1] The food should be clean and ripe. (Don't expect green or overripe fruit to taste anything but green or overripe after it's been dried.) [2] Juicy items should be cut up before they're dehydrated. [3] The individual pieces of food must be arranged on the tray or table in such a way that air can circulate freely around them. If you crowd the pieces together, mold can quickly ruin the entire batch.

Herbs Dry Well: Edible herbs have to be among everyone's favorite dryable foodstuffs. There's something invigorating about going out on a spring morning after the dew has dried to harvest nettles, comfrey, mint, and lemon balm. After bringing them inside, wash them lightly and blot the pickings on

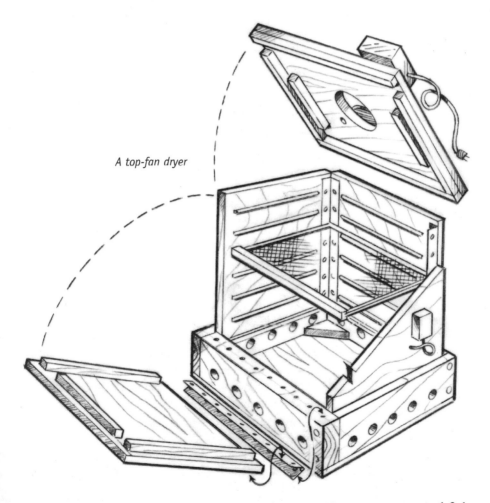

A top-fan dryer

a towel before putting them out to dry. You rarely need a food dehydrator to dry herbs: All you have to do is tie the plants in bundles and hang them in a dry place (such as the attic) for a few days. When the herbs are crackling dry, they can be crushed and put into jars or freezer bags and stored in a dark place. The seasonings can then be used in teas, or ground fine and added to soups, stews, or other dishes.

Fruits are Naturals for Drying: Virtually any kind of fresh fruit can be dehydrated satisfactorily. Pineapples and bananas, which can be bought year-round, are particularly good when dried, especially if they've been purchased in a very ripe condition and cut into thick chunks before being processed. These fruits have a sweetness and delightful chewiness that are hard to beat.

Few things are more fun to dry than the seasonal fruits: cherries (sour and sweet), peaches, apricots, apples, pears, and plums. It's a very satisfying feeling to have a year's supply of these delicacies in storage and to know that you didn't have to spend hours scalding, packing, and canning the fruit to get that supply.

Stone fruit: apricots, peaches, and plums need only be sliced in half and pitted prior to drying; no peeling is necessary. (Hint: The dehydrating goes a little faster if you pop each fruit half inside out by pressing on the skin side with your thumb.)

To dry pears, quarter the fruits and place them on the rack, skin side down. The same goes for apples, which you can also slice into rings, if you prefer. Coring is optional. Apples will turn brown (due to oxidation) when dried, but the color change doesn't affect the flavor.

To make your own raisins, pull seedless grapes from bunches and spread them out on the drying tray or table.

All of the above fruits should be "hard dried"; that is, they should contain no moist spots when done. Bacteria and mold can grow only where there's water. Hard-dried fruits can be softened by soaking them in water or juice before they're eaten, or they can be left lying out in the kitchen for a while to be softened naturally by allowing them to absorb some moisture from the air.

One of the most satisfying things you can do with your fresh fruit (or with softened dry fruit) is to make fruit leathers. These snacks sell for nearly a dollar a roll at the grocery store, but you can produce them for pennies at home. To make your own leather, [1] cut one or more kinds of fruit into chunks, [2] put the pieces into the blender, [3] blend until smooth, and [4] pour the puree out onto plastic wrap or wax paper to dry. (Note: As the sheet of pulp dries, it'll begin to curl up, so tape the corners of the "carrier sheet" down or put pennies on each corner to hold the plastic or wax paper flat.)

If the fruit is extra-juicy (as with most berries), you may want to add apple chunks, which are high in pectin, to the puree while it's still in the blender.

This will stiffen up the leather. (Or you can use one tablespoon of ground flax seed for each cup of blended fruit.) For added fun, try stirring small seeds or chopped nuts into the fruit blend before you dehydrate it.

When your leather is finally dry, peel the plastic or wax paper off its back, roll the sheet of pulp into a "scroll," and rewind the scroll in the plastic wrap or wax paper to keep for future use.

You can Also Dry Vegetables: In addition to fruits, many kinds of vegetables including beans, peas, peppers, beets, carrots, turnips, potatoes, yams, onions, squash, and cereal grains can be dehydrated. Corn can be dried on the cob (after which the kernels come off easily). Even the corn's silk can be powdered and added to soups for seasoning. Dried onion and leek tops, likewise, make fine condiments for use in soups and salads. Zucchini and cucumber slices can be dehydrated to make delightfully good-tasting chips suitable for dipping.

Many vegetable parts that aren't normally used: stems, beet tops, roots (in some cases), and squash blossoms can be dried and added to soups, stews, sauces, and broths, or unused parts can be ground into powder and blended with cheese to make delicious spreads.

Regardless of what you decide to dehydrate, remember that dried foods keep safely only as long as they remain dry. This means you should always store your dried goods in airtight containers (plastic bags or glass jars are best), away from bright light. If you follow this precaution, your dehydrated foods should remain dry and edible for many years.

Give Drying a Try: Drying foods at home can be a source of much joy and satisfaction, and it's a time tested way to [1] cut your yearly food bill, [2] free up valuable cupboard and freezer space, and [3] enjoy a greater variety of more flavorful foods. This simple preservation method can be a boon to your health and your finances.

A Root Cellar

A man-made cave dug into a hill and sealed shut is a naturally-cooled vault for preserving food in what was once termed "common" storage—as opposed to more involved drying, canning, or freezing. It is called a root cellar, and acts as a refrigerator in spring and summer and a freeze-proof pantry in fall and winter.

Not long ago, just about every family living in the world's colder climes had one of these harvest keepers. Nestled in the earth, away from the heat of the kitchen, a root cellar maintained a temperature just above freezing, and throughout the winter it provided a practical storage bin for root crops, apples, salted meats, cabbages, and other goods.

Of course, the heyday of the home root cellar ended a good while ago. When folks gained access to refrigerators and supermarkets, underground food storage seemed unnecessary and in most areas was abandoned.

With the revival of interest in practical, inexpensive ways of putting up food, more and more people are rediscovering the wisdom of constructing a place to store unprocessed, homegrown edibles. Even though building a cellar requires a fair investment in labor and materials, the finished shelter usually requires no operating energy and demands no maintenance beyond periodic cleaning.

A do-it-yourselfer in Three Lakes, Wisconsin, built an 8' X 8' X 20' root cellar, excavating the cavern into a hillside with a backhoe.

The bottom of the cellar was lined with sand for drainage. For the walls,

A root cellar dug into a hillside

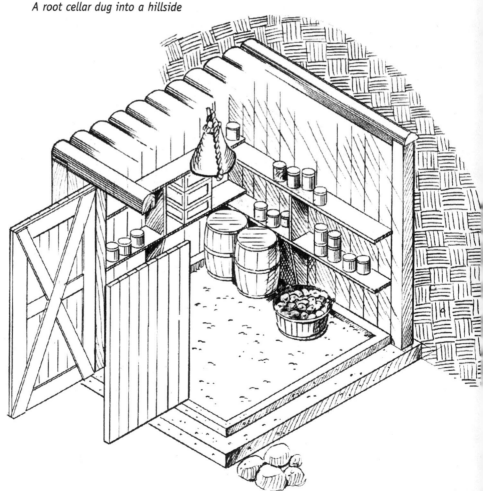

the builder laid a concrete footing that had an upwardly protruding inner lip. The L-shaped foundation would both support the weight of the cedar log walls and brace the base of those rounds against the tons of sideways "cave in" pressure inherent in an earth-banked structure.

Every cedar log was peeled and then cut square (on each of two opposing sides) to make sure that the vertically stacked timbers would sit level and stay in place. Ceiling logs were notched where they rested atop the wall logs so that, like the concrete base lip, the horizontal beams could help brace the sides.

Double doors, which were separated by an air space to keep out the cold, sealed off the front of the root cellar. The storage house is wired for electricity. When especially cold nights bring temperatures as low as 40° below zero, a single 25-watt incandescent light warms up the inside temperature a few degrees, insuring that the cached food doesn't freeze.

With the assistance of this "emergency" heater, the finished root cellar stays a few degrees above the ice-up point throughout the entire Wisconsin winter, and it maintains an even temperature during warm March thaws, when mourning cloak butterflies migrate over gray snow, or through sudden, stark May blizzards. Around midsummer the earth-sheltered space warms up to about 55°, but winter-stored crops are gone by then, and there are fresh vegetables in the garden.

A root cellar will eventually pay for itself by allowing its owner to store up food that is either homegrown or practically free for the picking at harvest time. Here is one example of economical food hoarding: you gather five or 10 bushels of unblemished apples late in the growing season (when they'd otherwise only fall and rot on the ground). The inexpensive edibles will keep for months in the cellar and provide you with a winter's worth of fresh fruit for eating, cooking, and making juice.

A root cellar is also a good place for aging game and storing smoked meats and cheeses. Such shelters offer complete protection from mice, raccoons, and other pests. The wife of the builder of this cellar uses it to store the huge potted ivies that decorate her patio in the warmer months but cannot live through Wisconsin winters. The crop holders are useful in summer, too, for storing wine, live fish bait, and other items that profit from a cool, protected environment.

All in all, it's plain to see that people who want the independence of being able to eat their own fresh, home-stored food should learn the deep, dark secret of building a root cellar.

Common Storage

Roots: Some garden produce and orchard fruits are self-designed to store themselves over the winter (with a little help but, for the most part, short of cooking/canning, freezing, or drying).

In the old days—before electricity—such methods were called "common" storage, as opposed to canning or more involved preserving techniques. Common storage includes salting and smoking or drying, or immersion in a preservative fluid bath such as a pickle brine, vinegar, or waterglass (a saturated solution of sodium silicate and water used to keep fresh eggs for up to 6 months).

The idea is to use plants' natural tendencies to keep them in an edible condition as long as possible.

The best candidates for common storage are biennial plants with a two-season life cycle. These naturally produce a stem, leaf clump, root, or tuber that survives over a single winter, then sprouts and goes to seed. This is compared to perennials such as trees that live for many years, or annuals such as radishes that do it all in one year: sprout from seed, grow, mature, and produce seed that overwinters in a dormant state.

The simplest method of common storage is just to leave a vegetable in the soil. Jerusalem Artichokes—watery tubers produced by a species of sunflower—are conventionally left in the ground because they lose water and rot if dug and stored for more than a few days. Though the tubers are watery, their fluid content does not freeze and rupture cells in winter, so they can be dug any time of year.

Parsnips, long-season carrots, and "winter-keeping" beet varieties such as Lutz-Green Leaf can also be left where they grew, but need a little more care. Leafy tops should be snipped off (but not so close the root itself is cut into). Then, the rows are covered with enough dry hay or straw mulch so they are at least six inches deep all winter.

In the Northern tier, winter-keeping root crops were once grown in a trench or a large cold frame and covered with a good foot of mulch. In modern times, the

(continued on page 137)

straw is covered with a thick black-plastic sheet...that will absorb the sun's warmth and keep the soil from freezing solid till the sun heats up in early spring. To harvest roots, the mulch is kicked back, and they are dug from the frosted soil with a garden fork. The quality of parsnips is actually improved by frost. Carrots and beets will lose sugar and can become woody and bitter by winter's end.

Winter soil conditions were duplicated in root cellars—basement rooms or separate below-ground rooms dug into hillsides or sunk in the ground. Soil teems with organisms that will introduce decay into any bruise or nick in a root, so root cellars were fitted with ground-level bins filled with moist (but not soggy) sawdust. Produce was dug carefully, topped, and brushed clean of soil (but not washed). Only the blemish-free were buried in the moist sawdust that was tamped snug around them to keep their moisture in and minimize air contact. Light was kept out of the root cellar, and temperature was moderated by nature to around freezing—40° was typical—almost year round. With good care, carrots' time clock would be slowed, so they did not sprout until the spring crop was nearly ready.

Potatoes are tubers produced to store water and carbohydrates to feed the plants that sprout from the "eyes" in the early spring. You've surely had potatoes

sprout in your kitchen storage bins and seen how they soften and mold as they contribute water to sprout growth. They sweeten as the starch is converted to sugar. If exposed to light, the skins turn green—which makes them mildly toxic.

To create ideal common-storage conditions for potatoes, the tubers are dug, brushed of soil but not washed, dried well, and stacked or bagged loose in a dark bin. The closer the temperature is to freezing, the longer the spuds will resist sprouting.

All common-stored goods must be overhauled periodically. Rot evidences itself as white or black mold or soft spots and must be eliminated (cut out

(continued on page 138)

the bad parts and use the rest) or the entire lot will be lost.

Apples: Apples are kept under conditions similar to potatoes, and hard-skinned, dark red keeping varieties will hold till spring in common storage. Never store apples with other produce. In the slow but inevitable ripening process, they produce ethylene gas, which initiates natural ripening in other produce as well; the saying: "one rotten apple spoils the bushel" is literally true. That's why you can ripen green tomatoes by putting them in a paper sack with a soft apple...and why only hard, sound apples should be stored.

In modern commercial storage, apples and vegetables are kept in the computer-age version of "common-storage": in vaults where temperature is maintained at just above freezing, light is excluded entirely, humidity is maintained at a constant high level, and oxygen and CO_2 in the atmosphere are replaced with inert gas—so the plants cannot "breathe." They are kept in suspended animation and will survive for well over a year with a minimal—but still noticeable—decline in aroma, flavor, and firmness.

The Cabbage Family: Most members of the cabbage family are conventional annuals that produce flower heads at season's peak (even if we do harvest them before the buds open), and aren't candidates for common storage. Thus, loose-leaf types such as raab broccoli as well as heading broccoli, cauliflower, and "broccauli" crosses must be canned or frozen.

Brussels sprouts store better. After a light frost, but not waiting for hard frost, pull the whole plant, shake soil from root, but do not cut off root or mini-cabbage at top (or you'll introduce rot into the stem). Pull all leaves and hang the whole stem upside down in a cool, windproof shed (not in the house cellar, or a natural "bad-cabbage" odor will drive you out.) Twist off sprouts as needed, and they will last beyond Christmas unless allowed to warm up or freeze all the way through.

Winter-keeping cabbages are bred to be late-developing, dry, and hard-

(continued on page 139)

skinned, thus long-lived in storage. Cut them as late as possible, remove loose leaves, and store—not touching—in loose straw. Traditionally (because of the inevitable smell), they were stored in straw-lined pits outdoors. In mild climates, they were stored in straw under overturned bushel baskets—one head to a basket.

A straw-filled bin in a shed is easier. As storage time passes, outer leaves will become soft and want to rot, so you must overhaul the cabbages every few weeks and remove leaves that show spots or changes in color at the stem-end. By the time your spring cabbage crop comes in, the stored winter cabbage will be peeled down to the (by then, yellow) inner leaves.

Making Kraut: To save a rot-threatened cabbage hoard (or to create your own hotdog relish any time), brew up some sauerkraut. To inoculate the brine with the correct breed of fermentation yeast, you need live brine from fresh kraut or fresh sour pickles from a deli. Bottled kraut may work, but canned won't work as all molds are gone. Natural wine-type molds from the blush on grapes or blueberries should do as well.

Get a large ceramic crock, a ceramic plate that fits the opening, a heavy rock that fits as well, a cabbage shredder, and Kosher (uniodized) or flaked pickling salt.

Remove all soft or discolored leaves, core out spots, and cut cabbages into easily shredded quarters. Hold in spotless containers in the 'fridge.

Boil enough water to nearly fill the crock, add salt to float an egg; cover and let cool to room temperature.

Scour and scald everything, rock included, to remove alien bacteria and molds that can "turn" the brew. What it can turn into we'll leave to your imagination.

While all equipment is still hot and your hands scrubbed or in boiled rubber gloves, shred cabbage over the crock till it is nearly full. If any shreds fall on the floor, leave them there. Pour in the kraut juice. Add salt water to cover, put on plate and rock. Keep in a cool place, covered with several layers of cheese cloth to keep dust and bugs out but let gasses escape. Don't stir, but skim off scum daily with a sterile spoon. When bubbling stops, clean all scum and inner rim of the crock. Leave in cool place. You can remove finished kraut as needed with clean metal tongs. Better is to pack sterile jars with kraut, top with boiling brine till overflowing, cap, and process in a hot water bath as with pickles.

Dried Stores: String tender, stringless green (snap) beans on thread. Hang them in the attic peak (not in bleaching sun), and the dry heat will turn them into "leather britches" that can be rehydrated and used in stews. Peas and beans

(continued on page 140)

can be allowed to mature on the vine. When they rattle in the pods, hull and store in weevil-proof jars or paper bags. Hot peppers can be allowed to leather-dry on the vine, then bunched and let cure to dry.

Winter-keeping type onions are left to mature in the field (to hasten the process, bend over tops when bulbs are fully grown). Pulled and cleaned, the stems are braided in long chains that will last indefinitely.

Squash for winter-storage (Hubbard keeps best, Butternut good; acorn-type okay) are bred to develop late in the season and produce a thick rind. Let yours mature fully in the field—to the point that the stem is completely dry three or so inches from the fruit. Turn in field so bottom cures. Collect, remove soil, and store in a dry place where air can circulate, keeping rind hard. Dry air is more important than temperature. Famous "No-Work" gardener Ruth Stout keeps her harvest in a box under her bed in her Connecticut home, and it lasts all winter. ∎

CHAPTER 6

࿔

Foraging: Free Food From Nature

Wild Greens of the West (and Elsewhere)

You can take to the countryside in late April or early May, most anyplace in North America, and find tender, fresh-sprouted wild greens in abundance. Imagine hiking the Rockies and feasting on copious quantities of miner's lettuce, watercress, yellow monkey flower, spearmint, dogtooth violet, wild hyacinth, plantain, salsify, burdock, and other delicious free fare. Some of the tastiest, most nutritious vegetables and herbs in the entire plant world are yours for the taking when you know where to find them and when to harvest them.

Waterleaf: One of the more abundant springtime "volunteer vegetables" is water leaf (*Hydrophyllum capitatum*), a delicate, leafy herb that grows in moist, rich, shade throughout the West at elevations ranging from sea level to 9,000 feet. (Two related species *H. canadense* and *H. virginianum* thrive in the northeastern United States, where the plants are sometimes called "John's cabbage.")

The nice thing about waterleaf is that the roots, stems, blossoms (when young), and leaves are all edible. The stems, in particular, are especially delightful, either in salads or pickled. Even after the plant's purplish flowers, each of which resembles a cat's paw, have appeared and the leaves are old, there's usually no bitter taste.

Try steaming enough of this plant's leaves and stems to make two cups of cooked greens. Then for 10 minutes simmer together one tablespoon each of vegetable oil and honey, the juice of half a lemon, two tablespoons of cider vinegar, two unpeeled, chopped or sliced green apples, and one teaspoon of mace or allspice. Combine the steamed greens with the hot, seasoned, cooked apples and serve the resulting "Sweet and Sour Waterleaf" as a delightful meal for two.

Nettles for Nutrition: Offhand you wouldn't think that the common stinging nettle with its thousands of bothersome needle-sharp hairs would be a good potherb, but it is.

When less than a foot tall, the sting nettle (*Urtica dioica*) is a delicious and nutritious spinach substitute. Its heart-shaped leaves are packed with protein, iron, vitamin A, and ascorbic acid.

Few plants, wild or otherwise, are as versatile as the weedlike nettle. Europeans have valued the spiny herb as a source of textile fibers for centuries. When dried to destroy the many stinging hairs, nettles make an excellent livestock feed, and when the cows and chickens are done with it, the plant returns to the ground as a nutrient-rich organic fertilizer. The dried greens also can be used to make tea.

You'll want to harvest nettles as you would the spiny fruit of prickly pears; that is, armed with heavy gloves, a pair of scissors, and a paper bag in which to carry the plant's tender tops. Once the foliage has been dried or boiled, it is safe to handle and to eat.

Nettle roots are edible, too, although they tend to be a bit fibrous. Chop and cook the roots, strain them to remove their fibers, and then for a marvelously savory soup, combine them with onions and milk, heat, and season to taste.

Nettles have a mild taste, and you may wish to combine them with more flavorful wild edibles such as older dandelions, dock, or plantains. Some cooks like to add onion tops and bulbs, Indian celery, sweet and hot peppers, and watercress to fresh nettles, cook everything in a small amount of water, and puree the mixture in a blender to create a creamy soup.

If you get a chance, try making some nettle rennet, too: dissolve two cups of salt in three cups of strong nettle tea. A teaspoon of the resulting liquid, when added to a pint of lukewarm milk, will set it into custard to be cut into curds for cheese as well as store-bought rennet does.

Next time you see a nettle plant threatening to sting your ankles along a hiking trail, don't cuss it...cook it! You'll be delighted with the results.

Miner's Lettuce: Miner's lettuce (*Montia per foliata*) was a favorite of the scurvy-plagued, vegetable-starved forty-niners. It's one of the most plentiful wild edibles in the western United States and is easily recognized. It's also one of the few native American plants that has been introduced into Europe, where it's known as winter purslane.

Miner's lettuce grows in moist, rich soils in forests, along streams, and at the bases of cliffs. You'll recognize the plant by its distinctive saucer-shaped leaves, which have the appearance of having been stabbed through the center by their supporting stem. At its tip, the stem bears one or more small, five-petaled flowers that are usually white, but occasionally pinkish .

The succulent, vitamin C-rich leaves and stems are delicious on sandwiches, and some say they are far superior to store-bought lettuce. Combined with watercress or other cresses, wild onions, and Indian celery, they make a delicious wilted salad, too. The greens are also good cooked, as are the plant's roots. When pureed they form the basis for a unique creamed soup.

Wonderful Watercress: Connoisseurs who savor the peppery taste of watercress (*Nasturtium officinale*) say they'd gladly trade any domestic variety of lettuce for this spicy member of the mustard family.

Watercress is naturally tolerant of cold weather, which means that the herb may be harvested year-round in many parts of the United States. (Watercress is sometimes found in protected streams in midwinter.) Thus, you should have no trouble locating successive crops of young plants. Even the older, flowering specimens, which can be quite peppery, are worth nibbling, seed pods and all.

Identifying watercress is no problem, especially if you're at all familiar with the high-priced version sold in supermarkets. Look for a low, floating plant with masses of glossy, rounded leaves and numerous threadlike roots in slow-moving rivers and streams or shady moist, seepy places in the woods. Pick the leaves and small stems, but leave the roots in place to generate more of the tangy greens.

When you do find a colony of wild watercress, make sure that the water in which the plants are growing isn't polluted. If you're uncertain whether the water is tainted, you can sterilize the cress by first soaking it for half an hour in halazone-treated water, then rinsing the leaves twice in clean water. (Halazone is available in most drugstores and sporting goods outlets. Follow the label directions.)

Many folks think of watercress as strictly a salad vegetable. But it is delicious when wilted in hot oil with sorrels, dock, miner's lettuce, purslane, dandelions, and other greens, and when served in other ways—on sandwiches, for instance, or boiled, or in soups.

A number of other cresses: winter, spring, alpine, mountain, and upland, to name a few, can be found in fields, on hillsides, and along roads and riverbanks throughout much of the United States. These species grow in more arid habitats and aren't as succulent as watercress.

Wild Lettuce: Many natural foods experts speak glowingly of the dozen or so species of wild lettuce, all of which—like domesticated lettuce varieties—are grouped in the genus Lactuca. Try some of these greens yourself, and you'll know why.

The two most common species of wild lettuce are *L. canadensis* (also called horseweed or tall lettuce) and *L. scariola* (variously known as prickly lettuce, compass plant, and wild opium). Both of these relatives of the sunflower can grow to a height of seven feet, both contain milky sap, and both are widely cursed as weeds.

Unlike cultivated lettuces, wild lettuce (regardless of species) becomes tough and bitter within a fairly short time, and the weedlike herbs should be harvested well before they reach maturity. Pick as much of the young plant as you can find; the leaves can be frozen for future use.

When harvested early, wild lettuce tastes like a zippier version of regular lettuce, and it's good in salads. The leaves, which have a slightly acrid taste, cook well in combination with milder potherbs, such as nettles, lamb's-quarters, and young dock.

Sow Thistle: Another lettuce-like wild edible that belongs to the sunflower family is the sow thistle (*Sonchus asper*). You'll find this prickly plant growing almost anyplace where wild lettuce thrives—along roadsides and streams, in meadows and vacant lots, and in similar weedy habitats.

Harvest Time: With winter barely past, you can pick waterleaf, stinging nettle, miner's lettuce, watercress, horseweed, wild opium and sow thistle. Later there will be such palatable wild edibles as curly dock, lamb's-quarters, sheep sorrel, wood sorrel, purslane, green amaranth, burdock, fireweed, mustard, and plantain. So what are you waiting for? Grab your gloves, pick up the shears, and head for the hills. Wild greens are ready to be harvested.

Wild Foods from Your Garden

You needn't hike hither and yonder to reap a bountiful harvest of volunteer vegetables. The fact is, you need not look any farther than your own yard or garden to find plenty of free-for-the-plucking wild plants.

It's entirely possible that the wheelbarrow load of "weeds" hoed and pulled from the yard and garden will be full of excellent soup and salad greens rather than just throwaways fit only for the compost pile. It's no accident that many wild plants also bear the name of a common domestic vegetable preceded by the word "wild." For instance, the leafy plant known commonly as lamb's-quarters is also called wild spinach.

The Secret of Cracking Hickory Nuts

A lot of folks think that hickory nuts—from a member of the genus Carya that is native to most areas of North America—are impossible to crack neatly, but if you strike one in just the right spot, the shell will fracture along clean lines almost every time, because of the interior architecture of the shell itself. A membranous partition called the septum divides the kernel in such a way that when a nut is struck near its stem end, where the thickest part of that membrane attaches to the outer hull, the shock waves travel along the septum and through the shell, causing the rugged casing to open like a hard-shelled flower into six separate pieces.

Foraging in Autumn: Hickory nuts usually begin to drop from the trees in early autumn as soon as they're loosened by rain or frost. If you want to forage a good supply, be sure to head for the nearest grove as soon as the nuts start to fall, because this wild food is a favorite of squirrels. The plume-tailed scavengers are skillful hickory hunters, and if you're not quick, they'll beat you to the scene and may plunder the entire crop before you have time to collect any nuts at all.

Take a bucket or sack with you on foraging trips (or just wear an apron with big pockets) and use a small stick to scratch around in the leaves under each tree. Most of the nuts you pick up will still be encased in their rough, dark hulls, which have to be removed before you can start cracking. Some gatherers stamp on their crop to dehusk the nuts, while others pick the sections of the outer coverings off carefully, one at a time. Whichever way you remove the hulls, though, don't throw away those hand-staining pods, as they can be used as a wood stain, fabric dye, or aromatic and bug-repelling mulch for your garden.

Once you've toted your harvest home, you'll need to sort through the pile and remove any wormy or rotten nuts. Discard nuts with discolored shells, grub holes, or a dry and wrinkled appearance. Rinse off all mud and debris and spread your hoard in the sun for a few days. It helps during this period to stir the nuts around every once in a while, so they'll dry out evenly.

The "Meat" of the Matter: Once completely dehydrated, the crop will be ready to be cracked open. First, assemble the few tools you'll need: a hammer, a nut pick, a brick, and a pan. Don't try to use a lever-type nutcracker for this operation, because it will crush the meats into fragments.

Place the brick on a hard, level surface and set the pan next to it. Right-handed folks should grasp a nut between the thumb and forefinger of the left

(continued on page 146)

(continued from page 145)

hand, with the (rounder) stem end pointing toward the right. Balance the nut on top of the brick (narrow edge downward) and aim your hammer at a spot about one-third of the way down from the stem end of the nut.

Whack that spot with a short, sharp blow, and the nut will pop right open. The shells may not split perfectly every time. The single most important factor will be the striking force of the hammer blow, which you'll have to learn to control through experience. As you open each nut, drop the meat-containing sections into the collection pan at the side of the brick. When you've cracked a good supply of hickories, you can use a pick to remove those delicious kernels. You can toss the shell fragments into the bird feeder. Feathered visitors love to peck at any tiny morsels you may have missed.

Eat 'Em Up: When you want to put the tasty crop to use, you can roast and enjoy the oil-rich nuggets raw, toasted, or added to cake and cookie recipes.

It's easy to roast the chewy pieces, either on the stove or in the oven. For range-top toasting, use a dry, unoiled pan or cookie sheet set over medium heat. Spread the nutmeats evenly across the pan and stir them often, until they turn light brown.

For oven roasting, warm the nuts in a shallow pan at 200°F until they're a golden color. You can make a wholesome nut butter from your roasted hickories by grinding the meats in a blender, along with enough safflower oil to produce the desired texture. Then salt to taste.

Hickory nuts can be used as delicious substitutes for expensive pecans or walnuts in bread and dessert recipes by using the same amount of the wild nuts as you would customarily use of the other varieties. ∎

Chances are, your backyard, lawn, or garden is well stocked with free edibles such as these few common good-to-eat weeds.

Lamb's-Quarters (*Chenopodium album*): Lamb's-quarters, also known as pigweed, goosefoot, and wild spinach, is a relative of spinach and one of the most widely distributed plants on earth. In years gone by, Europeans and Native Americans alike cultivated this leafy annual for its abundant yield of seeds, which contain an average of 16% protein (compared to wheat's 14%).

As a young green, however, it is delicious and surprisingly nutritious. The uncooked plants are richer in iron, protein, and vitamin B2 than both raw cabbage and raw spinach.

Mature plants stand from 2 to 7 feet tall and can be identified by their jagged-edged, diamond-shaped leaves, the undersides of which are powdered with coarse, whitish particles accounting for the Latin name album, or "white." The short leaf stalks may be either plain green or reddish-streaked. Both the stems and leaves of young plants are a mealy white.

While only the tender growing tips of mature Chenopodium are mild enough to eat, every part from the ground up is tasty when taken from plants less than a foot tall.

Some folks like to use this green in salads, but it's also excellent cooked as a substitute for spinach and is especially good when creamed. It is also quite tasty when wilted in hot dressing, as follows: Fry one small, diced onion in 1/2 cup of salad oil. Making sure the oil in the frying pan isn't hot enough to splash, add 1/4 cup of vinegar, 1/4 teaspoon salt, and pepper if desired. Throw in four cups of lamb's-quarters, stir-fry until limp, and serve.

Green Amaranth (*Amaranthus retroflexus*): A milder-tasting relative of lamb's-quarters that can be prepared in the same manner is green amaranth, also known as redroot, wild beet, and (coincidentally) pigweed—because foraging hogs (who know the good stuff) seek it out.

You'll recognize green amaranth by three main features: a stout, hairy stem; rough-to-the-touch, pointed oval leaves borne on stalks almost as long as the leaves themselves; and a crimson-colored root. Height varies, though the mature plant seldom grows more than 3 feet tall.

While some people suggest ways of preparing raw amaranth leaves, others recommend eating the leaves only after they've been cooked, because the foliage contains a substance called saponin. Used commercially as a foaming and emulsifying agent and detergent, saponin imparts to the raw leaves of green amaranth an odd taste and can cause digestive upsets.

Brief cooking will drive saponin out of the plant's leaves and create a vitamin-rich vegetable side dish that's sure to please. Because the plain, cooked greens have a very delicate flavor, you may wish to serve them with a stronger-tasting vegetable such as curled dock or with cheese sauce.

Boiled, wilted, fried, creamed, or steamed, green amaranth is an uncommonly delicious find.

Purslane (*Portulaca oleracea*): If you want a weed you can safely eat raw, try purslane.

A native of southern Asia, purslane is at present widely cultivated throughout Europe and the Orient for use as a salad green and potherb. In America, however, relatively few gardeners have discovered how flavorful and nourishing this small, ground-hugging plant can be.

Although purslane rarely grows taller than two inches, it can, and will, quickly spread its fleshy, reddish-purple stems and paddle-shaped leaves over a large portion of a garden. All above-ground parts of this semisucculent are edible and are rich in iron and calcium. Harvest only the tender, growing tips, though, if you want to keep your purslane productive all summer long.

The leaves or tips add a welcome and slightly acidic flavor to salads. In addition, the foliage is delectable, either boiled, or fried in butter with salt or pepper.

Purslane's texture is somewhat gooey or mucilaginous. If you find this disagreeable, try dipping the plant in a beaten egg, rolling it in a mixture of bread crumbs and flour, and then frying the vegetable until it's brown. The glutinous quality of the leaves is rendered unnoticeable by the procedure. This gooey property makes purslane an excellent substitute for okra in soups, sauces, and almost any recipe calling for a thickener.

Curled Dock (*Rumex crispus*): The docks are some of the hardiest, most widespread, most persistent weeds found anywhere. These plants are found practically anywhere you'd expect a weed to grow: alongside streams, roads, and driveways, and in pastures, vacant lots, and gardens.

Of the 15 *Rumex* species called docks, all are edible. None, however, is as well-known or delicious as curled dock (also called narrow-leaved dock and yellow dock). The plant's name refers to the fact that its slender, lance-shaped leaves, most of which sprout directly from the ground, have wavy edges. Often, these leaves reach two or more feet in length, while the weed's spindly flower stalks grow to four or five feet in height before they bear small, green blossoms.

Curled dock's glossy foliage is best if the leaves are more than a foot long, to the point of tasting bitter. There are two ways of dealing with this unpalatable pungency.

The first is to boil the plant through two waters. In other words, place the leaves in cold water in a pan, bring to a boil, and drain the hot water off. Then add more liquid to the container and cook the foliage until it's tender. By doing this you are pouring some vitamins down the drain, but the steaming-hot greens that remain in the pan are among the best-tasting of all wild, foraged vegetables.

A second effective way to rid dock leaves of their astringency is to cream them. To do this, mix a tablespoon of flour with a tablespoon of melted butter in a pan, add two cups of chopped dock leaves and 1/2 cup of milk to the butter and flour paste, and cook, stirring constantly, until the sauce thickens. The result: a gourmet's delight without the bite.

Sheep Sorrel (*Rumex acetosella*): A close relative of curled dock and a frequent inhabitant of neglected gardens is sheep sorrel, also known as sourgrass.

Although the light-green, arrowhead-shaped leaves of sourgrass are a bit acid tasting and shouldn't be eaten in excess, this shouldn't keep you from using small amounts of the foliage to add zest to your salads, soups, and other dishes. Place a few leaves of *acetosella* (literally, "small vinegar plant") in a salad as a substitute for vinegar dressing.

The crisp tartness of sheep sorrel makes it a perfect accompaniment to fish. Verify this for yourself by including some chopped sourgrass leaves in your favorite seafood sauce, or the next time you bake a whole, stuffed fish, add a small quantity of sorrel to the stuffing mix.

Sheep sorrel may also be substituted for rhubarb in pie recipes. Just cook the sorrel leaves, combine them with the remaining ingredients, and pour the resulting mixture into a pie shell. Then top with a layer of crust, pop the whole thing into the oven, and bake according to the recipe's directions.

Another sheep sorrel dish, puree, goes back many years. The timeless instructions say to boil three pound of the leaves until tender, drain them, and press the cooked foliage through a sieve until they're smooth. Then pour the pureed greens into a saucepan containing two tablespoons of butter, and simmer while stirring for 10 minutes. Finally, add more butter or milk or cream as desired, and salt and pepper to taste.

Wood Sorrel (*Oxalis acetosella* and other species): This fragile plant, held by some to be a descendant of the original shamrock, grows in shady areas alongside houses and fences. It can be recognized by its familiar triple heart-shaped leaves. Most of the dozen species of *Oxalis* known as wood sorrel bear yellow flowers, though some have white blossoms and others have violet or pink blooms. Regardless of the species, the pointed seedpods of wood sorrel are always good for a refreshing, lemony nibble on a summer day.

Wood sorrel is similar in taste to sheep sorrel. Thus, one plant can replace the other in many recipes. However, because the wood sorrel's stem can be stiff and hard to chew even after cooking, you'd be well advised to harvest only the leaves from *Oxalis* species.

You'll find that raw wood sorrel leaves add a delightful flavor to sandwiches, and that the shamrock-like foliage makes a decorative and tasty garnish.

Food Is Where You Find It: You can use any of the plants described here alone or mixed as soup greens or the base for a puree. Also, it's no chore to store the wild edibles for year-round use. All you have to do is blanch the greens by placing them in a small amount of boiling water for two minutes, cool the foliage quickly in prechilled water, pack the victuals in airtight containers, and put them in the freezer.

Give the lamb's-quarters, purslane, amaranth, curled dock, or either of the sorrels described here a try. Add an extra measure of nutrition to your meals and watch your grocery bill go down at the same time. It makes good sense to stop thinking of garden weeds as ornery pests and to begin accepting them for what in many cases they actually are: natural, free foods.

Bright Berries of Summer

Wild berries! Nothing's as likely to set a mouth to watering and a body to thinking about pies and jams and jellies and other such excruciatingly delicious treats. And there's no better time than midsummer for gathering nature's fruits from fields and forests, roadsides and city streets, meadows and open

slopes. Myriad types and varieties can be found in virtually any corner of North America, and you shouldn't have much trouble locating at least one tasty species not far from your own back door. When you do, try your best to get as many of the bite-size morsels past your mouth and into a collecting bucket as you can (a formidable test of willpower, to be sure), and remember to return later to the same spot if you see any flowers of fruit yet to come. By carefully observing where and when each variety in your region ripens, you may well be able to go berrying from late spring until the first few weeks of fall.

Blackberries: Blackberries are the forager's delight and the eternal bane of botanists, who thus far have only been able to pin down the number of individual species to "somewhere between 50 and

390." True blackberries are borne on thorny upright canes (as opposed to trailing vines) and can be found throughout most of the continent, including even Arctic regions, along roadsides and hedgerows, and in abandoned meadows. Rich in vitamins A and C, the fruit which is preceded by large white flowers in early spring can usually be harvested from late June to early August and beyond. Pick the berries when they're really sweet (one or two days after they've turned black).

Cranberries: The American cranberry (*Vaccinium macrocarpon*) thrives in peaty bogs and, similarly semimarshy areas from Nova Scotia to North Carolina and westward to Minnesota. The coast of Massachusetts and other relatively cool regions near large bodies of water are particularly prime territory for this small shrub, which is easily identified by its thick oval-shaped evergreen leaves and nodding pink or red flowers that blossom between June and August. The tart berries (best when cooked with honey, for sauces and jelly) turn ripe-red during September and October and cling to their branches throughout winter. They're especially good when picked after autumn's first frost.

Strawberries: Although roughly half a dozen species of wild strawberries (genus: *Fragaria*) grow in our part of the world (ranging from the Arctic Circle to Florida and west to California), the fruit is found in greatest abundance in the Northeast and eastern Canada. The plants sport three coarsely toothed leaves, produce small five-petaled white flowers in the spring, and bear fruit (which is most often red, but sometimes white) between May and July. Look for this sought-after forager's prize in open woods and clearings, on exposed slopes, and along roadsides, stream beds, and railroads. Harvest them soon after sunrise, when they're still glistening with the early morning dew.

Huckleberries: If you pop an especially dark "blueberry" in your mouth and promptly bite down on 10 stone-hard seeds, you can be sure that what you really have is a huckleberry. This fruit's unfortunate preponderance of pits, however, is but a small obstacle, overcome by straining the pulp through a sieve, to folks who've come to savor its unique and somewhat spicy flavor. Most species of huckleberry (genus: *Gaylussacia*) are small shrubs that favor acid soil, grow from a foot to three feet tall, and range throughout most of the eastern, southern, and northwestern states. Look for the almost-black-skinned fruit from June to September in oak woods, bogs, sandy or rocky areas, and clearings.

Gooseberries: Gooseberries are relatively common in moist woods throughout Canada and across the northern border states of this country, sometimes occurring as far south as Colorado in the West and New Jersey in the East. Mountainous regions from Massachusetts to North Carolina may also be the home of this tart round fruit. There are several species of gooseberries (genus: *Ribes*), each of which ripens to a different shade of reddish purple. The globe-like berries are usually picked when green, though, and flavored with honey or some other sweetener in pies, jellies, and sauces. The shrublike plant stands from two to four feet tall, displays greenish or purplish flowers in May and June, and produces a bounty for the resourceful forager during July and August.

Dewberries: For practical purposes, most foragers distinguish dewberries from blackberries (both of which belong to the genus *Rubus*) as "the ones that grow on trailing vines rather than on canes." The consensus is that dewberries are the choicest of blackberry-like fruits. They're bigger, fatter, juicier, and tastier. Look for the telltale white flowers of this ground-hugging plant in the spring, and be prepared to harvest its bounty beginning in mid-June, or about two weeks earlier than the "ordinary" blackberries in your area are ready for picking. The dewberry favors dry soil, and it ranges from the eastern United States as far west as Oklahoma. Watch for sharp thorns on some species.

Currants: All species of wild currants, which ripen during July and August, belong to the genus *Ribes* and grow on small shrubs that sport maple leaf-shaped foliage and favor cold, wet woods. Most varieties of the fruit are smooth, but a few are covered with short "bristles," and nearly all exude a slightly disagreeable odor resembling that of skunk cabbage till cooked . Red currants range throughout southern Canada, along the Rockies to Colorado and the Alleghenies to North Carolina, and in parts of New Jersey, Indiana, and Minnesota. Black currants, which are relatively rare, can sometimes be found in moist forests from Nova Scotia to Virginia and west to Kentucky, Iowa, and Nebraska.

Blueberries: Blueberries (genus: *Vaccinium*) are one of the world's most widespread fruits. They occur from the tropics to northern Alaska. The two most abundant species in the United States are the low-bush blueberry, which rarely exceeds a foot in height and ranges from New England west to Minnesota, and the high-bush variety, which can reach a height of up to 6 feet and grows throughout the Atlantic coastal plain from Maine to Georgia and west to Lake Michigan. Both ripen between July and September and thrive in areas of acid soil, particularly burned-over fields and old pastures. Less common types can be found from the mountains of the West Coast to the swamps of New Jersey.

Raspberries: The wild red raspberry (*Rubus strigosus*) is found in dry or rocky areas from Newfoundland to British Columbia, south in the Alleghenies to North Carolina, and in the Rockies to New Mexico. The tangy fruit is borne on canes that grow from two to five feet tall and are covered with many weak, bristly spines. Look for the promising three- or five-petaled white flowers between May and July, and make a mental note to bring a bucket back with you several weeks later (mid-July to September) when the canes will be laden with plump, ripe-for-the-picking berries. You'll have to add commercial pectin to the fruit if you intend to put it up as jam or jelly.

Mulberries: Nobody ever has or ever will "go round the mulberry bush" because the red mulberry (Moruirubra) is not a bush at all, but a tree, found in fields and along roadsides (and even city streets) throughout the eastern United States and west to the Great Plains. The fruit ripens over several weeks during July, when the elongated berries turn deep purple and can easily be shaken from their branches into a blanket spread over the ground below. You can dehydrate mulberries for winter storage by drying them between window screens in the sun. Be advised: you'll have to battle the birds for the ripe juicy fruit, as it is a favorite with our feathered friends. If you run across a mulberry tree on a hike, don't pitch your tent beneath its branches thinking to reach up and pluck breakfast next morning. The birds'll beat you to the pick'ns and will leave purple splotchy reminders of their repast all over your tent.

Elderberries: The sweet or common elder (*Sambucus canadensis*) is a 4- to 12-foot-high shrub that grows along road-sides and in open fields and woods throughout the eastern half of the United States and Canada. In July, the plant produces umbrella-shaped clusters of tiny white flowers called "elderblow," that makes a delicious treat when fried in batter like fritters.

The blooming flower heads fill the air with a heady perfume and by early August give way to equally numerous bunches of berries. When green, the fruit can be pickled and used to flavor sauces as a substitute for capers. Most foragers, however, wait until September when the berries have ripened to a mildly astringent, sweet deep purple and virtually beg to be picked by the handful.

Black Raspberries: The wild black raspberry (*Rubus occidentalis*, some-times known as "thimbleberry") is more widespread than its red-colored cousin and is a bit more hazardous to harvest. The canes' strong, sharp thorns have left many a berry picker scratched from the ankles up. You're most like-ly to find this outrageously tasty species along roadsides and fence rows and in neglected fields from Quebec to Ontario and south to Georgia and Missouri. The plant seems to have a special liking for old tree trunks and rocky places, so keep an eye out for such spots when you're searching. Black raspberries ripen during July and early August. Harvest them when they're plump and heavy with juice.

Domesticating Wild and Feral Fruits and Berries

This sound familiar? You are out hiking and run across an old apple tree with a few misshapen fruit hanging from a gnarly branch. You pick one of the sorry-looking fruit and take a bite—and discover a rich, tart apple-flavor you've never experienced before. Or, in a sunny meadow, your eyes light on a glint of bright red or purple in the grass. You bend down to discover a grand spread of wild strawberries or dewberries so sweet and juicy they melt in your mouth. Or, crossing a low wall, a bramble snags your backpack; you turn to disengage the thorns…and discover a whole tangled thicket of black or red raspberries in all stages of ripening from white to dark glistening red, black, or purple.

You needn't wait wait for luck-of-the-hike or fortune-of-the-foray to savor those wild and feral (escaped from cultivation) fruits. So long as you have the landowner's permission, you can snip a few whips or dig a few roots and trans-plant the wildings to your own land. Offer them a few benefits of cultivation and savor their luscious output from your own backyard.

You may be rescuing a rare—maybe even a near-extinct—strain of pioneer fruit abandoned to the wild. And sad to say, so much rural land is being urban-ized, next time you decide to go hiking you may find your favorite hike-snack apple trees and berry plants bulldozed away, because, as it goes in the song: "…they paved paradise and put up a parking lot."

Adaptable and Hardy: No wild edible-fruiting plant species are even remotely endangered, and all will transplant and thrive in home gardens, since such varieties are typically very hardy. In fact, in northern sections of the coun-try where winter temperatures reach well below zero, many tender commer-cial varieties won't bear or may even fail to survive, while transplanted native berries and fruits, born and bred to withstand the rigorous weather, are strong and productive.

Be careful to select only healthy stock; wild plants often harbor diseases that don't much bother them, but that can attack and devastate less robust commercial strains.

Leaf curl, orange rust, verticillium wilt, or other diseases might spread from wild brambles to fancy hybrid raspberries and blackberries. So, plant wild cousins as far from the domestic bushes as possible. For the same reason, locate the transplants well away from tomatoes, peppers, eggplants, potatoes, apple trees, or maple trees.

There are three (seasonal) stages in domesticating wild fruits and berries. First, as the fruit develops during the growing seasons in their original habitat, mark the healthiest, most productive with day-glow surveyors ribbon tied to a cane or branch. In the fall, work organic matter into the soil of the beds that will receive the native plants and correct pH balance to around a moderately sour 6.0 if necessary. In late winter or early spring before the sap rises, go forth with a shovel and burlap sacks, dig up the prizes, and immediately replant them in the new location.

Succulent Strawberries: The large, commercially grown hybrid strawberries were developed from native North American wildings, but they have never matched the delectable, aromatic flavor of their undomesticated ancestors. The perennial wild strawberry (genus: *Fragaria*) is among the most delicious of all fruits, but sample the berries a season before transplanting because some, the wood strawberries (*Fragaria vesca*), are practically tasteless.

Wild strawberries are so vigorous and transplant so easily that it's difficult to make a mistake with them. Fill the new bed with well-tilled, slightly sandy, compost-enriched loam and make sure the pH range is between 5.8 and 6.5. Because the plants can't tolerate standing water, good water drainage is more important than either pH levels or soil composition. So, drain wet land or build raised beds to guarantee your new plant-guests will have dry feet.

In early spring before the plants have flowered, dig up the most robust, brightly-leaved strawberry plants with a trowel, keeping plenty of soil around the roots to lessen the shock of transplanting. Pick off dead leaves, old runners, and any sod plants that cling around the plant crown. Leaving 12 inches between plants, set them out in rows two feet apart, being careful not to cover the crowns with earth. During the first season after transplanting, pick off any flowers that appear, and in the late summer, arrange runners around plants. Limit runners to two per plant. These prunings assure heavier fruit production in subsequent years.

In order to meet their early ripening schedule, the plants almost always put out blossoms before the last of spring's treacherous weather is over. Therefore, in the North they do best if planted on a slope that's above frost pockets if they're to give the highest possible yields. Even so, should the temperature take a plunge, you should cover the plants to protect their tender blossoms.

Keep weeds out of the bed and by late August, you will have a dense mat of flourishing dark-green plants, which promise a good yield during the coming summer. In late fall, cover with an organic mulch.

Plants will push up through the mulch next spring and bear for you. After the first few fall frosts, rake the bed vigorously to remove old plants, mulch the bed with straw or dry calamus or cattail leaves. When spring comes, remove the covering and await the next bountiful harvest.

Versatile Elderberries: One of the most useful woodland plants is the elderberry; the flowers and fruits can be used to make superb wine, jelly, fritters, pies, muffins, pancakes, chutney, and a deliciously refreshing nonalcoholic drink. In the Northeast, several kinds of elderberries grow wild, but the common elderberry (*Sambucus canadensis*) is the most familiar.

Transplant these bushes in the spring by digging up plants of a manageable size and packing the roots in moist mulch before taking them home. If a bush is tall and rangy, prune it back by half and then plant it an inch deeper than it grew in the woods.

Common elderberries enjoy damp habitats and tend to spread vigorously if not cut back. The best place to plant one is in a moist area near a compost heap, for they're reported to help speed the formation of compost and produce a fine humus around their roots.

The easy-to-care-for wildings are prey to very few insects and diseases, but more than 43 species of birds place elderberries high on their list of delicacies, so be prepared to use protective nets as the fruit ripens.

Zesty Wild Apples: Wild apples might be either neglected, old cultivars found in abandoned orchards or seedling crabapples descended from domestic trees. Since apple seeds don't propagate true to type, the majority of wild trees revert to the characteristics of their ancient crab-stock ancestors and produce small, tart fruits that make excellent pies, jellies, sauce, and a superior tart cider.

Young trees growing in the wild can be transplanted to develop into mature specimens (though you won't know what their fruit will be like till it appears), or they can be used as rootstock after a year of adjustment to their new locale. Whichever purpose the seedlings are used for, the transplanting must be done while the trees are dormant.

Before uprooting a wild fruit tree, trench as above and prepare a roomy hole to receive the seedling and replace any hardpan or poor earth with rich topsoil. As soon as the tree's dug up, wrap its roots in burlap or plastic and rush the sapling to the prepared planting site.

Once there, snip off any shovel-frayed roots, spread the rest out on the bottom layer of rich, well-worked soil, and position the tree about an inch deeper than it grew in the wild. Build up the earth around the roots, pat it firm, and tamp down the final layer of soil to make a two-inch-deep water-holding depression all around the tree. After that, give each new transplant a bucket of water, which should soak the earth and help collapse any hidden air pockets.

Top-pruning is also important, both to balance root loss and to conserve the tree's vigor during its period of adjustment. Slice off any crossed, dead, and obviously weak or badly angled branches flush with the trunk, prune the remaining limbs, and cut the top half way back. Finally, paint the pruning wounds with a special tree sealer or nonleaded paint. If the weather is dry, water the trees every few days. Don't add any fertilizer during the first season. Strong substances could injure trimmed and weak roots.

If the wild seedling is to be used as rootstock, wait at least a year before making the graft so the tree can recover from transplantation shock. Because they're suited to your climate, established wild apple seedlings can provide especially hardy rootstock for your grafting experiments. All apples are related through the genus *Malus,* so all are compatible for grafting. Be sure, though, that the trees from which you choose scions can also tolerate the region's weather. It's useless, for example, to expect a warmth-loving Granny Smith scion to survive a cold Vermont winter because it's been grafted onto a northern New England tree's rootstock.

Black and Red Bramble Fruit: Both wild blackberries and raspberries should be transplanted in the spring while the bushes are still dormant. While they are both members of the genus *Rubus,* these two fruit-bearing cousins seldom grow together in the wild and should not be planted near one another because raspberries can be an unaffected carrier of anthracnose, a disease that can destroy blackberries.

A few of the approximately 122 species of blackberry sport small prickly spikes along the canes, but the most common wild species protect themselves with stout, fierce thorns that can tear the skin and draw blood. With the plants set in orderly rows, harvesting the fruit is much less hazardous than picking the berries in a clump of wild bushes. The thorns on raspberries are less threatening.

Pruning is needed for the canes of both these plants when they are moved, but raspberries should get a less radical cutting than blackberries. Cut raspberry canes back to just above the first bud on each cane, but not more than six inches above ground level. Blackberry canes should be cut back to the roots. Yearly pruning of old, unproductive growth will keep your brambles healthy and your yields high.

The bushes should be set about 30 inches apart in well-prepared soil. To minimize the chance of any fungal diseases spreading in the patch, leave six to ten feet between the rows. Try to pick a spot that is similar to the one where the bushes were growing in the wild. Raspberries will need frequent waterings in dry weather, and a hay or grass-clipping mulch will help retain the moisture in the soil and keep weeds in check.

Outdoor Playthings from the Woodlot

Most toys produced these days seem outrageously expensive, easily broken, and unnecessarily complicated. But just watching youngsters' reactions to the world around them can provide the inspiration and instruction to create play things out of free, readily available materials.

Horse Swing: While taking a stroll through your woods one day, you might spy a young tree with a beautiful curve at its base. The bottom of the trunk can make a sturdy and graceful swing.

To convert the trunk to a swing, first cut it and carry it home. Back at the house, strip off the bark—quite an easy task while the wood is green. Then, using a brace fitted with a one-inch bit, bore two parallel holes through the swing-to-be, one at each end of the trunk.

Next, saw a pair of one-inch-diameter lengths from a straight hardwood branch, each about eight inches longer than the width of the log. With the bark removed, blunt the ends. The stubs should fit snugly in the holes with an end protruding on either side of the log. Ropes are then attached to the ends of the cross pieces to suspend the swing.

The hanging horse can be used safely by any child old enough to hold himself or herself in place on it, and the height of the swinging steed can easily be adjusted to suit the length of the young rider's legs by letting out or taking up the rope it hangs by.

Bark Pipelines: The remainder of the tree used to make the horse swing can be stripped and cut into fenceposts, a process that will produce a pile of curled

(continued on page 159)

The adventurous may wish to experiment by transplanting other untamed fruits. Wild cherries, serviceberries, blueberries, native plums, and others can be moved from their happenstance homes to a cultivated plot.

Wild Yeast for the Baking

The leader of a survival-school camping expedition in the rugged terrain of the Pacific Northwest routinely distributed to each member of the party a ration of whole wheat flour sweetened with a lump or two of raw sugar. This basic food served as a supplement to gathered wild fare. In the evening, the flour

bark. A 4-year-old can construct a water engineering project using these left-overs, and though such a homemade aqueduct might seem just a toy, bark-strip conduits have been used by pioneers and homesteaders for channeling water to a house.

Bark Boats: Another project using bark will turn small scraps 2 to 2-1/2 inches wide and 3 to 4 inches long into little Viking ships.

First, use a nail to press holes into the bark at any points where you want to locate masts. The uprights are made from thin sticks whittled to a point on one end. Trapezoid-shaped pieces of paper or big leaves can serve as sails. Just slip them onto the sticks and mount the masts in the nail holes.

When you blow on the little sails, the small bark boats slip prettily across the water, and there are almost always a few exciting capsizings to watch.

A Rustic Play Platform: The next time you have to cut down trees near your house, you might leave a foot or so more stump than you ordinarily would. These will make sturdy foundations on which you can build rustic play platforms.

Set a stump-high log (or two) six feet from two serviceable stumps (one stump) to make a triangular shape. Anchor in place with large rocks or long wooden spikes. Then, spike 2 X 4s in place running between stumps to form a triangular base. Old boards can be nailed across these two beams, and a sturdy railing and a small ladder added.

This rustic "playform" is far enough above the ground it will give children the feel of a tree house—but is near enough to the ground it is safe. And, it can become a pirate ship, a goblin's cave, or a knight's castle in little kids' imaginations. ■

---

would be mixed with water, and the resulting paste shaped into a kind of tortilla and cooked in the hot coals of the fire. Such "ash cakes" tasted good the next day, and by the third day were still edible. However, by the eighth day in the woods, everyone hungered for fresh-baked tender, crispy-crusted leavened bread. Little did they know that the means of satisfying their craving was growing all around them.

On one of the daily foraging hikes, a biochemist in the group picked a handful of ripe Oregon grape berries and explained to curious onlookers that the white powder covering the fruit was a fungus commonly known as yeast.

Wild yeasts grow nearly everywhere, continually releasing spores into the air. If a single spore lands where there's moisture, sugar, and warmth, the simple plants will begin to grow and multiply—thriving especially well on the sweet skins of berries and grapes.

As the hiking scientist explained, the same yeast that ferments the sugars in the juices of grapes and other fruits will serve as a leavening agent when mixed with dough—as early prospectors discovered.

The prospectors' bread starter was made by combining equal amounts of flour and water and allowing the mixture to sour in an earthenware pot for three to five days. Yeast would be found and added, and the dough would become a bubbling mass or "sponge" with a pleasant, slightly alcoholic aroma.

Legends about the prospectors in California and Alaska indicate that they guarded their sourdough bread starter more closely than they would a poke of gold. The perpetually fermenting yeast culture was the wellspring of every meal, and it meant the difference between feasting on fresh bread and choking down a weevil-infested, rock-hard biscuit.

The leavening agent was kept growing by constant use and replenishment of the flour and water. A prospector would protect the brewing mass from the below-freezing northern temperatures by wrapping the sourdough crock in his bundle or by placing the pot in a pouch that could be tucked under his long johns, where body heat would keep the yeast alive. (Legend says that if the winter winds howled too fiercely, some gold seekers would hole up in their cabins and slurp down the nectarous liquid or "hooch" that formed on the surface of the well-fermented starter. The potent brew would keep the miners happy until the weather cleared!)

It's no wonder that the sour starter soon lent its peculiar homebred aroma to a prospector's cabin and clothing. Eventually the starter and the bread it produced became so well-known that the gold miners themselves took on the name of "sourdoughs."

It would hardly occur to most of us to forage for yeast in view of the ready availability and low price of the packaged commercial product and in light of the time consuming nature of sourdough baking. However, being in the middle of the forest with plenty of time on her hands, the leader of this expedition set her sights on making a batch of wild yeast sourdough. Her attempt was successful, so the next time that you're away from civilization and have a yen for real sourdough bread, you may want to try her method.

A Backwoods Backery: It's easy to spot the powdered blue berries of the Oregon grape (*Berberis aquifolium*), a fall-ripening, hollylike evergreen shrub that grows profusely in the mountain ranges of the Pacific coastal area. In the east, wild grapes and blueberries host their own species of yeasts. On both coasts, juniper berries and the bark of the aspen are other good sources of wild yeast, which appears in the form of a powdery white coating. When harvesting aspen bark, be especially careful not to harm the tree.

To prepare the "sponge," put a handful or two of the berries or bark in a scalded quart jar or crock, add two cups of whole wheat flour, and stir in two cups of lukewarm water. Next, loosely screw the lid onto the container to allow the gas from the fermenting process to escape and at the same time to protect the yeast culture from contamination. Keep warm near the fire or in the foot of your sleeping bag and wait for the prolific yeast to multiply.

After two days, tiny bubbles will appear in the mixture, and you'll know that the yeast is working. (A whiff of the fragrant concoction will leave no doubt as to whether the procedure is successful; it will smell like a miniature brewery!)

Remove the berries or bark promptly once the yeast is brewing, because an undesirable flavor may be imparted to the dough. And the starter may spoil if the berries are allowed to ferment in the mixture. They are no longer needed as a source of yeast, because the culture can now perpetuate itself.

Now, armed with a vigorous starter, you can set to work to produce some loaves of real sourdough bread. Before mixing the batter, check again to make sure no berries or bark remain in the sponge. In a large bowl, combine one cup of the starter with six cups of whole wheat flour, and add just enough water to make the mixture easy to handle. The next step is to knead the dough thoroughly, adding about four more cups of flour in the process until the mix becomes stiff and no longer sticks to the sides of the bowl. Shape the dough into two loaves and set them by the fire to rise, which may take three hours (or a little longer) on the warm rocks.

You can put that time to good use, however, by building a stone oven. A primitive cooker can be fashioned by setting a large flat rock directly in the coals of the fire, then forming three sides with inch-thick stone slabs and covering the top of the enclosure with a final stone. During baking, the heat can be regulated by piling up or scraping away the coals around the sides of the oven. The sourdough should cook to perfection in about an hour.

You'll find that the flavor of these golden loaves of wild yeast bread is more robust and a bit more sour than that of baked goods made with package leavening, and it's a far better taste than you'll find in the airy loaves found on supermarket shelves.

Once you have treated your taste buds to the hearty flavor of genuine sourdough bread, you'll never want to be without a crock of starter again. So go ahead. Gather a crop of yeast-bearing bark or berries and brew your own sourdough sponge in the kitchen or in camp.

A Feast from the Ocean Shore

Clam chowder so rich you can savor the taste of the steam and mussels so delicate they defy description don't have to mean an enormous bill at an exclusive seafood restaurant. These and other delicious foods are free for the taking to almost anyone within foraging range of an ocean, and it doesn't take days to fill a kettle.

Expensive equipment is unnecessary to pursue and harvest a bounty of shellfish. A good field guide, the desire to spend the day surrounded by the sounds and smells of the beach, and a willingness to brave water, mud, sand, and rocks are about all a person needs to get started.

Bountiful Bivalves: Bivalves, mollusks with two-hinged shells, make up the bulk of most people's seashore scavenging because they're readily available and fine eating. Even a novice forager can harvest plenty of these creatures without difficulty on the first trip out.

Before getting down to specifics, however, a few words of caution are in order. Most mollusks feed by siphoning in water and straining out and absorbing the small bits of food that they happen to suck in with the liquid. This, unfortunately, means that if the water is contaminated, these creatures can become tiny storehouses of poison. Always make sure of the water's purity by contacting the local health department before collecting and eating bivalves from any beach, tidal flat, or other coastline location.

Calling the area's state fish and game department office to determine seasons, size and bag limits, and licensing requirements is also a good idea. Most local sporting goods stores can sell you a permit if one is needed, and they can usually supply you with a yearly tide table. The latter will help you plan your expeditions around the prime foraging times, which in most areas are from two hours before until two hours after low tide.

Finally, never eat any shellfish that isn't unquestionably fresh. A general rule is to discard each and every bivalve that doesn't resist your efforts to open its shell or that doesn't close itself more tightly when touched.

Mussels: The quickest way to make the collecting sack bulge is with a passel of tasty mussels.

Members of the genera *Mytilus* and *Modiolus* (varieties of mussels) can be found along just about any portion of the North American coastline, east or west. Westerners should limit their gathering to a season running from November through April, since during the rest of the year, the bivalves found in their area may ingest microscopic dinoflagellates that can cause illness in humans. The old rule to harvest shellfish only during months that contain an "r" should do nicely for folks on the East Coast.

Once the season begins, a sharpened tire iron or heavy-bladed knife and a gunnysack are the only tools needed to go musseling.

Finding a bed of delicious mollusks to dig into should present no problem. Locate a rocky area near the low tide line, and if mussels are present, you'll be hard pressed not to walk on them. In large colonies where the shellfish are packed together like mosaic tiles, it's obviously an easy matter to pry off enough for a filling, delicious meal.

While foraging for mussels, have a look around the rocks for a clump of the long-stemmed, white-shelled goose barnacles, which are closely related to crabs, though they look like a cross between a mushroom and a gander. These bizarre creatures of the genus *Mitella* on the West Coast and *Lepas* on the East Coast have a flavor like lobster and are easy to collect. Scrape the black stems off their rocky perches and try for a compromise between getting the maximum amount of stalk and the minimum of grit and sand.

The mussels can be steamed right on the beach in a large kettle, and the barnacles can be popped into the water right along with the mollusks. Their white-shelled tops can be discarded after steaming, the stems cut open, and finger-sized pieces of meat pried out. Furthermore, since their taste is similar to that of the clawed crustaceans, goose barnacles can be substituted in any recipe that calls for crab or lobster.

Those patches of gravel surrounding the masses of stone that harbored the barnacles should be foraged too, as they're often the homes of small clams and of several types of mollusks called cockles.

Along the Atlantic coastline "cockle" usually refers to members of the genus *Cardium*. On the Pacific shore, however, the term is applied to mollusks of at least four different genera. Confusion is seldom a problem, though, because in local usage "cockle" most often seems to translate as "good eating clam." See what the area residents gather, double-check with your field guide, then have a go at foraging on your own.

You'll be thankful, as many a sore-backed digger has been, that cockles have no breathing siphons at all. Because of this, they must limit their below ground travel to within an inch or two of the sand's surface. A clam rake, a hoe, or a shovel should be the only tool needed to gather the tasty little rascals. However, because of the rocky nature of the sand in which cockles are generally found, even a small amount of digging will be anything but easy. And after leaving the seaside, remember that a freshwater rinse will greatly extend the life of your foraging equipment.

The West Coast's Large, Economy-Sized Clams: The Pacific Ocean is a huge body of water, and some of the clams that inhabit its North American coastline are nothing less than giants. The most common of these monsters is the horse clam (*Schizothaerus nuttalli*), found in mud and sand flats from Alaska to San Diego.

It isn't necessary to wait for a particularly low tide to snare a few of these whoppers, which run up to four pounds each. The only real job, after sighting the spouts from their squirt holes between the low and high water marks, is digging them out. Even when they're spraying water three feet into the air, these clams may well be buried a yard deep in the sand. Dig the giants out anyway; when properly cleaned and prepared, they're more than worth the effort.

The flavor of horse clams and other bivalves found in muddy sand can be improved by storing the shellfish alive in a cage sunk beneath the surface of the ocean or in a large, shaded tub of seawater for about 48 hours. If you add cornmeal to the water in the tub the critters will replace any silt in their bodies with the grain. This simple treatment will make most bivalves taste better, even species that the local diggers may think are inedible.

No discussion of clams, at least in California, would be complete without a mention of the pismo. This, the Golden State's most famous mollusk, is a tourist attraction in its own right and is found in open, sandy areas from Half Moon Bay near San Francisco all the way to southern Mexico. The pismo clam (genus *Givela*) supports an entire digging industry, complete with chauffeured boat rides to prime beaches and shoreside equipment rentals. Unfortunately, despite rigid size and bag limits, the pismo's population is threatened in popular clamming areas. It should be looked upon as a special treat rather than a regular source of wild food.

Clams can be steamed right on the seashore, the same way mussels and barnacles are prepared, and with any of these shellfish it's easy to collect a great many more than can be eaten in single a post-foraging feast.

Taking Some with You: Since shellfish spoil rapidly if left uncooked, it's best to go ahead and steam the entire day's harvest on the spot and carry any cooked but uneaten meat home to the freezer for use in chowders, soups, and other seafood recipes.

Steaming is the simplest and easiest way to cook shellfish and requires only a kettle equipped with a tight-fitting lid, some water, and a driftwood fire. White wine can be substituted for the water to make a flavorful treat .

Heat just enough liquid to cover the bottom of the pot and not boil away before the morsels are done. Add the shellfish and cover the kettle. Clams and mussels will be done after about 20 minutes of steaming; they are ready when the shells open wide. Barnacles take about the same amount of time.

Served with butter, French bread, and wine, all three of these seashore delicacies produce an excellent meal.

Out in the Water: Not all the coastal treats are found on exposed areas of rock or beach when the tide is out. Fish, crabs, and shellfish other than the mollusks, clams, and barnacles mentioned earlier must be pursued in waters along the coast.

When it comes to pulling in fish for the frying pan, the lowly cane pole (about 14 feet of bamboo), some string, a bobber, a sinker, and a few small hooks are all you really need.

The two most consistently productive types of shoreline saltwater fishing seem to be angling in tidal pools and off wharfs. Since many (but by no means all) of the fish you're likely to tie into in such areas are relatively small, the fastest way to fill your stringer or catch bucket is by using a tiny hook in the No. 6, No. 8, or even No. 10 size range on the end of your line.

Other anglers may look askance at your minuscule grapplers, but you'll have the last laugh. Bait up with rock snails, mollusks, and little sea worms foraged near your fishing site and proceed to haul in as many big ones as the people using larger hooks are catching, plus a healthy assortment of the small, tender, tasty fish that the other folks can't catch at all.

Smelt (*Osmerus mordax*), for instance, average only about six inches in length, but you can catch them by the bucketful when you find a school. It's hard to name any fish, regardless of size, that has a more delicate and delicious flavor when fried in browned butter.

These feisty little fish are abundant in most coastal waters of the United States. They look like miniature barracuda and have an appetite that matches their vicious appearance. They'll grab most anything you drop in front of them.

Another fish that can keep your bobber dancing if you live along the eastern seaboard between North Carolina and Labrador is the harbor pollack (*Pollachius virens*). This member of the cod family often grows to more than two feet long and isn't at all shy about latching onto a foraged bait. Locals frequently look down on this plentiful fish because of natural back spots and its many tiny bones, but a fillet taken from this cod's meaty back above the rib cage is both bone-free and wonderfully tasty.

Tie half a dozen of these fillets in a piece of cheese cloth, lay the package in the bottom of a sizable kettle, and add two quarts of water, one tablespoon of salt, and the juice of one lemon. Bring the water to a quick boil and simmer for five minutes. Remove and unwrap the pollack, and serve the fillets hot with a dill or anise sauce. This fish doesn't taste "fishy" and is also excellent fried, baked, or broiled, especially when seasoned first for an hour in a marinade made of one large finely diced or ground onion, two tablespoons of salt, two tablespoons of vinegar, and one teaspoon of mace. Rinse the fillets in cold water after their soak and then fry, bake, or broil them.

There are, of course, literally hundreds of other species of saltwater fish that you can harvest along the shoreline with a pole and line. Despite the fact that some are a little offbeat, most are delicious when cooked slowly until their meat just flakes. Don't, for instance, overlook shark, which has a taste and texture much like cod and is frequently sold in the market as grayfish. Another not to throw back is the ray. Cut off the wings of a common skate (*Raja erinacea*) close to the body, slice them into strips parallel to their "airfoil," peel off the skin, pop out the cartilage in the middle, and cube the remaining meat. Dip it in a mixture of beaten eggs and either bread or cornmeal crumbs, and deep-fry it; you'll think you're eating scallops.

Crabs: The heads of the fish you catch have their use too: as crab bait. Few crabs can resist a fresh fish head, chicken neck, or chunk of salt pork. Tie the bait to a line, add a sinker, and toss the rig into the muddy water along shorelines, estuaries, and tidal streams where crabs are known to lurk. When you think a crab's latched onto the bait, pull the line in very slowly and easily and slip a dip net under the crabs that will cling to the bait all the way to the surface.

That's the way individuals, couples, and entire families go after the luscious blue crab (*Callinectes sapidus*) up and down the East Coast, and they sometimes come home with baskets full of the tasty crustaceans.

The same approach works just as well on the West Coast with the Dungeness crab (*Cancer magister*) and its Pacific seaboard relatives, even though most folks in that part of the country seem to prefer to catch their crabs in store-bought ring nets and crab traps.

Unless they live in polluted water, all true crabs are edible, and as long as you obey the pertinent game laws, you can enjoy any of the critters that are big enough to take a nut pick to. Drop the crustaceans alive into boiling water (it's the quickest and most humane way to kill them), leave them until their shells are bright red, and then pick out and eat their meat, hot or cold, with melted butter or a light white sauce.

Some Western Mollusks: The West Coast intertidal zone from northern California to southern Mexico is the home of the often ignored owl limpet (*Lottia gigantea*). These huge gastropods, whose shells look like squat tipis and are often more than three inches across, are abundant in many areas and can be gathered at low tide by popping them off their rocky perches with a sharpened putty knife .

As with all univalves, only the owl limpet's fleshy foot, which yields a steak about two inches across, is eaten. Tenderize the cut of meat by pounding it and storing it in the refrigerator overnight before it's cooked. Then dip the steaks, of which you'll need several for every eager eater, in an egg-and-bread-crumb or cornmeal batter and fry them to a golden brown. The flavor will wake up even the most jaded taste buds.

Other West Coast limpets and *Acmaea testudinalis*, an East Coast variety, are generally considered to be too small to bother with. As the late Euell Gibbons pointed out in his writings about foraged foods, however, that idea is nonsense. They might not be big enough to eat as steaks, but the meat of almost any limpet is worth going after for chowders and soups.

To prepare one of those chowders, put a quart or more of limpets into a covered kettle with one cup of water and steam for 10 minutes. Remove the limpets, saving the broth, and as soon as they are cool enough to handle, remove their meat and discard the shells and viscera. The meat is then ground in a food chopper with a medium blade, returned to the broth, and placed over a low heat.

Next, dice one large onion and four slices of bacon and fry them together until the onion is translucent. Add two cups of diced potatoes, cover everything with water, and boil the mixture until the potatoes are soft. Then stir in the limpet meat and broth, and immediately add one quart of milk and one-quarter teaspoon of finely ground black pepper. Allow the mixture to simmer while you blend one tablespoon of flour into one fourth cup of milk and slowly stir this mixture into the chowder. Continue stirring the soup as it simmers for approximately ten minutes, and serve it with crackers on the side.

Another East Coast family of related mollusks, the chitons or sea cradles, are also quite tasty, though they are only about 2 inches long, and few people ever give them the chance to reach the dinner plate. It's a different story, however, on the West Coast. All the way from Alaska down to Baja California, a forager can find the giant sea cradle (*Micelle stelleri*), which reaches a length of 13 inches.

The brick-red, giant sea cradles can be found at low tide along rugged beaches. The vegetarian animals often hide under overhanging ledges and are sometimes difficult to see, but it's not unusual to stumble onto dozens of them clustered together along the low water mark of rough northern California beaches in the spring.

Chiton meat has a tendency to develop a strong fishy smell within two hours of the time the animal's caught. However, when they're cleaned immediately, the steaks packed in ice, and the meat cooked as quickly as possible, sea cradles are so delicious that you may want to get right up from the table and begin picking your way through slippery coastal rocks in search of more.

If you want to collect your seafood without any competition, watch for various members of the whelk family. These marine gastropods look so much like snails that few folks ever give a thought to eating them.

The best whelk pickings are found on the East Coast from Newfoundland to Florida and around the Gulf Coast all the way to the tip of Texas. Look for the 3- to 4-inch-long waved whelk (*Buccinum undatum*) along the upper East Coast south to the Carolinas; the 12-inch-long knobbed whelk (*Busycon carica*) and six inch-or-longer channeled whelk (*B. canaliculatum*) off the sandy shores from southern New England to Florida; the six-to nine-inch lefthanded whelk, some times called the lightning whelk (*B. contrarium*), south from Cape Hatteras, and the 3- to 5-inch-long pear conch (*B. spiratuni*) from Hatteras, south around the tip of Florida and westward to Texas.

If you're a snorkler, you can probably find all the whelks you want, anytime you want, by checking the ocean's bottom 12 to 18 feet down, off any sandy beach that sports a few washed-up whelk shells. They can also be found by walking the shore after a heavy storm and picking up those fresh, live specimens that have washed onto land, often by the bushel.

Whelks can be broken open with a hammer and the fleshy foot, the edible part, cut out. This meat can then be pounded or rolled, seasoned, and fried to a light brown. The foot can also be ground or diced.

Whelks can be pickled by boiling a pailful of them in heavily salted water until they can be slipped from their shells with a pin or a nut pick. Discard the viscera above each mollusk's foot and pull or slice off the operculum, the horny plate that closes the shell. Then place one packet of crab boil and three bayberry leaves in the bottom of a quart jar and pack the container loosely with alternating layers of cleaned whelks and finely sliced onions. Finally, fill the jar with boiling vinegar, seal it, and allow the meat to soak for a few days.

Once you've discovered how good whelks can be, you may also want to go after moon shells, which look like miniature whelks. Look for the Lewis moon shell (*Lunatia lewisi*), a grayish-brown 5-incher, on sandy bottoms from British Columbia to Mexico; the 1- to 3-inch-long Recluz's moon shell (*Polinices reclusianus*) from California to Mexico, the northern moon (*Lunatia heros*) from Newfoundland to the Carolinas; and the shark eye (*Polinices duplicatus*) from Cape Cod to Texas.

All the moon shells are good to eat. They're generally found in the same places that you'll find whelks, and you should look for their rounded burrows in the sand as you walk along a beach at low tide. Their feet are both savory and tender when prepared properly. Slice them into half-inch-thick steaks, pound the meat, separate the slabs with wax paper, and store the pieces in the refrigerator for 24 hours. Dip the steaks in egg, roll them in bread crumbs, and fry the meat to a light brown.

Only the Beginning: There is much more to be taken along the edge of the sea, of course. There are oysters, scallops, seaweed, sea eggs, beach plums, bay berry leaves, grunions, blennies, lancelets. All delicious and free for the catching.

Produce a Fish Crop in Cages: The great single advantage of cage culture is that it permits raising fish in bodies of water that are unsuitable for aquaculture, bodies in which large nets and other methods of harvesting are not feasible.

Public (or Large Private) waters: Harvesting of fish from public waters is usually restricted to sport fishing methods, and private ponds that cover more than an acre can present formidable difficulties to harvesting the fish with nets. However, such environments are often ideal for cage culture.

Multipurpose Ponds: In ponds built to attract wildlife, offer recreational fishing and swimming, or just provide scenic beauty, converting that entire body of water to intensive fish culture may be difficult and would certainly compromise other uses. However, with cages, you could easily produce several hundred pounds of fish without hampering your ability to enjoy the pond in other ways. Also, the cages may even attract wild fish, and thereby enhance sport fishing.

Ponds with More Than One Owner: Suppose your land fronts on a private body of water that's shared by a number of owners. Since each family probably has its own ideas about how best to enjoy the pond or lake, it could be difficult to get all the owners to agree on an aquaculture management plan. However, you could keep a few cages floating off your section of the shoreline without interfering with your neighbors' activities.

Very Deep Ponds: Deep bodies of water such as quarry pits usually aren't as productive as conventional aquaculture sites, but the same sites are often good for cage culture.

Brushy ponds: Some ponds are so full of brush, logs, or other obstacles that harvesting with nets is all but impossible. As long as there are patches of open water, however, such locations can be used for cage farming.

Kinds of Fish: Although most fish probably can be raised in cages, experience to date suggests that anyone more interested in production than in experimentation should select from one or more of seven varieties:

Channel Catfish (*Ictalurus punctatus*): Some people are prejudiced against eating these whiskery fish, claiming that "scavengers" aren't fit fare, but in the South, folks know better. In fact, the well-developed taste in that area for catfish largely supports this country's principal fish culture industry, which is centered in the lower Mississippi valley. More than 50 million pounds of cultured catfish are sold annually, and perhaps 2 percent of that total is grown in cages.

The channel catfish is a handsome creature. Young fish, those up to about a foot long and covered with round black spots, were formerly thought to be a distinct species and were known variously as willow cats, lady cats, squealers, or fiddlers. Although the channel cat can now be caught in most of the United States, almost all commercial sources are located in the southern and central states and California.

Rainbow Trout (*Salmo Gairdner*): The American Fisheries Society currently recognizes 14 species of trout as being either native or successfully introduced to North America. Most of these are important as sport fish, but only the rainbow trout is widely grown for food. Rainbows are able to tolerate slightly higher temperatures than most trout, and they seem reasonably content in the crowded circumstances typical of intensive fish culture.

The rainbow is indigenous to the Pacific coast drainage areas of North America but can now be encountered almost anywhere trout of other kinds are found.

Bluegill (*Lepomis macrochirus*): the bluegill is probably the best known of the 11 sunfish species. It's always been widely distributed throughout the United States and southern Canada and is now found almost everywhere. It's better suited to most aquaculture purposes than other types of sunfish, primarily because of its large size and its adaptable feeding habits.

You can distinguish bluegills from related species by glancing at the opercular flap (the small, soft tab on the rear edge of the gill cover). If the flap is short and dark blue, and not edged or spotted with a lighter color, the sunfish is probably a bluegill. Other distinctive characteristics include a dark blotch at the rear of the dorsal fin and sharply pointed pectoral fins.

Commercially available hybrids, which are usually crosses between the bluegill and the green sun fish (*Lepomis cyanellus*), have been the subject of some controversy among aquaculturists. The different hybrids seem to vary in performance, but in general they grow more rapidly than either of the parent species. They are expensive, however, and small-scale growers can't expect to produce their own hybrids.

Blue Tilapia (*Tilapia aurea*): The many species of tilapia, originally native to the Near East and Africa but now spread throughout the tropics, are among the world's most important food fishes. When Saint Peter and his companions cast nets into the Sea of Galilee, they were fishing mainly for tilapia, which are some times marketed as "Saint Peter's fish." In recent years tilapia have also become important for culture in green houses and other heated environments, as well as for seasonal culture in the temperate zones.

The blue tilapia is about as beautiful a fish as you could hope to raise. A male in breeding condition, as he is most of the time, is suffused with iridescent blue, particularly around the head, and his fins are edged with brilliant crimson. Blue tilapia have won more than a few prizes at aquarium shows.

You can obtain various species of tilapia from aquarium shops, but you'll get a better price and some assurance that you're not purchasing a miniature species if you buy from an aquaculture dealer.

Not only is the tilapia valuable as a food fish, but if a few are kept in a cage with other fish, they reduce the time spent cleaning algae from the inside mesh of the cage.

Mirror Carp (*Cyprinus carpio*): Though it was originally brought here as a food fish, the common carp isn't very popular in this hemisphere. However, in Europe, Israel, China, Japan, and other countries, it has become the most popular of aquaculture species.

In North America, wild carp are found nearly everywhere there's sufficiently warm water, except in the Florida peninsula. Few of the select food varieties are available in this country, but it is worth the trouble to look for the mirror, or Israeli, carp, which has only a few large, scattered scales. It's an even more adaptable eater than the wild type, and has a higher height-to-length ratio. If you can't locate carp stock elsewhere, you might want to contact bait dealers, as they sometimes sell small Israeli carp as minnows.

Eels (*Anguilla rostrata*): The American eel is a catadromous fish. Its life cycle reverses that of the anadromous salmon, as eels live in fresh water and spawn at sea. Therefore, the controlled breeding of captive eels is for all practical purposes impossible. However, in many estuaries along our Atlantic coast, young eels, or elvers, can be collected in numbers sufficient to supply eel-culture systems. For this reason, though an occasional large eel will turn up in a body of water hundreds of miles inland, eel culture will probably always be a coastal enterprise.

Furthermore, eels aren't the easiest creatures to keep in cages. The young fish may slip through the mesh, and adults often become adept at crawling up and out through cracks. Their exceptional food qualities, and the fact that they have the lowest percentage of dressing loss of any fish, do make them worth the trouble, though.

Brown, Black, and Yellow Bullheads (*Ictalurus*): The bullheads, with their large heads, stocky bodies, square tails, and usually sluggish movements, conform more closely to most people's conception of a catfish than does the channel cat. While bullheads are native to the eastern two-thirds of the United States, they are now found in almost all parts of the country.

The differences among the three major bullhead species are not easy to distinguish, yet it's very important for the cage culturist to know which type of bullhead is being dealt with. In brief, a yellow bullhead (*Ictalurus nalalis*) has whitish or yellowish barbels (whiskers), a long anal fin with 23 to 28 rays, and small serrations on the inside edge of its pectoral fin's spine. The brown (*Ictalurus nebulosus*) and black (*Ictalurus melas*) bullheads both have black, dark brown, or darkly spotted barbels. The brown bullhead has a medium-length anal fin with 22 to 24 rays and stout serrations on the interior pectoral fin's spinal edge. The black bullhead has a distinctly short anal fin with 16 to 22 rays and a smooth, or barely serrated, pectoral fin edge.

Obtaining Fish: There are three ways to obtain your fish stock: Buy them, catch them, or breed them. You should be able to locate dealers who sell channel catfish, rainbow trout, hybrid sunfish, Israeli carp, and even some of the tilapias. You may also be able to find folks who deal in some of the other species, but don't count on it.

You may well be able to locate free fish for stocking, particularly bluegills and bullheads, which are rapid reproducers that can quietly overpopulate a body of water if they're not kept in check. Many farm pond owners will be glad to relieve their fish population crunch by letting you haul away some of their stunted stock. Such fish will resume normal growth patterns when they're again placed under favorable conditions.

Taking your starting supply from public waters is usually illegal, especially if you're after such prized game fish as trout. Still, it can't hurt to check with a local fishery biologist concerning any unwanted surpluses of bullheads or carp, which can generally be caught with seines, cast nets, or traps baited with liver, fish, or meat offal.

Among the fish discussed here, bullheads, nonhybrid sunfish, and tilapia will readily reproduce in any pond in which they can survive. Channel catfish and carp are a bit more particular about their breeding grounds, but most home growers should be able to get them to reproduce. However, many backyard aquaculturists consider trout too tricky and time-consuming to breed. Breeding hybrid sunfish requires specialized skills.

The Cage: Once you've gotten access to a body of water and are confident that you'll be able to line up a supply of fish, it's time to build your cage. You could, of course, buy a fish box, but commercial cages often cost three to five times as much as homemade units. Rectangular cages seem to work best. Home growers planning to manage one to six boxes will probably do well with 3' X 3' X 6' structures.

Although you can make the cage walls out of almost any sort of mesh material, nylon webbing that is sold in hardware stores and is often used to keep leaves out of rain gutters works well. Flexible nylon mesh is easy to work with, slightly buoyant, long-lived, and chemically inert. Wire, on the other hand, may be less expensive initially, but it's also much heavier than nylon, so extra flotation is needed to compensate for the added weight. Also, it usually has sharp ends that can injure people and fish, and the mesh corrodes in water. There are many sad but true stories about bumper fish crops that fell through rusty cage bottoms at harvest time.

Whatever the material, using the largest mesh capable of preventing new baby fish from escaping will allow good circulation, reduce cleaning labor, and save some money.

The cage will need a rigid top frame made of either treated wood or aluminum tubing. You can frame all of the underwater sides of the cage as well, or you can make a basket cage by simply lashing the sides together with nylon rope or twine. Basket cages are lighter, easier to store, and less expensive than full-frame ones, but they take longer to construct and don't hold their shape as well.

The other three essential cage components are the flotation devices, a top, and a feeding ring. It takes one cubic foot of an ideal flotation material like polystyrene foam to support a 50-cubic-foot full-frame, nylon-web cage. Also, the floats must be attached in such a way that the top of the cage sits at least four inches above the water.

The cage will require a solid top that's hinged or removable, because most fish prefer shade to sunlight. Such a lid will also help deter theft, predation, or high leaping escapes. The feeding ring is simply a band of fine mesh, such as mosquito netting, that prevents floating feeds from slipping out the sides of the cage. You can stitch a length of this material around the inside of the cage at the water line, construct a floating wood framed feeding skirt, or cut a hole in the cage's lid and trim that with netting to make a feeding well.

Siting Cages: The ideal site for a cage will be a spot where the water is

Nutritional Value of Foraged Food

PART 1

Because of the skyrocketing prices and questionable nutritional value of many commercially available foods, a multitude of Americans not only employ organic gardening as an alternative source of wholesome edibles, but they also supplement their homegrown diets with free-for-the-finding wild foods.

Although most foragers have assumed all along that wild fare—free of additives and genetically unchanged—is naturally wholesome, the increased public interest in wild food plants has created a demand for some hard facts on how nutritious these edibles are.

While many wild plants contain substantial amounts of nutrients and do not contain the additives usually found in supermarket fare, the untamed edibles can absorb toxic chemicals from the soil, the air, and water. Anyone foraging for food, then, should be careful where they pick. Plants along the roadside, for instance, can absorb pollutants from vehicle exhaust, and there is no telling what chemicals might exist in plants growing over a landfill or downstream from an industrial facility. Agricultural sprays can also land on and taint wild edibles.

How Good They Are: Having taught courses in foraging for some years, Robert Shosteck had been challenged many times with the query, "How do you know this plant is nutritious?" In most cases, he could only quote the author of a book on wild foods as his source. As often as not, this writer referred to the work of an earlier writer who may well have based his statements on folklore.

This lack of solid data led Shosteck to work up a systematic collection of all available scientific research on the subject and then to compare each particular wild edible with the Recommended Daily Allowance (RDA) established by the National Academy of Science's Food and Nutrition Board. The RDA represents the suggested requirement for nutrients needed by normal, healthy people.

A typical male adult, for example, needs 5,000 I.U. (International Units) of vitamin A per day, and he can get much more than that in only a cup of cooked dandelion greens! Or take that bane-of-the-farmers, amaranth: 10 ounces of the leaves or tips of this prolific plant can provide an adult's daily calcium needs plus almost all the iron requirement of men and half that of women, while only 3.5 ounces of the greens will meet the daily needs for vitamin A, thiamine, and ascorbic acid.

You see, then, that you can assure yourself of a well-balanced diet by com-
(continued on page 174)

(continued from page 173)

bining produce from your garden with wild edibles in season. Beyond that you can freeze, dry, can, or pickle many of your surplus foraged foods for use later in the year.

Caution: The listing of a plant doesn't necessarily mean that it's edible under all circumstances. People should inform themselves fully by consulting a good field guide as to any wild food's safety before consuming it, since frequently a plant may be poisonous at one stage in its development and edible at another, or as with domestic rhubarb and potatoes, one part of the plant may be edible, while other sections are poisonous.

In order to get some overview of the various nutrients covered in the list, a listing of plants and nutritional categories is in order. First are the foods that provide the most calories. Most folks have no trouble consuming enough starches, sugars, and fats for their energy needs (on the contrary, such elements are in oversupply in the average North American's diet), but among the wild edibles, only nuts, seeds, tubers, and a few fruits provide such "energy to burn" in significant amounts. Most wild foods have less than a gram of fat per 100 grams, and they're often low in carbohydrates as well, usually containing only several grams. This means that you can fill up on many wildings without putting on weight.

Most people also get enough protein in their diets from meat, poultry, fish, and dairy products. However, if you're a vegetarian or want to supply part of your minimum daily need (50-63 grams of protein) from vegetable sources, the following plants will provide five or more grams of protein for each 100 grams (about 3-1/4 ounces) consumed.

Soybean	35. 1
Sunflower seed	24.0
Butternut	23.7
Black walnut	20.5
Beechnut	19.4
Wild rice	14.1
Hickory nut	13.2
Filbert	12.6
Garlic	6.2
Alfalfa	6.0
Nettle	5.5
Pawpaw	5.2

PART 2

Nature's Nutrients: Wild foods can also play an important role in satisfying your body's daily vitamin and mineral requirements. For example, the average person needs a minimum of 800 to 1,200 milligrams (mg) of calcium, the body's most abundant mineral, every day. Here's how a few wild plants stack up in comparison with milk (the most commonly mentioned, and a highly touted, calcium source) in milligrams per 100 grams of food:

(continued on page 175)

Lamb's-quarters	309
Rape	252
Mallow	249
Soybean (dry)	226
Filbert	209
Shepherd's purse	208
Mint	194
Dandelion	187
Watercress	151
Knotweed	150
Water primrose	144
Cow's Milk	118

Iron is usually obtained from meats, shellfish, and whole grains. Adult males need 10 mg of this mineral daily; females, 15 mg, and children, 10 mg. Here's a sampling of wild foods and the amounts of iron they offer per 100 grams as compared to beef liver, one of the best supermarket sources:

Primrose-willow	12.7
Mallow	12.7
Soybean	8.5
Water primrose	8.0
Sunflower seed	7.1
Butternut	6.8
Black walnut	6.0
Amaranth	5.6
Curled dock	5.6
Alfalfa	5.4
Shepherd's purse	4.8
Fame flower	4.8
Beef liver	8.8

Liver is among the best "conventional" sources of vitamin A, while deep yellow and dark green vegetables supply carotene, which the body can convert into this important nutrient. Adult males need 5,000 I.U. of vitamin A daily, while females require 4,000 units. The following wild edible plants contain more than either of those I.U. requirements in a 100-gram serving:

Dandelion	14,000
Dock	12,900
Lamb's-quarters	11,600
Peppergrass	9,300
Pokeweed	8,700
Violet leaves	8,200
Nettle	6,500
Mustard greens	5,800

PART 3

Three of the B vitamins: thiamine, riboflavin, and niacin are usually obtained from meat, milk, whole grains, and especially from the organ meats. But since adults require a daily minimum of only 1.5 mg for men and 1.1 mg for women of thiamine, a good serving of many wild foods can help to fill the need for this nutrient. The following plants contain from 0.25 mg to 2.0 mg per 100 grams, and the amount they have is compared to beef liver:

(continued on page 176)

(continued from page 175)

Sunflower	2.00	
Arrowhead	1.60	
Pecan	1.00	
Pokeweed	0.80	
Soybean	0.66	
Filbert	0.46	
Wild rice	0.45	
Lamb's-quarters	0.44	
Burdock	0.25	
Dandelion	0.25	
Shepherd's purse	0.25	
Beef liver	8.80	

Better Health for Free: In the past, some people were justifiably skeptical of unsupported allegations regarding the nutritional content of many well-publicized wild foods. However, now that the scientific evidence is in, there's no reason not to forage a substantial proportion of your diet in spring when the greens are young and the nut harvest in the fall. You can eat better, stay healthier (just getting outdoors to find the plants is a good start), and watch your food budget shrink instead of constantly growing. ■

about six feet deep. Shallower locations will normally have reduced water circulation, and some deeper spots are subject to turnover, a sudden reversal of water layers that brings oxygen-starved bottom water to the surface. Caged fish that are caught in a turnover may be killed.

Try to choose a site that's exposed to breezes but protected from high waves and motorboat traffic. Consider, too, that if you can set your cage off the end of a dock, you won't have to take a boat out to feed the fish. Should you need to put the enclosures in open water, secure them with at least one anchor fastened at each end of the cage with nylon lines. Always put the cages out and make sure they float properly before stocking them.

Stocking: A delicate, indeed critical, moment in any aquaculture operation is stocking, the transferring of the captured or purchased fish to their permanent home. You should always transport your stock in large, double plastic bags that are half full of water and have plenty of air inside.

Begin by floating the fish-filled sack in your cage, and checking the water temperatures of the enclosure and of your container. Unless the two temperatures are nearly identical, wait for them to equalize, a process that usually takes from 15 to 45 minutes, but can be speeded up by carefully exchanging small amounts of water between the sack and cage. If you try this, however, be sure you change the water temperature gradually. Too drastic a jump can either kill the fish outright or lower their resistance so much that many will die later on.

When the two temperatures have equalized, submerge the bag, tilt it sideways, and allow a few minutes for the two fluids to mix. Only then should you move the bag to encourage the fish to leave it.

In general, it's best to stock cages when the ambient water temperature is slightly below the range desirable for growth. That would mean introducing trout into 50°F to 55°F water, tilapia in 70° to 75° ponds, and the other species discussed here in 60° to 70° water. Consequently, in most cases you'd probably want to stock your cages in the spring. However, in many areas larger, more vigorous stock is often available in the fall. If stocked then, these fish can be kept through the winter and finished out during the following spring and summer. If you live where hard freezes are not a problem, you can even stock young in the fall for over wintering. Remember, though, fish set out in autumn won't grow appreciably during the cold months. The cost of purchased fish will depend on their size. Smaller ones are naturally less expensive, but if possible, it's best to stock the largest young fish available because they'll outgrow their little kinfolk and will have a higher survival rate.

Feeding: Fish in cages have very limited access to natural food. The cage culturist is responsible for providing a diet that is complete both quantitatively and nutritionally.

Most American fish culture is based on processed commercial feeds. These are somewhat expensive, but the rations are both effective and convenient, and beginning cage culturists have enough to learn without trying to create their own feeding schemes.

Most ready-made fish food is tailored to the requirements of either channel catfish or rainbow trout, the two major conventional aquaculture crops, and is thus only partially suited to other species. Such feeds also often lack certain trace elements, since pond-raised fish for which foods are created are expected to gather minor quantities of natural organisms. However, some manufacturers do offer special cage culture feeds that are nutritionally complete.

The other characteristic essential to any feed used in cages is that it float; sinking rations will be largely lost through the bottom mesh.

Commercial feeds range in size from meal to 3/16-inch pellets. You can pretty well gauge the size you'll need by the mouths of your fish. Since that size will change as your stock grows, and because the feed doesn't store well, you should always buy the smallest convenient quantity at one time, and keep those rations tightly covered.

The best time to feed is usually at dawn. Later in the morning or at dusk are second choices. As a rule, you'll want to give your fish 3 percent of their total body weight at each feeding, and feed them six days a week. To determine the total weight of your fish, simply catch and weigh a sample periodically, and use this information and the number of fish in the cage to calculate the group's weight.

To gain some idea of the kind of feeding schedule you'll have, make a few calculations using the "end point" method. To illustrate how this works, let's suppose you begin with 200 bullhead fingerlings that weigh a total of 2-1/2 pounds. Assume that you want to raise them to an average of 1/2 pound each, thus yielding 100 pounds of fish using the 3-percent-weight-a-day feeding rule, you would then give them 0.03 X 2.5 = 0.075 pounds of ration the first day. Furthermore, on the last day before harvest, you'd be feeding 0.03 x 100 = 3 pounds of feed. If you have some idea of when that harvest date will occur, a good time is just after the date your water temperature falls below that needed for optimum growth, you can then count the number of feeding days between stocking and harvesting, and calculate an approximate weekly feed allotment that gradually increases from 0.077 to 3 pounds a day. Be sure, however, to allow for the fact that fish put on weight most rapidly at first, and more slowly as they grow.

Natural Feeds: With the exception of the sun fish, which can be reared on a 100% processed food diet, all the fish mentioned here will eat some commercial feed even though they really don't make good use of it. Of course, all fish will eat available natural foods.

Nocturnal flying insects can be attracted to the space above a cage by a light that costs only a few cents a day to operate. The bugs then drop into the water and become food for the fish in the cage. Although almost any species of fish will eat insects floating on the surface of the water, among the fish best suited to cage culture are trout and bluegill, particularly relish downed bugs. At least one commercially available type of light comes equipped with a fan to pull in the insects and blow them down onto the surface of the water.

Earthworms can also be used to supply caged fish with natural meals. A special feeder can be constructed by simply punching a few holes through a thin block of polystyrene foam. Worms are spread on top of the block, and it is placed on the water in the cage. The worms will crawl down through the holes, and the fish will make a meal of them as they reach the water under the foam block.

If you have a source of unwanted fish, meat scraps, or offal, you can use these leavings by grinding, chopping, or boiling them. Any food particles that are so small they might pass through the mesh should be placed in a large container and lowered into the cage.

Although most of the fish discussed will not eat leafy matter, tilapia are quite fond of plants, and Israeli carp will take some. Most soft aquatic plants, comfrey, purslane, carrot tops, and hairy vetch can be used. Serve the vegetation by tying it in bunches and suspending it in the cage.

You may not be able to provide much natural food, but keep in mind that even an amount totaling less than 1 percent of your fishs' total diet may improve their growth or flavor, or even enable you to switch from a complete commercial feed to a less costly supplemental one. Remember to allow for water content when calculating feeding rates or ratios with natural feeds. Commercial products are relatively dry. Insects contain approximately 75% water. Fish, meat, and worms are about 85% water, and green plants contain 90% to 95% water.

Maintenance: Inspect your cages daily. When necessary, clean the mesh so any accumulated algae growth won't inhibit water flow. (A toilet brush mounted on a long handle works fine for this purpose.) You should also examine the fish to see that their feed is being eaten and that they're in good health. If food is being wasted, cut back on the amount, skip a day's serving, or change their diet. If your stock remains off its feed after you've taken the above measures, check the fish for disease.

Harvesting: Mass harvesting of cage-cultured fish is the simplest process imaginable: Just lift the cage and take out the crop. To catch only a few fish for dinner, you can drive some into a corner with a shallow, square-cornered dip net and scoop them out.

The Payoff: Though the cost of operating a caged fish operation will vary from one area to another, there is little doubt that even a small-scale setup can produce clean, protein-rich meat for a fraction of the prices at a supermarket.

❧

CHAPTER 7

Raising Livestock

Comparing the Best Backyard Livestock

Raising small and medium-sized meat animals from babes to butchering is no more difficult, and a lot less time-consuming, than cultivating a garden, and is possible in areas as limited as a large backyard or an urban lot. However, choosing the species that will best suit your needs is crucial to small space meat production.

Although reducing the grocery bill is important, other factors are bound to influence your choices as well. Advantages and disadvantages of the five most popular types of livestock should help you make the final decision as to what you'd like to raise.

Before building any pens, hutches, coops, or sties, be sure to check local restrictions and laws regarding the types and number of animals that may be kept in your community.

Chickens: These most popular of barnyard critters can be highly efficient meat or egg producers. A broiler may yield nearly a pound of meat for every two pounds of feed and a good laying hen will supply about a dozen eggs for every five pounds of feed. Dual-purpose breeds will give a fair supply of both products.

Chickens aren't fussy eaters and are good foragers. They'll eat everything from meat scraps and bugs to weeds and kitchen leftovers. However, they can devastate a garden, so guard your crops by fencing in either the vegetables or the birds.

The smaller breeds are well suited to a small-space operation. Stout fences aren't required (the appropriately named chicken wire is usually the least expensive and easiest enclosure material to use). The birds will, however, learn to fly over five- or six-foot barriers, so you must either fence over the top of your pen or clip the chickens' wings to keep them earthbound. In addition, predators may well try to raid your flock, so be sure your coop's fencing and flooring are strong enough to deter rats, owls, coons, opossums, and canine prowlers.

Be forewarned that chicken coops in an urban neighborhood (even if permitted by law) tend to cause more human commotion than does the appearance of a few rabbit hutches. Neighbors are often concerned that the birds will get loose and dig up their prize petunias, that the flock will create odor and fly problems, or that you'll decide to keep a rooster, forcing them to put up with a living alarm clock. Although these difficulties can be prevented by proper management, you might be wise to sound out the folks next door and prepare them for their new neighbors. (The promise of an occasional gift of fresh eggs might be one good way to make the introduction.)

Rabbits: Quiet, clean, and prolific, rabbits are the most nearly ideal animal to raise in a small space. If they're kept in all-wire hutches and the manure is cleaned out regularly from under their cages, they are odor-free and won't attract flies. Rabbits also give an excellent return for the amount of feed and labor invested. The litters from one 10-pound doe, kept in a 30" by 36" hutch, can yield up to 80 pounds of meat a year. In addition, the pelts, although generally not strong enough for clothing, can be used or sold for trim on coats.

In spite of all the good things to be said about rabbit raising, the species does have one serious disadvantage. The gentle creatures are vulnerable to attack by predators, so unless you build your hutches or fences strong enough to keep prowlers out or enclose your rabbits in a shed or garage, your stock will be easy prey.

Sheep: Calm, quiet, almost odor-free, and easy to keep penned, sheep are a good addition to nearly any meat-producing homestead, especially rural households with an acre or so of unused pasture. Sheep are excellent grazers. In season they can be raised entirely on good grassland without supplemental grain. When pastured exclusively, they're probably the most economical animal to raise on your backyard farm. You can harvest about 100 pounds of meat and eight pounds of wool from each adult ewe, and an acre of lush pasture will support four or five ewes and their lambs. (Some European breeds, by the way, are raised for milk in addition to meat and wool.)

Sheep don't require much regular caretaking, either. They do need to be shorn every year, however, and this can be a problem for the backyard homesteader. Shearing must be done correctly if it's to produce a quality fleece for spinning, and few small-flock owners have the time to learn the skill. Since it may be difficult to find a professional shearer who's willing to work on just a few animals, you should contact in winter, well before the shearing season begins, someone who shears larger flocks in your area and arrange to have your sheep included in the shearing schedule.

Labor requirements for your backyard flock can also be high at lambing time. Ewes will need to be watched (and assisted, if necessary) to be certain they care for their lambs properly.

You'll have to guard the timid creatures against predators unless you have the resources to invest in a Komondor or other European sheep-guard dog (raised to believe they are sheep, and valiant protectors of a flock against any danger).

Overall, though sheep require less daily maintenance than do either rabbits or chickens, raising them demands more livestock husbandry skills than managing those smaller species. The pasture, for instance, must be managed to prevent overgrazing, and your flock will require a good veterinary care program.

Goats: Perhaps the most intelligent, and certainly the most companionable, of backyard livestock animals, goats are highly efficient milk producers and good friends to have around the homestead.

A good doe will yield a gallon of milk each day from a feeding of three to four pounds of grain and a few pounds of hay. Fresh goat's milk tastes similar to cow's milk, yet many people who can't drink cow's milk can tolerate goat milk (which makes it a salable product). Then, too, although the popular breeds in this country are not usually raised for meat production, the meat (called chevon) is delicious, and tanned hides from the animals can be used for rugs and vests, jackets, and other garments.

For all these reasons, many new homesteaders think a goat is the first animal they should have for their farm, especially after they've had a chance to play with an adorable little kid. But before you run out to purchase your own goat, it's best to be aware of the disadvantages of keeping the beasts. First, a dairy goat must be milked twice a day, seven days a week through her entire 10-month lactation period. This is a caretaking requirement many homesteaders might find too confining. Second, although goats don't require much space, they are difficult to keep penned, and third, in addition to their fence-jumping tendencies, some of the little fellows are pretty good noisemakers. Neither the second nor the third quality will endear you or your goats to the neighbors.

If you intend to get the highest and most economical milk production from your goat, or any dairy animal for that matter, you must have a good understanding of its nutritional needs during lactation and dry periods, and provide good veterinary care. You should know, too, that the tiny fat droplets in goat's milk, unlike those of cow's milk, are mixed throughout the liquid. Thus the butterfat doesn't rise naturally to the top (it can be separated mechanically), which means that making butter or cheese is a bit difficult.

Probably the hardest aspect of goat raising, though, is culling a favorite doe no matter how poor her milk production is because the creatures are so lovable to have around. But if you're not willing to get rid of your caprine companions, it won't be long before one cute doe, at one to three kids per year, multiplies into a sizable herd.

Pigs: Among the best waste-to-meat converters, pigs will turn kitchen scraps, garden greens, grains, roots, surplus eggs, or offal from other butchered livestock into hams, pork chops, bacon, and fresh side meat. In other words, swine can be the finest garbage disposal available. Alternatively, when fed a well-balanced store-bought diet, a good hog will gain a pound for every 2-1/2 to 3-1/2 pounds of feed.

Pigs don't require much room. You can raise one or two from weanling to market weight in a pen 16 feet square. For backyard meat production, pigs should be purchased as weanlings in the spring and raised through the summer to their market weight of about 220 pounds each. Using this method, you'll avoid the considerable husbandry problems associated with handling newborns, piglets, and those 400- to 500-pound boars and sows. All you'll have to do until butchering time is feed and water your stock twice a day and clean out the manure as often as needed.

Most pigs are not jumpers, but they will try the best of fences at ground level so your enclosures must be absolutely "hog tight" at the bottom. Commercial hog panels, each of which consists of 16' of 32"-high welded wire, are just about the ideal fencing for a backyard pigpen.

Along with the tendency of pigs to root their way out of captivity, pig raising has other drawbacks, such as the work involved in butchering a 200-pound hog. There's even the problem of trying to find room for 100 pounds of meat in your freezer. The biggest disadvantage to these otherwise excellent meat producers, however, is the public's general reaction to the aroma. Be sure to consider your neighbors before you set up a pig sty behind your house.

Take Your Pick: While these are some of the objective pluses and minuses of each of the five best minifarm animals, don't forget that one of your chief considerations should be your personal preference. The homesteader who really enjoys a particular species of livestock will give them more care and attention. The animals, in turn, will be more comfortable and therefore more productive. So if, for example, you like the soft clucks of a flock of chickens but find the thought of raising pigs distasteful, don't let cold economics alone determine your choice.

There's one final consideration. It's possible that the hardest part of livestock raising for you would be butchering the animals you've nurtured since birth. If this is an insurmountable problem, you would do better to limit your operation to milk-producing goats (you can sell their offspring) or egg-laying chickens.

A Home Chicken Flock

Chickens can be ideal animals for the beginning homesteader or backyard farmer. A small home flock will provide fresh eggs and chemical-free tasty fried, roasted, or stewed chicken—for a fraction of the commercial cost if you let them "free-range" for most of their food.

Homegrown meat won't reach your dinner table laced with growth hormones, antibiotics, and whatever else goes into mass-produced poultry these days. And the eggs will be fresh, with rich, yellow yolks that stand up all fat and sassy in the frying pan.

A backyard flock can also provide a good supply of manure for the compost pile or garden, and you can even use your friendly fowl for pest control, especially in the fruit orchard.

Perhaps the most attractive aspect of having chickens, is that the birds almost raise themselves. To establish your flock, you'll have to build a small coop with a fenced outdoor run, obtain the birds, and keep them supplied with fresh feed and water. If feed and water fonts are large enough, you can leave the flock for several days...say, during a long-weekend vacation. For longer periods, a neighborhood teen can tend them.

Varieties: Today, thanks to the ingenuity and selective breeding efforts of scientists and poultry fanciers, the birds are available in all sizes, shapes, colors, and feather patterns. There are more than 350 breeds. However, chickens can be divided into four main classifications: egg layers, meat types (broilers), dual-purpose birds (egg and meat producers), and exotic or exhibition breeds.

The most common egg-layer, the White Leghorn, will produce a good-sized white-shelled egg 250 to 300 days a year. But don't expect this variety to grow into a fat fryer or plump roasting hen; leghorns are mainly feathers and egg-factory, barely tipping the scales at four pounds of stringy flesh, no matter how much you feed them. Only hens are kept.

Broilers such as the Rock-Cornish cross are bred to convert feed to flesh most efficiently; the birds most often found on supermarket fresh meat counters are eight-week-old broiler-type birds, either male or female. Roasters are allowed to reach 11 to 15 weeks of age before being butchered. The gourmet Rock-Cornish Hen is a bird (of either gender) slaughtered at only a few weeks of age.

A dual-purpose hen such as a Rhode Island Red will lay about 200 to 250 brown-shelled eggs per year and the cockerels (young males) will grow to five to six pounds at six months.

Exotics aren't bred for egg or meat production but for their colorful plumage. Polish Cresteds, the "Turken" or Bare-neck (a turkey-look-alike chicken breed) and the various miniatures—Bantams—are primarily show birds kept to ornament the barnyard and be exhibited at State Fair competitions.

House and Run: Chickens need a weatherproof, varmint-proof shelter and an outside run. Besides four walls and a roof, your birds' coop should have a roost for the sleepyheads to doze upon and a secluded place for the hens to sit while laying their eggs.

Chicks will need about half a square foot of indoor floor space per bird until they're six weeks old. Adults require three square feet each, but if an outdoor run is provided, this figure can be cut in half.

Every bird should have 10" of roosting space. A limb that's about 2" in diameter works well as a perch, or you can round the edges of a length of 2 X 2 board. Place the roosts 24" above the floor, spaced 13" to 15" apart.

Hens prefer covered nest boxes to hide in while they're laying eggs, so make a number of simple open-faced shelters, each about 12" square with a perch in front, and situate them 24" off the floor. Not every hen needs her own private nest. They'll bicker when two want to lay in the same box at the same time, but one nest box for every four biddies should be plenty. Or build a single large nest the same size as four one-hen nests in a square. Put in a single opening but build a long roost in front.

As you build your coop, keep in mind that ventilation and sanitation are both extremely important. For that reason, the easier the shelter is to clean, the better. Always keep plenty of fresh, dry loose litter on the floor; there are a number of inexpensive materials that can be used, including sawdust, woodchips, straw, ground cobs, old hay, and leaves.

Several times each year scrub all the roosts, nest boxes, feeders, and waterers with a solution of one tablespoon of chlorine bleach per gallon of water. You'll find your cleaning chores easier if you put a shallow wire-covered pit beneath the roosts. Make a wood frame covered with 1/2-inch wire mesh for the lid. The pit will collect the droppings, which can then go directly into the compost pile. If a cleanout door is built into the coop wall at the rear of the manure pit, it can be cleaned without entering the coop and disturbing the hens. Many fanciers also build such doors at the rear of the nest boxes to harvest eggs the same way.

A portable coop (that is, a shelter on wheels) will enable your poultry to serve more than one function. With a movable house, it's easy to transport the chickens to a fresh pasture every week or so. On each site, the birds will scratch and dig, and eat many of the pests that are getting ready to attack your garden. As they feast on greens and bugs, the hens will deposit a layer of fresh fertilizer. In essence the birds act as miniature farm implements, removing weeds, turning the earth, killing the bugs, and fertilizing the soil.

If space is available, you can let your chickens run the range. By choosing their fare every day, free-roaming birds are able to balance their own diets. Giving them the run of some pastureland is easier on your budget than having to purchase all their food, but most range chickens need to have their diets supplemented with commercial feed containing 5% to 15% protein. When hens are laying, they also need a calcium supplement. A container of crushed oyster shells is best.

Unconfined chickens can take daily dust baths, which will help keep the birds free of mites. One word of caution, though: roamers can be active and aggressive garden destroyers. They will scratch up new-sown seed and eagerly devour your succulent, newly emerged seedlings, so either fence their pasture in or fence the birds out of the garden.

While you're building enclosures, assure protection from predators. Make the run and the coop rat-proof and strong enough to keep out roaming dogs,

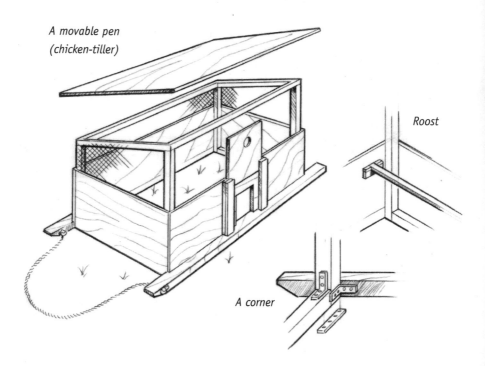

A movable pen
(chicken-tiller)

Roost

A corner

raccoons, coyotes, and other predators from breaking in or digging under the fence. A two-foot-wide band of small-mesh welded wire, secured to the lower portion of the chicken-wire fence and extending at least six inches underground, should do the job.

Health: A healthy, normal chicken is bright-eyed, alert, and active. In contrast, a sick bird will have dull, expressionless eyes and will sit with its head drooping and its feathers fluffed out. The vent of a good layer will be pink and moist; if she's quit laying for any reason, it will be dry, puckered, and yellowish. A hen that's broody (one that either is trying to hatch eggs or thinks she is) will often look about the same as a bird that's ill, except her eyes will be bright and beady. She will fuss and make a strange kind of cluck. It'll take a little time to learn to distinguish between a chicken that is actually sick and one that is merely broody. If you want to hatch your own chicks, let a broody hen sit on a clutch of eggs (so long as you are keeping a good young rooster to assure they are fertile).

Most folks get started by buying day-old chicks in batches of 25 and raising them at home. You can purchase all roosters or all hens, depending on whether you want meat or eggs. If you don't particularly care about the gender of the birds, you can buy them as-hatched "straight-run" which are sold just as they come out of the eggs, with about an even mix of males and females.

Sexed chicks will cost more than straight run; pullets (young hens) of egg breeds and cockerels (young males) of the broiler breeds bringing a premium.

You will have to brood day-old chicks under a heat lamp for a month till they grow large enough to fend for themselves. Brooders as well as special feed and water fonts are sold in the same feed stores or mail order catalogs from which you can select your birds.

If you'd prefer not to raise the chicks yourself, it's possible to purchase older birds that'll be ready to lay eggs a few weeks after you receive them. These "started pullets," as they're called, are usually from 18 to 20 weeks old and will cost five or six times as much as day-old chicks.

Don't buy laying hens from a newspaper ad. These will usually be older biddies past their egg-laying prime and not worth their feed. They can also bring in disease and parasites.

Cycles: A hen has only one year of peak egg production. After that she'll molt and stop producing. In about six to eight weeks the hen will regrow her plumage and begin to lay again but will produce at least 10 percent fewer eggs than during her first laying season. A nonproducing chicken will eat every bit as much as a good layer—which may prompt you to manage your flock in the following manner:

In the spring, purchase a straight-run batch of day-old dual-purpose chicks. When they reach 20 to 24 weeks of age, butcher the roosters and expect the hens to begin laying.

The following spring, buy a replacement batch of day-old, dual-purpose babies and begin again.

During the second and each succeeding year, when the time comes to kill and dress out your 20- to 24-week-old roosters, you can butcher the previous season's hens (for stewing purposes). By the time you've put the roosters and old hens into your freezer, the new young biddies will be about to begin laying.

A good hen in peak egg production will lay about once every 30 hours. She'll produce best, however, when she's exposed to 14 hours of sunlight every day. In the fall, when the sunshine hours decrease and egg production conse-

An Egg Candler You Can Make

"Don't count your chickens before they hatch" is one proverb poultry raisers learn to take literally. The frustrating and time-wasting experience of trying to hatch an unfertilized egg under a hen or in an incubator can be avoided with a homemade candler that allows you to see inside unhatched eggs. Not only can infertile eggs be distinguished from fertile ones, but the freshness and purity of those infertile eggs can be checked.

Candler Construction: The main component of this little lantern is a metal can with a lid. A coffee can or any similar canister with a tight-fitting lid will do. To make the candler, position an ordinary light fixture inside the can, punch a few mounting holes in the container's bottom, and secure the fixture with a couple of small bolts and nuts. Make one other opening in the bottom of the canister for the light's electric cord. On the free end of this wire, attach an electrical plug, and then add an in-line switch to the cord.

To make a hole for illuminating the eggs, cut a 1-1/2"-diameter hole in the container's lid. A 2-1/4"-diameter cork gasket glued around that opening prevents an egg from cracking if it accidentally bumps the can while being examined. If you have a hard time finding cork gasket material, felt or rubber can be used for this part.

Four legs attached to the side of the candler allow horizontal viewing. These are easily made by cutting two 6"-long strips from thin sheet metal and bending each strip to form a pair of legs. Secure them to the can's side with sheet metal screws or pop rivets.

Punch a few holes in the container's sides for ventilation, and coat the outside with high-temperature auto engine paint as a finish. When the paint's thoroughly dry, screw in a 40-watt light bulb, plug the device in, and darken the room. With that, you're ready to start candling eggs.

Glowing Reports: It's best to test the fertility of white eggs around the fourth day after they've been laid. Dark ones, on the other hand, give the most accurate results after about a week. Any dirt on the shells should be gently brushed, not washed, away. To check for signs of fertility, carefully place an egg's wide end to the candler opening so that the entire oval is illuminated. In a fertile, hatchable egg there will be a fine network of veins running out from a dark center. "Clears," those with no visible embryonic development, are ones that were never fertilized, while the few with small blood spots could be either fertilized eggs in which the embryo has died or infertile eggs that have picked up a bit of the hen's tissue.

(continued on page 189)

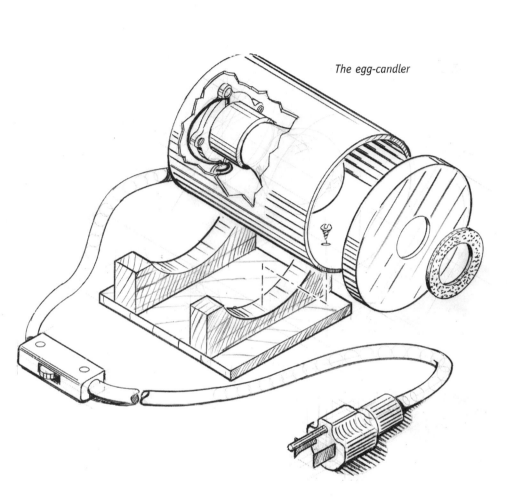

The egg-candler

Candling can also be used to check the quality of eggs going to market or to the kitchen. Here again, the oval is held with its broad end to the light opening. However, in this case, the egg is given a few quick turns so that the contents rotate within the shell to promote fuller viewing. A fresh egg will have an air space 1/8" or less in depth and a yolk that's free of foreign particles, blood rings, large spots, and other defects. You probably won't want to sell the eggs with blood spots, as most buyers consider them unsightly, but if you merely remove the specks with the tip of a knife, they'll do just fine for your own table. ■

quently tapers off, you can keep the hens producing by setting up an inexpensive light timer and keeping the coop illuminated for the recommended 14 hours per day.

Keeping a backyard flock of chickens can be a very rewarding experience. You'll be treated to fresh, wholesome food and have the opportunity to watch the fascinating social interaction of your birds. A rooster isn't necessary to get eggs, but having one in the coop does seem to lend an air of completeness to the flock, and you will be treated to the early morning crowing chorus that has wakened people for centuries.

Raising Rabbits

Even if your backyard is no bigger than 30 square feet, you can produce 200 pounds of homegrown meat every year by raising rabbits.

Domestic rabbit meat is a tasty, amazingly versatile food. Its flavor is often compared to that of chicken, and like the barnyard fowl, rabbit is good fried, baked, stewed, cooked in casseroles—any way you'd use chicken or veal. The mammal's firm, fine-grained fat-free flesh actually makes for more healthful eating than does chicken, as rabbit has more protein and fewer calories per pound.

Rabbits are a wise choice for the small livestock fancier for other reasons: They are easy to raise, feed, and care for. They're also quiet, an important consideration for folks who are rearing animals in a populated area.

Preliminaries: You can expect a good doe to yield four to five litters with six to nine youngsters a batch per year. Each of the young animals should reach a weight of 4 to 4-1/2 pounds at the standard butchering age of eight to ten weeks. At that age they should dress out to between 2 and 2-1/2 pounds. Therefore, a single doe can contribute 60 pounds or more of meat for your larder in one year, which isn't a bad output from one 10- or 12-pound animal. What's more, unlike a steer, which yields all its 500 freezer-filling pounds at one time, your rabbit meat will be produced in meal-sized portions throughout most of the year.

You won't need to throw out your rabbits' innards, either. Slice the kidneys in half, deep-fry the segments, and serve them as hors d'oeuvres. Rabbit liver can be cooked and chopped up into a tasty sandwich spread, or fried with mushrooms and bacon. Even the remaining viscera from your butchered fryers can be utilized: It makes a tasty treat for pigs. But, don't feed it to your dogs. They'll develop a taste for rabbit and be more prone to try getting into the cages.

Rabbits produce more than meat. You can shovel their high-quality manure straight onto a vegetable plot. Rabbit manure has more nitrogen and phosphorus than does horse, cow, or pig manure.

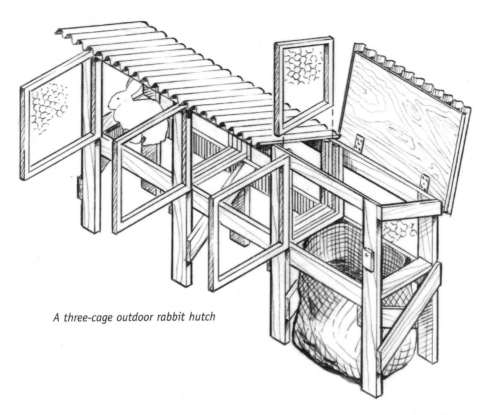

A three-cage outdoor rabbit hutch

You could also set up a ground-level bin under your elevated rabbit hutches and start a worm farm in the collected droppings. Furthermore, the rabbits' pelts make excellent hats, collars, and mittens.

Always remember, though, that you are the real market for the bounty your bunnies produce. Sure, you might eventually want to try your hand at commercial breeding, but no one should undertake such an enterprise without enough experience to understand fully the labor, costs, and marketing possibilities involved.

Build a Good House: Don't plan to build an outside run. Domestic breeds descend from European hares that dig; they will tunnel out overnight. They really don't need a lot of space to hop around in, but if they're to be as healthy and productive as possible, each adult animal will need a hutch that's at least 3' long, 2-1/2' deep, and 1-1/2 or 2' high. You can construct the sides and top of a rabbit hutch out of small-gauge chicken wire, but be sure to use only sturdy and easy-on-the-furry-feet 1/2" X 1" galvanized hardware wire for the cage floor. The entire box can be framed on the outside with wood or metal, but note that rabbits will chew on any exposed wooden members they can reach.

The hutch should be constructed so that it stands well off the ground, but build a strong fence around the legs or predators can get in underneath. Even if they don't work the bottom wire loose, their efforts can give the rabbits a fatal scare.

Your hutch will also need a door about 14" square, which is large enough to place the nesting box through and to let you reach every part of the cage's interior. You can build the portal from a piece of welded wire and should hinge the door to swing inward.

Rabbits tolerate adverse weather and harsh climates fairly well, but you should construct a sloped hutch roof to shed snow and rain, and in areas where harsh winter gusts occur, build some form of windbreak. The animals actually suffer more in hot weather than they do in cold, though. Prolonged exposure to heat can be fatal to your animals, so be sure the rabbitry is positioned so it'll get adequate shade during sweltering midsummer days.

Along with a good hutch, you should supply your rabbits with a feeder, a waterer, and a nesting box. The food container can be nothing more than a heavy earthen crock or a coffee can fastened to the side of the cage. On the other hand, you might prefer to buy one of the commercial automatic feeders that attach to the outside of the hutch and are, therefore, difficult for the rabbits to contaminate.

A waterer can be as plain as a frequently cleaned and replenished dish, or as elaborate as a commercial drip waterer. You can construct a homemade automatic device by suspending a filled and inverted bottle over a watering pan. Just make sure the jug's lid is slightly under the pan's water level.

Finally, each doe will need a nesting box to use when she "kindles," or gives birth. This maternity ward can be built out of wood and should measure about 20" long by 12" wide by 12" high. Also, fasten a 6"-wide wood strip across the bottom of its otherwise open front-end to keep the newborns from rolling out. Leave the top partly open to allow ventilation.

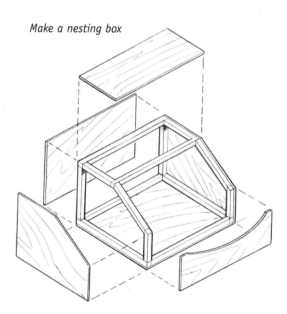

Make a nesting box

Know What to Look For: When you begin to look for your starter rabbits (most rabbit breeders start out with two does and one buck), you'll soon learn that the long-eared animals come in many different breeds and sizes. Lop-eared breeds and the miniature breeds are darling and good for pets—not eating. Angora rabbits produce a fine wool that can be plucked, spun, and knitted into wonderfully fuzzy sweaters.

However, most rabbit raisers across the country agree that the midsize (10 to 12 pounds) New Zealand White and California varieties make about the best backyard meat breeds.

You'll want to make sure that any animal you buy is healthy, so examine each rabbit closely before making a purchase. The inside of the animal's ears should not have the dry scabs that are caused by ear mites; its hocks and feet should be free of sore spots; its nose shouldn't be wet, runny, or crusty; and its droppings should be firm and round. If the animal looks fit in these and other obvious respects (does should have eight or more nipples, for instance), you can be sure you've found a healthy one.

Also, never lift a rabbit by its ears. Always pick it up by gently grasping a handful of skin at the scruff of its neck and, at the same time, placing a supporting hand under its bottom.

Choose the Best Animals: Purchase only bucks and does with excellent production records or youngsters bred from such prolific propagators. In addition, you can tell a lot about what sort of offspring your breeding stock will produce by examining the potential parents. Most of a rabbit's meat comes from its hind legs, so gently squeeze the rear thighs to judge how plump and meaty those areas are. Give a squeeze test to the back between the animal's pelvis and ribs as well. This loin muscle section should be long, wide, and firm.

Culling: It's an easy matter to remove the poor producers, negligent mothers, and seriously uncooperative breeders from your rabbit herd: Simply butcher and eat them. Even the most productive parents will decline after five or six years, so your older animals should also be regularly culled.

Feed Them Correctly: Water is the single most important element in a rabbit's diet. A doe and her litter will consume a full gallon each day, so keep plenty of clean water in the hutches at all times.

Protein is the most critical food ingredient in assuring superior growth and production. Adult rabbits require a diet with at least 12 percent of the valuable food stuff, while nursing mothers and growing youngsters need a 20 percent protein ration. A rabbit on a protein deficient diet will grow more slowly, and if it's a doe, she may bear fewer young and produce less milk.

Most rabbit raisers rely on commercial feed, which provides plenty of vital protein and a completely balanced diet as well. Putting together a do-it-yourself rabbit feed that includes all the correct amounts of digestible nutrients, protein, minerals, vitamins, and sheer food energy—but doesn't contain poisonous weeds, molds, or other toxins—is too difficult a task for the average person.

You can, of course, supplement your critters' meals with an occasional helping of root crops, green vegetables, and bits of hay, though you should note that greens will give young bunnies a severe case of diarrhea. Keep in mind that any time you add such a treat to your rabbits' ration, you will undoubtedly be decreasing the percentage of protein in the animals' overall diet.

Baby rabbits should be given free access to all the feed they can eat to help them grow as quickly as possible, but don't overfeed your adults, because obesity is one of the most prevalent causes of infertility in both male and female rabbits. An adult buck or "dry" doe should be fed about three to six ounces of pellets a day, a pregnant female needs five to ten ounces daily, and nursing mothers may require as much as 20 ounces. It's best to tape ration sheets right to your feeders so you know how much food each animal should get.

One last note about rabbits' eating habits: You may notice that the critters are "coprophagous"—in other words, they eat what seems to be their own fecal matter. It isn't; rather, it is half-digested food the first time through and the rabbit's way to masticate cellulose-containing vegetation twice—just as cattle regurgitate food and "chew their cud." This "recycling" process is a necessary part of the animals' digestive cycle that breaks down cellulose and provides, among other essentials, niacin and riboflavin, so don't interpret the habit as yukky manners or a sign of ill health. On the other hand, don't worry if you never see coprophagy, because rabbits tend to engage in this and most other feeding practices at night. They are able to maintain this habit even in wire-bottomed cages.

Be Aware of Your Animal's Cycles: All rabbit raisers should pay close attention to their animals' reproductive life patterns. Mature rabbits can breed year round—typically with the buck being brought to the doe's cage. Does don't ovulate until 10 hours after they're bred, so every mating union should be a fertile one, providing neither animal is overweight and the buck has not been exposed to too much hot weather. As with many animals, excess heat causes short-term sterility in male rabbits.

You can tell whether a doe is pregnant by giving her a checkup two weeks after her mating. At that time, place the animal on a table, restrain her with a one handed scruff-of-the-neck grasp, and palpate her belly with the other hand: Squeeze gently and slide your hand from the lower rib cage back and up to the pelvic region, feeling carefully for any marble-sized placentas.

A doe usually gives birth 30 to 32 days following conception, so place the nesting box in the animal's hutch no later than 27 days after her mating. You'll be able to wean the fast-growing youngsters within two months after their birth. The doe can be re-bred before this separation, but be sure to give her a good two weeks' rest between the end of caring for her past litter and the birth of the next offspring.

Keep Meaningful Records: If you can imagine the difficulty you'll face in trying to keep track of when to wean and when to mate and when one doe is due to kindle and which of your rabbits came from which doe, and in doing all this while those busy rabbits are multiplying faster than electronic calculators, you'll readily understand the need for keeping accurate records. Without the information they'll contain, it's impossible to tell which rabbits are the most, and which the least, productive.

You can design your own buck and doe breeding forms or use ready-made record-keeping charts. If your flock starts getting really large, you may even want to tattoo each rabbit's ear for identification.

Caring for the Youngsters: Newborns don't need much human attention because their mother will take care of everything except providing the nest box. That's your job. Be sure to give the nursery a good supply of clean straw or wood shavings—3" or 4" in summer and twice that amount during the winter.

Barnyard Livestock Requirements

REQUIREMENTS:	CHICKENS	RABBITS
Housing: floor area/critter	3 sq ft (1-1/2 sq ft with run)	24"X30"X36" wire cage
Furniture	hanging dry feeder vacuum waterer grit bowls	nest/kindling boxes feed bowls water fonts
Roost space	10" to 12"	none
Fenced run	poultry wire	none
Water/critter	1/10 gal/day	1 gal./day
Feed /animal	1/2 lbs chick 3 lbs starter 100 lbs grow or lay per yr	100 lbs per litter
Ratio male/female	3:25 to breed no males for eggs	1:10
Harvest	225 eggs/yr broilers at 5 wks. roasters at 14 wks.	2 lbs meat from 4 lb bunny at 10 - 12 weeks
Feed:meat ratio	2.5 to 3:1	4 to 5:1

Then put the box in the hutch three or four days before the doe is due but not any earlier than that because she may turn her delivery room into a toilet. Fill the nest box with clean hay; the mother will line the nest with her own belly fur to make the home even more comfortable for the expected youngsters.

The day after the rabbits are born, check the box and remove any dead newborn. After the little ones are three or four weeks old, remove the nest box itself and let the new residents get used to the hutch. Before the portable nursery is brought back for a new batch of youngsters, it must be thoroughly emptied, cleaned, and disinfected.

Help Your Animals Avoid Disease: If you buy and raise good rabbits, feed them correctly, and keep your rabbitry clean, you'll avoid 99.4% to 100% of all rabbit disease problems.

However, there are a couple of persistent health bugaboos that may require particular attention. For example, ear mites, which hide in the crevices of your hutch and love to nibble the insides of rabbit ears, are often a problem. You can control these pests by putting a few drops of mineral or olive oil into your rabbits' ears once every six weeks or so.

In addition, the rough wire floor of the hutch can sometimes produce sores, scabs, and even inflammation on the animals' feet, especially their hocks. You can help remedy that problem by placing flat 6" X 10" boards over part of the cage bottom away from the animals' favorite toilet corners so the rabbits can rest their weary toes.

Once you've tried raising these prolific animals, you'll be surprised that more folks don't do likewise.

Basics for the Backyard Beekeeper

As long as there are flowers that bear nectar in your area, you can become a beekeeper and successfully manage one or more hives to produce all the fresh, unadulterated honey you and your friends can use. This holds true even if you live in the middle of a large city. In fact, many urban beekeepers maintain hives on apartment house roofs or in attics. Before getting into beekeeping in a city or anywhere else, however, you should check state and local ordinances.

Stings: Many people don't have beehives because they're afraid of being stung. That concern is not unfounded; if you keep bees, you will get stung. Many times you'll visit them and not receive a single poke, and other days you may acquire one or two light "tip" stings that don't even swell. Then again, odds are that someday you'll make a careless mistake, such as working with insects under unfavorable weather conditions, and get stung by several of the 30,000 to 100,000 flying honey-gatherers.

A sting hurts a little, but most beekeepers build immunity. A minority of people are allergic to bee stings, and their sensitivity may increase with time. If you experience allergies of any kind, get tested before taking on bees. In addition, there's a technique that can be used to reduce the amount of venom absorbed from occasional stings. Simply use a fingernail or some other thin-edged object to scrape the stinger out immediately; otherwise, its venom sack will continue to pump poison into the flesh for a minute or more. Don't try to grab the stinger with your fingers as many people do, or you'll squeeze even more venom into your system.

That beekeeper's trick will reduce the damage inflicted by stings. But, of course, the goal is to get stung as little as possible while tending hives, and the following tips should reduce the number of stings you receive .

First, wear a snug, bee-tight veil and light-colored clothing: White cover-alls are excellent for beekeeping, blue jeans are poor. Eliminate any entrance spaces between your garments and skin by tucking your pants legs into your socks and by wrapping rubber bands around your shirt sleeves. Do not wear wool. And consider not wearing protective gloves. During the first few months you may feel more comfortable if you do don them, but eventually you'll probably find that it's easier to work a hive without crushing bees when you're bare-handed.

Second, do not wear clothes that have previously received stings. When bees strike, they release a banana-scented pheromone to alert their comrades and entice other bees to sting the same area. So wearing garments that are still scented with that alarm odor is literally asking to be stung.

Third, always use a smoker. The portable bellows/fire box combination, a standard piece of beekeeping equipment, enables the beekeeper to puff plumes of smoke into the beehive. For some reason, perhaps because bees believe they're getting ready to flee a forest fire, they engorge themselves with honey whenever they smell smoke and become much less aggressive toward intruders. A smoker is also useful for temporarily covering up the scent of pheromone if you do get stung.

Fourth, whenever possible, visit the bees on a warm, sunny, windless day when plenty of nectar-bearing flowers are in bloom or as beekeepers say, when there's a honey flow. On such occasions many of the insects will be out working in the fields, and the stay-at-homes will be so busy with their own labors that they'll hardly notice your presence.

Fifth, don't block the hive entrance with your body. Tend the bee house from the side or back.

Finally, try to make all your movements calm, even, and efficient. Don't alarm the insects by moving jerkily or hastily or try their patience by taking more time than you should. Such poise may not come naturally at first, but with experience the skills and demeanor involved will soon improve. Also, if

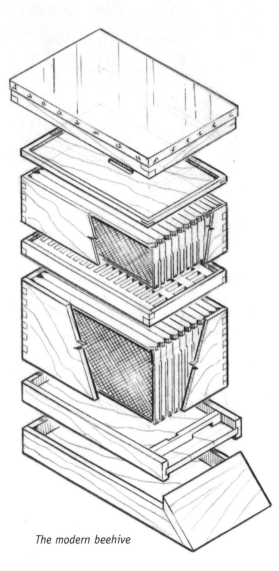
The modern beehive

at all possible, it's best to get some experience working with other beekeepers; a lot of their self-assurance will rub off on you.

The Hive: The modern beehive, devised in 1851, incorporated two vital features that are considered standard today: movable, interchangeable frames and uniform "bee space."

The fact that all the interior parts can be easily taken out and moved about is what makes precise and nondestructive manipulation of the hive possible. Since all the internal pieces of equipment are separated by the 5/16" "bee space" that bees naturally prefer as passageways, the insects usually won't be tempted to close off their "halls" by sticking the hive parts together with extra wax or bee glue (propolis).

The basic parts of the bees' home are a hive stand, a bottom board, inner and outer top covers, and open boxes or supers that make up the body of the hive. Inside every one of the bee-housing boxes are eight to 10 frames, with each of these removable rectangles containing a thin sheet of beeswax imprinted with hexagons the size of a worker bee cell. Such foundation sheets give the bees ordered starting points for drawing out either egg or honey cells.

The main hive body or brood chamber, sometimes called a deep super, is 9-5/8" high and is used to house the queen and her eggs (brood). Many beekeepers like to keep two brood chambers on each hive.

The shorter boxes or supers are only 5-3/4" tall. They're stacked on top of the brood chamber(s) and used primarily for storing honey.

Kinds of Bees: The membership of a hive colony includes one queen bee, thousands of worker bees, and a number of male drones. The queen, the longest-lived member of the colony, resembles a worker bee but has an enlarged abdomen. After a few youthful mating flights, she spends the rest of her life, which may be as long as seven years, in the hive performing one function: laying eggs—more than 1,500 a day during the peak of each season.

The worker bees are all females that lack fully developed reproductive organs. These industrious insects run the hive: They feed and clean up after the queen; they gather honey, pollen, and water; they keep the internal temperature of the hive constant (they can both cool and heat their enclosed environment); they feed the larvae; and they build all the honey and brood comb.

In contrast, the drones do no work in the hive. They eat honey while waiting around for an opportunity to mate with a young queen (their sole purpose in life).

Bees can be obtained in three different ways: by mail order, by buying a working hive from a local beekeeper, or by catching a wild swarm.

Catching a swarm isn't really as difficult as you might imagine. Usually seen hanging from tree limbs, posts, or shrubs, the tight, homeless clusters of bees tend to be remarkably mild-mannered. Still, anyone who's never handled bees before or doesn't want to depend on the chance of finding a swarm may prefer to start out by purchasing bees.

It's often possible to buy a strong, established colony from a local beekeeper. Such a working community should contain about 50,000 bees along with a complete hive. And if subsequent weather and honey flows permit, you ought to be able to harvest 50 to 100 pounds of honey your first season.

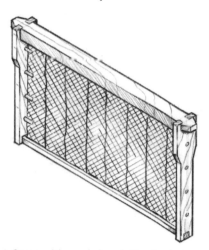

Many states require that such purchases be examined by a bee inspector, who can be contacted through the county agricultural extension service. The examiner will inspect the colony for signs of highly contagious bee diseases, such as American foulbrood. If you don't have an inspector look into your hive,

A frame with comb-foundation in place

you should have read enough to be able to spot problems yourself, and should ask the seller to go through the hive in your presence.

Some beginners start their colonies with mail-ordered packages of bees, and this is surely the safest way to be sure you're buying the kind of bees you want. (There are several varieties of *Apis mellifera*, but the vast majority are variants of the "Italian" strain.)

If you choose to go the package route, however, you should place your order as early in the year as possible, because most bee suppliers become quite busy in the warm months. The package, which will be shipped four to six weeks before the first spring bloom, will contain a healthy, mated young queen, two or three pounds of worker bees, a can of syrup for the insects to eat en route, and complete instructions for both installing the colony in the hive and feeding its members until the first honey flow. This method costs less initially than buying a working hive, but since you'll be starting out with a small nucleus, your new bee community may not make any honey beyond its own wintering food needs during the first year.

Comb or Liquid: After your bees are in place and prospering, you should consider adding your first honey super to the hive. But before you can take this step to expand a colony's lodgings, you'll have to make another fundamental beekeeping decision: whether to harvest comb (chunk) or liquid (extracted) honey.

Chunk honey is produced in frames that contain thin, chewable foundation. The foundation used for honey that is to be extracted must be thicker and reinforced with either preset or hand-inserted wires so that it will be sturdy enough to withstand the pressure of the honey extractor that spins the viscous liquid out of its combs.

Beginners will probably encounter less trouble and expense starting off using comb foundations. By doing so, they'll be able to harvest the honey by cutting it, comb and all, out of the frames. Then, liquid honey can be separated from the yield by smashing all the comb cells with a kraut chopper or a beater from an electric mixer and letting the honey drain out through a small mesh screen lined with cheesecloth.

Heating and then cooling the leftover comb shards in a double boiler will yield some more honey. This will be topped by a solid layer of yellow beeswax. Don't throw that substance out! You can either use it for making wonderful candles or save it until you accumulate enough to sell to bee-supply companies, other beekeepers, or craft shops.

Because bees use a lot of honey and energy while building their combs, you can harvest about 50% more honey from your hive if you extract the sweetener and reinstall the intact cells in the hive instead of cutting the combs out altogether. Ah, but there's a rub: The smallest hand-cranked extractors cost more than all the other combined start-up expenses for a single-hive operation.

However, if you want the increased yield possible with extracted honey without the full expense of purchasing the necessary machine, you might be able to share the purchase cost of an extractor with some other small-scale beekeepers, or you may be able to pay with honey so that a nearby commercial apiarist will do your comb/honey separating.

A Visit to the Hive: To give you a better feel for what it'll be like to tend a flock of insect livestock, imagine that it's a sunny day in June. Wild flowers are blooming like crazy, the hive seems to be prospering, a honey super was added two weeks ago, and you're a mite curious as to just how well those bees are doing. In short, it's a perfect day to inspect the apiary.

Having donned bee-tight garments and started a steady fume-producing flame in the smoker, approach the hive from the side and watch for a moment. Yep, there's a good honey flow on. Plenty of bees are flying in and out of the wooden home... and the ones coming back are so laden with nectar, which will be converted to honey inside the hive, that they almost droop their way through the air.

Put the tip of the smoker in the mouth of the hive's low entrance and put a couple of clouds into the brood chamber. The bees near the entrance will buzz around a bit, but soon most of them will go into the hive

A minute later, lift off the hive's outer cover and blow smoke down the narrow hole in the inner lid. Wait for a short time after this, then using the hive tool, an inexpensive crowbar implement that's an indispensable beekeeper's aid, pry the inner cover's corners loose and take the thin top off.

Using your hive tool as a lever, carefully pry up one corner of a spare frame until you can grab the wooden rack's top edge with one hand. Then pry up the opposite top corner, grab that end, too, and pulling slowly so you don't crush any workers, lift the entire bee-covered frame out of the hive. Some of the cells you examine are capped with white beeswax (indicating the presence of ready-to-harvest honey). Most of the hexagonal units, though, are unsealed and contain clearly visible honey. Since such ambrosia needs further curing by the bees, this indicates it's not yet time to make the first harvest.

After carefully replacing the frame, give the entire super a few puffs with the smoker and then start prying that honey-holding box free from the brood chamber. Even though the super may have been on the hive only a short while, the bees will have already stuck it tightly to the brood box, and you have to free all four corners carefully with your hive tool and then slowly twist the upper story sideways to break the gummy seals.

When not laden with honey, the super's not very heavy (if full, it would weigh at least 40 pounds), so you'll be able to lift it off easily and set it on the over-turned outer cover. You then grab the smoker again and give the bees at the top of the brood chamber a few brief puffs.

One by one, now, pull out a few separate frames from the central hive room. Except for the less occupied outer racks, each frame you examine is, as some beekeepers say, "slam full of brood." A large semicircle of dark convex cappings will cover much of the surface. Some cells will contain uncapped white larvae, and honey or pollen will be stored in the frames' corners.

You may not happen to spot the queen as you forage through the chamber, but rest assured that since the colony is so full of fine brood, the hive is obviously healthy and "queen—right." Don't bother the bees by needlessly searching for her but carefully reassemble the hive and head back home.

Returning to the scene a week later, you'll find the honey crop is 80 percent sealed and ready to harvest. You could leave a "one-way bee escape"—a gateway that lets bees out but not in—under the super, walk off and reap insect-free racks in a day or so. But if you've just got too much of a hankering for some homegrown honey to wait, pull out the sweet-filled frames one by one and sweep all the bees off them with a soft-bristled brush and take the golden gatherings home.

Beekeeping's Vital Season: Every beekeeping season has its annual tasks. Summer work includes jobs such as adding supers and harvesting the honey. Fall is the time to make sure your bees have all their winter stores built up. And before winter hits, you need to add some hardware cloth to your hives' entrances to keep out mice and start assembling gear for next year.

But the most crucial beekeeping season is surely the spring. Having made it through the winter on their own supplies and being ready to begin foraging anew, many colonies are then faced with a few change-of season weeks when no harvestable flowers have bloomed. If the nectar-gatherers don't have enough stores to see themselves through this period, you'll need to provide some sugar or honey syrup and perhaps some pollen or pollen substitute. Otherwise, the bees may have survived the winter only to starve in the spring!

The warming weather after a long winter brings yet another threat to the colony's productivity: swarming. In the wild, bee colonies reproduce annually by division. Many of the workers and the old queen emerge from the hive and fly off to find a new home. If your bees swarm, a new queen and some workers will be left behind to carry on. But much of your best winged livestock will have flown the coop, so the hive will probably not produce a good honey crop that season.

Although you can take some hive-saving steps, you won't prevent all swarms from occurring. You might, however, balance your losses with gains, since spring is also the season to catch stray runaway clusters and thus increase the number of hives in your apiary.

The danger of swarming, and the quality and number of bees that do desert the hive in such instances, decreases as spring turns to summer. As an old nursery rhyme notes: "A swarm in May is worth a load of hay. A swarm in June is worth a silver spoon. But a swarm in July isn't worth a fly."

Sweet Rewards: If you take up beekeeping and manage your little honey-makers with care, you'll have the pleasure of learning about one of nature's most intriguing phenomena. The intricate patterns of bee behavior provide continual discoveries to the most experienced apiarist.

Although there's commitment and labor required of the beekeeper, as the colony's caretaker you'll probably feel humble when you compare your efforts to those of your partner. As long-time beekeeper Richard Taylor has artfully phrased it: "The truly monumental work of apiculture is always done by the bees themselves."

Breeds of Sheep

Sheep can be grouped in any of several ways: by their suitability as meat producers, by the length or quality of their wool, by their facial color, or by their adaptation to altitudes. The most useful grouping is classification by wool grades. The latest method of classification by wool grade uses the micron (just under 1/25,000 inch) as a standard, and then rates wool by the average diameter of the fibers in a given lot: The finer the wool, the smaller the micron number.

The micron system appears to be more technically accurate than its predecessors, and there is some effort being made to establish it as the standard for describing wools in the United States. Few people, however, have a "feel" for micron measurement, so the sheep listed here are categorized as having fine, medium, or long wool.

Fine-Wooled Breeds: The fine-wooled breeds in the U.S. include the American Merino, Delaine Merino, Rambouillet, and Debouillet. Like the Spanish Merino from which they're all descended, these varieties are noted for fine, tightly crimped wool that has a heavy, greasy covering called yolk. When refined, this combination of secretions from the sebaceous and sweat glands becomes the smooth, oily product we call lanolin.

In recent years the meat-producing capabilities of these breeds have been improved, but if putting lamb chops on the table is your aim, there are better meat types available. On the other hand, ewes of the fine wooled types will often breed out of season, a definite advantage for the owner who's interested in maximum productivity.

No other breed has contributed more to the development of other sheep types than has the Merino. Early examples of this breed had thick wrinkles along their entire bodies, a characteristic that breeders later discovered produced wool of inferior quality. Called "type A," these sheep are rarely seen today, having given way to the less wrinkled varieties known as "type B" and to the virtually wrinkle-free "type C," or Delaine Merinos.

All the Merinos are hardy and long-lived, and they possess a strong flocking instinct. Their fleece is extremely fine and therefore difficult for any but an experienced spinner to manage, but it does yield yarns of very high quality.

The Rambouillet, a direct descendant of the Spanish Merino, is the largest of the fine-wooled breeds. The animals are commonly used in crossbreeding programs, and it's been estimated that at least 50 percent of all the sheep in the United States have some Rambouillet blood in their background. The Debouillet, for example, is a Delaine/Rambouillet cross.

Rambouillets are considered dual-purpose (meat and wool) sheep. They have superior long, dense, fine wool that's very popular for spinning. Most rams of the breed sport large spiral horns, though some strains are polled (hornless).

Medium-Wooled Breeds: The most popular medium-wooled breeds include the Cheviot and North Country Cheviot, Montadale, Dorset, Tunis, Hampshire, Oxford, Shropshire, Suffolk, and Southdown. The last five examples in this list are sometimes called the "Down" breeds, a reference to the hills and downs of southern England where they originated.

All the medium-wooled sheep were developed for meat, and their fleece is rated somewhere between the extreme fineness and density of the Merino and the coarseness and open quality typical of the long-wooled varieties of sheep. Most of these breeds have dark faces and dark legs.

The smallest and oldest of the Down types, the Southdown is said to produce the finest mutton of any sheep. Its compact, wide, deep body was used as the foundation stock for all other Down breeds. The young reach market weight quickly, but the ewes, which are just average milkers, are not prolific. Southdown wool is relatively short and can be used to make a fine yarn.

The original Shropshires had a wool "cap" extending down to the muzzle, but because this contributed to an ailment known as wool blindness, breeders have worked to develop a clean-faced variety. Long-lived, hardy, and prolific, Shropshires have the heaviest fleece of the mutton types, but the wool tends to be short and varies in quality from fine to medium grade.

Oxfords, the largest of the medium-wooled sheep, are the result of crossing Hampshires and Cotswolds in the mid-1800s. Oxford lambs weigh nine to 12 pounds at birth and reach market weight early.

A very popular breed used extensively for cross breeding is the Hampshire, which is a heavy milker and often produces twins. The lambs are born dark and gradually turn white, retaining dark legs and faces. Because of their large size (they're second only to the Oxford among the Downs), Hampshires need good pasture and feed, and won't thrive if left to forage on poor ground. The ewes sometimes experience lambing problems because of the large head and shoulders typical of the young ones.

The thin, black-faced, black-legged look indicative of the Suffolk strain can be seen in many of the crossbred sheep raised on the western ranges in this country. Unlike the Hampshires, Suffolk lambs have small heads and shoulders and give little trouble at lambing time. Members of the breed are active foragers, too, and their meat has less fat and a finer texture than does that of most other medium-wooled breeds.

Both the rams and ewes of the original Dorset breed had massive horns. Recently, however, a polled strain has been developed. Dorsets will breed out of season, are noted milkers, and are active, thrifty foragers.

The Cheviot, with its distinctive white face, erect ears, Roman nose, and small size, is easy to identify. This hardy breed originated in the rugged hills of Scotland and is quite suitable for small farms. Cheviots produce a medium-grade fleece that is prized by many spinners because it doesn't need carding—combing so fibers are straight.

Larger than the original Cheviot, the North Country Cheviot strain is also calmer in temperament. The fleece of this interesting breed is of medium grade and excellent for spinning.

Montadales originated in America in 1932 and are the result of cross-breeding Cheviots and Columbias. They are an attractive and hardy dual-purpose, intermediate size sheep with good medium fleece.

Easily recognized by its red or tan face and pendulous ears, the Tunis originated in North Africa. Like some other desert sheep, it has fatty tissue in its tail and can call on that stored energy when forced to go without food for extended periods. Popular in the South, the Tunis was nearly wiped out during the Civil War but staged a comeback in the late 1890's. It's once again growing in popularity.

Long-Wooled Breeds: The long-wooled breeds: Cotswold, Border Leicester, Lincoln, and Romney, for example, were developed primarily for mutton. They are typically the largest sheep, and 225- to 350-pound rams and 175- to 275-pound ewes are common among them. Their wool is generally very long, open, and coarse, and it's frequently used in carpets, wall hangings, and outerwear. Heavy rains may cause the fleece to part and allow the sheep to get wet to the skin. When that happens, the wool is undamaged, but the animals sometimes become ill as a result of their drenching. These strains tend to mature slowly and are likely to become fatty, but their large size often makes them desirable for crossbreeding.

One of the oldest breeds, the Cotswold has a tuft of hair on its forehead and long, lustrous, naturally curly wool that many spinners find pleasant to work with.

Developed in the country along the border between England and Scotland, the Border Leicester has the erect ears and Roman nose of the Cheviot and wool averaging between 8 and 12 inches long. The fleece is coarse and has considerable luster.

The Lincolns are the heavyweights of sheepdom and also grow the heaviest fleece (up to 30 pounds from one ram), which is usually from 10 to 15 inches long. The wool is lustrous, long-wearing, and difficult to card. These animals are somewhat sluggish and slow to mature, but when used for cross-breeding, they add size and staple (a term for fiber length and diameter).

In full fleece, Romneys are noted for their beautiful faces and coats. Unlike that of some other long-fleeced varieties, their wool is relatively fine, dense, and much desired by hand spinners because it doesn't need carding. Romneys are quiet, particularly resistant to foot problems, and known for high milk production.

Breeds such as the Columbia, Corriedale, and Targhee are the result of attempts to produce larger ewes that'll yield more wool and heavier market lambs than do other types. Their fleece is usually of medium to fine quality, and many such breeds have adapted well to western United States range conditions.

The Columbia was developed from a Lincoln/Ram bouillet cross in the early 1900s. It's a tight-flocking, dual-purpose sheep that does well on range or farm.

Barnyard Livestock Requirements

REQUIREMENTS:	SHEEP	GOATS
Housing	15 to 20 sq. ft. shelter per adult. Pasture with 20 sq. ft. shade/adult	the same the same
Furniture	Hay rack, feed bin, salt lick, waterer. Lamb creep/heat.	the same Milking platform
Fence	3' welded wire or	10' deer fence or chain link
Water	2 to 3 gal./day	2 to 5 gal./day
Feed	3 to 6 lbs. hay/day (15 bales/yr.)	3 to 4 lbs. hay/day (10 bales/yr.)
Yield/female	8 lbs wool/yr. 1 or 2 lambs/yr.	1 gal. milk/day 1 or 2 kids/yr.
Meat	60 lbs/100 lb. lamb Shearling hides	50 lbs/90. lb kid Leather hides

A New Zealand breed resulting from a cross between Lincoln and Merino sheep, Corriedales generally produce more pounds of wool and lamb per pound of ewe body weight than any other range type. They're fairly prolific, adequate milkers, and tight herders that produce wool noted for its brightness, softness, distinct crimp, and ease of handling. Their fleece can be worked without carding.

The Targhee, so called after the national forest of the same name, is an American breed developed in Idaho around 1926. These sheep are prolific (often having twins or triplets), large, and resistant to both internal parasites and hoof problems.

Other Breeds to Ponder: The Scottish Highland (or Scottish Blackface) is a very old breed and is one of the most common sheep in Britain today. Members of this breed tend to be small, horned, and oddly mottled with black on their faces and legs. Highland fleece is 15 to 18 inches long and quite springy. It's used to make carpets, tweeds, and mattress stuffing. The sheep also produce excellent mutton.

Multiple births are the Finnsheep's claim to fame. The ewes may have litters of anywhere from three to seven lambs. Finnsheep are fine-boned and medium sized, and they produce a very lustrous, light fleece.

The Karakul is the only true black sheep, and all the other dark types are mutations of various white breeds. Karakuls are the source of broadtail, Persian lamb, and half-Persian furs, terms that refer to the pelts of lambs at various stages of growth. Adult Karakul sheep have long, coarse outer hair with a fine undercoat. Usually born black, they do lighten in color as they age, and may turn to various shades of brown, blue, gray, or even white.

The Navajo is quite possibly a descendant of the Spanish Jacob (or Piebald) sheep. The breed hasn't been standardized and therefore occurs in a wide range of sizes, shapes, and colors, and with a varying number of horns: The rams may have from one to four.

The Barbados Blackbellies are hair sheep with practically no wool. A long cape around the neck and shoulders does have fibers that can be spun, however. Barbados are used in crossbreeding to add hardiness, multiple births, and are important for hand spinners' color variety. The sheep will also breed out of season.

A How-to Look at Raising Goats

Raising goats for milk can help the homestead budget stay in balance, but there are several things a person should know before becoming a small-scale goat herd. Selecting and buying stock, providing shelter for the animals, and maintaining a healthy herd are vital areas where the tips of experienced goat raisers can keep the beginner from stumbling into any of several easily avoided pitfalls.

For Beginners: Though some people feel it's best for novices to buy only one or two young female goats, you'll end up with a better herd by starting out with five or six. Three or maybe four goats are a practical number for a person to milk twice a day. Working any fewer than three animals means the time spent setting up to milk, cleaning utensils, hauling grain and hay, and so forth really isn't economically used. On the other hand, milking five or more goats can leave the owner exhausted.

With a starter herd of five or six doelings, you can select the three best producers of that first year to keep and still have a couple of young does to sell that'll bring a premium because they're "in milk" and have their kids at their sides. Then you can keep the very best of the unsold female kids until the next year to see how she turns out. If she looks as if she'll be a better milkmaker than another animal in the herd, keep her. If not, sell the doe to someone who is less critical.

However, it's easy to become trapped in the creeping spiral of goat inflation. "Goatflation" occurs when an owner starts out with one or two animals, fully intending to limit the herd size to that number but not realizing that the kids will be too cute ever to sell. Well, that kindhearted goat herder just naturally keeps the youngsters. The third year is a replay of the same scenario: the owner soon has eight to 10 milking does, all too "valuable" to sell or cull. And so it goes, until the goat fancier has so many animals to take care of that there's time for little else.

The key, then, is to decide how many goats you want to milk and, no matter what, to stick to that maximum number by selling every excess milker. Be firm with yourself, because once you get rid of the ones that don't measure up to your standards, you'll be tempted to keep the rest, even if you still have too many.

Sharing the Wealth: Now that you've decided on the perfect herd size and have sworn to keep absolutely no more than a certain number of milkers, there's one more task to be taken care of before starting off on a buying spree: rounding up some folks who like goat's milk. The problem with dairy goats is that they're prolific producers. Just keeping one nanny will give you a gallon of milk per day, enough to leave most families awash in goat's milk.

Many goat owners have spent a lot of time and effort devising ways to use all that excess liquid. Some owners have even tried selling their dairy products to friends or neighbors. At present there are very few licensed commercial operations in the country that are financially successful at peddling goat's milk or other products. This fact, sad but true, should tell you there's a rather limited future in the sale of goat's milk.

One way to distribute your milk is to supply your own household and another family or two. Ideally, these other folks will be more than just customers; they'll also be willing to take their turn at getting their farm fresh milk right from the source. After all, you may not mind milking, but you very well might get tired of performing the ritual twice a day, every day of the week.

That's why swapping works well: Friends get free milk in exchange for milking your nannies once or twice a week, which gives you a nice break from the chore.

Buying Tips: If possible, when it comes time to pick a goat, buy a youngster about four to six months of age. By this time the doeling should have outgrown her gangly teenaged appearance, so by looking at her body size and type, you can get a fairly good idea of what kind of producer she'll be. She should weigh 60 pounds or so and be ready to breed that first fall. If she's too small (generally under 60 pounds) or too young, don't buy her. Look for an unbred doeling, because then you'll be able to select the buck to which she's going to be bred.

A second goat-shopping choice would be to head out in the spring and look for a promising kid. True, you'll know better what an older animal is going to look like as an adult, but for that very reason a tyke should be less expensive.

With only rare exceptions, don't shop for an adult doe. Purchasing a full-fledged milkmaker is too much like buying a used car: There's a good chance you'll end up with someone else's problems, plus you'll have to pay a lot more for a grown-up than for a younger girl. Bear in mind that most livestock owners rarely, if ever, get rid of their best and most trouble-free producers.

Furthermore, buy only registered purebread animals with American Dairy Goat Association (ADGA) papers, not mixed-breed or grade, unregistered young goats. Of course, you can expect to pay more initially for a purebred youngster, but it more than makes up the difference when you're able to sell her offspring at registered prices.

Also, it's a good idea to buy the breed that's most common in your area. By sticking with the most popular variety, you'll find a receptive market for the offspring you'll be selling later.

Selecting an Animal: Being able to choose a fine dairy goat is especially important, because unlike a feeder pig or calf that you'll butcher down the line, you'll be living with your decision (and her offspring) for many years to come. The best way to learn what a decent goat looks like is to attend some judgings at local goat shows or at a county fair. Spend enough time there looking at good examples until the image of an ideal goat is firmly established in your mind.

In addition to knowing a good goat's general physical attributes, you should pay attention to specific crucial qualities.

Size is the most important characteristic in determining how much milk the animal will produce over her lifetime. The rule here is the bigger the frame, the better. Look for a long, tall doeling with a deep, widespread chest. The prospect's belly should look like the cross section of a barrel. However, be careful not to confuse size with heft; the creature under consideration should be big but refined, not coarse and thick-boned.

This lean, angular look is an elusive quality that livestock owners refer to as "dairy character." In general, the more of this trait that a beast carries on a large body, the more milk she'll produce over her lifetime.

After determining that a prospective purchase is big and well formed, look at her teeth and legs. To have a long and fruitful life, the doe will need to eat and to carry herself to the feeding trough, hence the need for structurally sound teeth and legs. The animal's lower incisors should touch squarely on the upper dental pad, not in front of or behind it. Her legs should appear to drop straight down from her body when she's viewed from the front and the back, and her forward and rear pinnings should have the correct angle at the hock, hip, shoulder, and pasterns.

A healthy udder will be firmly attached to a doe's belly by broad rear and fore ligaments. It should also be symmetrical and evenly divided from side to side with a firmly attached median ligament. And the teats need to be properly shaped. They should be hand size rather than huge or pendulous. Teats of the proper size are easier to milk, leave more room for the milk-producing part of the udder, and are less prone to mastitis. The milk canals (the passages through which the liquid passes) need to be large enough to allow milking with an easy, rhythmic squeezing of the fingers.

Admittedly, udder evaluation is a little difficult when you're sizing up a doeling that's never been milked. However, you can get a better idea of how that animal's udder will probably turn out by checking its mother's apparatus.

Actually, you should evaluate both of the prospect's parents if possible. Once you've given a doe a thorough once-over, you'll have pretty good grounds for guessing how her babies will look when they grow up. Remember to pay special attention to the mother's size, her undercarriage, her teeth, and her mammary system.

Even more important than a mother goat's appearance, though, are her milk-production records. How much milk does she yield annually, and how many kids does she usually have at one time? Pay particular attention to the animal's length of lactation as well as to the overall pounds of liquid produced. You'll want a doe that's going to keep you in milk throughout her entire ten-month lactation spell, not one that pumps out a lot of milk for four or five months and then dries right up.

Home Sweet Home: Where to keep your newly acquired charges turns out to be less complicated than many would-be goat owners want to believe. A simple three-sided shed that keeps out the wind and the rain and offers about 15 square feet of bedding space for each adult goat is the best kind of shelter. The open side of the shed should be aimed south to catch the sun's warming and cleansing rays. Enclosing a goat barn or adding heat to it increases the chance for bacteria to grow and flourish. Bacterial pneumonia, in fact, is quite prevalent among kids kept in stuffy barns. So the most desirable approach is to keep the shelter simple and draft-free, yet well ventilated.

Choosing the right kind of fencing for your goat pen is every bit as simple as erecting the right kind of shed. The best kind of fence for goats is one made out of commercially available stock panels. Slippery caprine Houdinis can wiggle through welded wire fences and can squeeze under or through electric strands, and some goats have even learned how to take advantage of the timed pulses to make a shock-free escape.

Popular Dairy Goat Breeds

Perhaps this "goat field book" will help you decide which of the common breeds might best suit your family.

French Alpine: French Alpines attain a minimum height of 30" and a weight o f about 135 pounds. One of the hardiest of all goat breeds, they are very ruggedly built and can be any of an almost endless variety of color combinations. "Alps" will sometimes produce as much as 5,000 pounds of milk per lactation period (37 to 48 weeks long).

Toggenburg: Toggenburgs hail originally from the Toggenburg Valley in the Swiss Alps. They're small (about 26" and 120 pounds), sturdy, vigorous goats, and in spite of their size, the animals can produce 3,500 pounds of milk in a lactation period.

La Mancha: La Manchas are a recently developed American goat, derived from a cross between a Spanish breed and other varieties. They reach a minimum height of 28" and a weight of about 130 pounds, and in a lactation period are able to produce close to 2,500 pounds of milk. Their most outstanding physical characteristic are ears so small that they appear almost nonexistent.

Saanen: Saanens, also from Switzerland, are very popular and can produce up to 5,200 pounds of milk per lactation. A mature adults will be 30 inches tall and weigh 135 pounds. They are a placid breed and distinguished in appearance by their white costs.

Nubian: A large breed with floppy ears and a Roman nose, superior milk producers and meat animals, they will grow to 140 pounds and produce up too 4,000 pounds of high-butterfat milk per lactation. Stubborn but affectionate. ■

In contrast, goats can lean or stand against stock panels without beating them down or pushing them over, and the sectioned barricades are tall enough to contain all but the most rambunctious breeding buck. The only disadvantage of such fencing is its cost, but since nothing else quite does the job, stock panels are worth the expense.

Bring on the Kids: Rather than keeping a buck around the homestead for breeding purposes, it's usually better to get together with half a dozen or so other nanny owners in your community and pool all of your resources to buy one exemplary buck that can serve all of your does. Then see if you can't talk one of those other goat lovers into boarding (with the expenses shared by everyone, of course) "old whisker face" on his or her farm. Naturally, you'll have to go to the trouble of hauling your does over to this benevolent neighbor's barn at breeding time.

If you can't find someone magnanimous enough to care for a collectively owned buck, consider utilizing artificial insemination (AI). This method is well suited to goat raising and is the best and least expensive way to upgrade your herd. Semen from some of the top breeders in the country is available for as little as $10 to $50 a unit. Unfortunately, it's sometimes hard to catch the females in heat, but you'll have to in order to use artificial insemination. In fact, some gals won't come into season unless there's a male goat on the premises. However, you can fool them. During the fall breeding period, take an old rag and wipe it on a buck's head where the horns should be and along its hocks. Then hang the dripping-with-maleness cloth where the does can smell it. In 48 to 72 hours, your ladies should be in heat.

Milking: To avoid the risk of having unwanted barnyard fumes taint your fresh milk and to allow your self more comfort, you might want to milk your does in an area that's separate from their pens.

Milking stands, easy-to-construct goat restrainers, can be placed almost anywhere, and they can turn a potentially back-straining job into an easy sit-on-a-stool task. Since milking time rolls around twice a day, that's quite a plus.

Don't worry about how your animals might take to using one of these stands. If you milk at the same times each day and make sure there's always plenty of food in the bin for them to snack on, the does will quickly adopt a routine, hop right up, and munch away peacefully while you do the milking. As a bonus, such a structure can serve the purpose of holding your animals when you need to trim their hooves, vaccinate them, or perform any other chore for which they might otherwise be unwilling to stand still.

Before milking, clean each doe's udder with a fresh paper towel saturated in disinfectant. Then direct the first few streams of milk into a black strip cup to check for the stringy material or cheesecake chunks that are signs of mastitis, an inflammation of the mammary glands. If the milk is okay, continue to work, straining the liquid through a clean cheesecloth into a sanitized metal container. In place of cheesecloth, some sources advise using tin or stainless steel strainers that are specifically made for your pail, or even disposable strainers. When you're finished milking, but before you send that little mama back to her pen, dip each of her teats in a specially prepared solution (from the vet or mail order supply house) to help protect her against mastitis.

With that done, pour the milk into sterilized glass containers with lids and place the covered jars in a refrigerator. To insure that the milk stays fresh as long as possible, some folks place the containers in an ice bath before refrigerating them. If put directly into the icebox, unpasteurized milk will remain fresh-tasting for at least three days. Simply date each jar, and when day number three rolls around, give the old milk to the pigs or dispose of it otherwise.

Are you wondering what you'll do with your regular and sizable supply of nice, fresh goat's milk before day number three? Well, it can be used to produce delicious yogurts, custards, and ricotta cheese. Goat's milk also adds a delicate sweetness to almost any bakery or candy recipe.

Kid Care: Of course, the production of milk is triggered by pregnancy, which means that come spring you'll probably have some youngsters to care for. However, that extra work can be quite worthwhile, because if the mamas give birth to a good crop of quality kids, selling them could yield enough money to feed your milkers for a year. With this in mind, then, you'll want to do everything possible to make sure that your valuable kids remain robust and healthy.

Start your kid-care program by seeing to it that each youngster gets a healthy dose of colostrum, the mother's first nutrient-rich and antibody-laden milk, within the first 12 hours after birth. From then on, the little guys and gals will need to have their mother's milk fed to them three times a day, from a soda bottle or similar container fitted with a special lamb's nipple. Of course, you could let them nurse from the doe herself, but if you do, you'll probably find that they're much harder to wean. Besides, almost any kid will take to a bottle with no problem, as long as its mother is nearby to provide company and reassurance.

During the first week, feed your young animals six to eight ounces of milk three times a day and then increase the dosage to 10 to 12 ounces. Be careful not to overfeed, though. Once the kids are about two weeks old and while they're still nursing, you can help them start to develop their rumens, that is, their adult stomachs, by providing them with access to tasty grains such as cracked corn and rolled oats, and fresh, leafy hay. Be sure, also, to put a new section of hay in their midst daily and to change the grain regularly to accommodate any particularly fastidious eaters.

In addition to maintaining an appropriate feeding schedule for your kids, you'll need to see to it that the youngsters have ample pen space and adequate shelter. Though stock panels are effective goat fencing, during your kids' first month you can make do by putting up a 32-inch hog stock-panel fence, which you can easily step over. Also, you can save yourself a little more money if, instead of building sheds for the kids, you house them in old 4' X 8' wooden packing crates equipped with lots of regularly changed straw bedding.

The young goats can all be penned together on one lot until they're ready to be weaned at three to four months. Then move them onto another section of ground. However, do not put your juveniles in with the adults until the youngsters reach breeding age—six to eight months old. Also keep in mind that next year's kids shouldn't be kept on the same terrain as were this season's. In fact, you should wait at least three years before using the same ground for goat turf again. By rotating the kid lots in this manner and keeping the offspring away from the grown-ups, you can all but eliminate the goat-killing disease coccidiosis. As a further precaution against this disease, burn the packing crate sheds as soon as the kids have outgrown them.

If you've decided not to board a buck, you can slaughter all the male kids immediately after birth or within six months after they're fattened up. Perhaps this sounds harsh, but adding chevon to the freezer is one good way to fight the rising tide of goatflation.

The Three Prime Feeding Periods: There are three nutritionally critical periods in a goat's life: a kid's first few months, a mother's first two months of lactation, and a doe's dry months. If you maintain adequate records so you'll be prepared for such periods before they come around, and feed your animals according to their needs during each of these times, you should be able to keep your critters pretty healthy.

During the initial months of lactation, a doe will produce the maximum amount of milk she's capable of. Therefore, in order to fuel her internal factory sufficiently, she has to eat the best grain and hay available. Generally, you can figure that a lactating female should get about one-third to one-half pound of grain for each pound of milk she yields in a day. However, when she's at her peak, it can be nearly impossible to satisfy all her energy requirements. If that seems to be the case, just be sure that during this time you give her the best grain and hay (preferably alfalfa) you can afford, and that you allow her plenty of time to be able to eat as much of her food as she can pack away.

The grain mix should be from 16% to 18% protein if it's fed along with a low-protein hay (such as timothy or prairie hay). But should you be feeding a high-energy hay (like alfalfa), you'll be able to get by with a grain that's only 12% to 15% protein. You can figure that an average milker will need about 1,000 pounds of hay a year and roughly 1,000 pounds of grain. This should work out to be approximately 1/2 pound of grain for each of the 2,000 pounds of milk she gives. Better producers will, naturally, need additional feed.

The third dietary prime time in a goat's life occurs during the two months prior to kidding. You can do a lot to insure that your doe has an easy delivery, healthy babies, and a problem-free lactation just by keeping her in good flesh without letting her get downright fat and by making sure her calcium intake is low during this period. A pregnant doe will put on kid pounds, but watch her ribs right behind her shoulders. She shouldn't put on so much fat that they disappear. In general, if you feed a doe a couple of pounds of grain each day and all the hay she wants, her developing babies will stay healthy and her figure will remain fit and trim.

Then, in order to keep your mother-to-be's calcium intake in line, feed her a mineral mix that doesn't contain that substance. Also, feed her only a low-calcium, non-leguminous hay, such as timothy or prairie hay. After the kids arrive, switch to a mix that does have calcium in it and put her on a better quality hay.

Always keep in mind that goats need lots of water and exercise. One doe can drink as much as two to five gallons on a cool day, so make sure there's plenty of fresh water available to your herd at all times. You might also want to take your does for an out-of-pen stroll, preferably every day. However, even the trek from the yard to the milking area is better than no exercise at all.

Medical Aspects: Now that your goats are eating well and are getting a lot of exercise, it's time to attend to their medical needs.

Kids need *Clostridium perfringens* C and D plus tetanus toxoid when they reach six to eight weeks of age, followed by a repeat dose of each a month later. Furthermore, adult animals need an annual booster of both these vaccinations 30 days prior to kidding.

Goats must be wormed in the spring and fall, or more often if the herd is confined to a small area. If you use a variety of anthelmintics (worm medicines), the parasites will be less likely to develop a resistance to any one substance. The easiest wormers to administer are those that are available in paste form. Boluses (huge pills) are nearly impossible to get down a goat's gullet (more than the first time), and wormers that are added to the feed are often ignored.

A vitamin E/selenium injection should be given to a doe 30 days before she's due to kid if you live in a region with soil typified by a selenium deficiency. The youngsters should receive a shot when they're three weeks old.

No matter how proficient a backyard doctor you are, you should still take advantage of the knowledge and experience of a veterinarian once a year (vets still make barn calls). This can help pinpoint existing or potential problems, and the vet can assist you in setting up a good health care program for your animals.

Picking the Right Goat for You: Solomon said, "Thou shalt have goat's milk enough for thy food, for the good of thy household, and for the maintenance of thy maidens"...a statement that, besides extolling the beverage producing attributes of these caprine creatures, goes to show the generous beasts

An All-Weather Solar Watering Trough

Getting up early on bitterly cold mornings to chop through a thick layer of ice on the barnyard watering trough makes the economic advantages of raising livestock wane more than a little. Commercial automatically heated troughs are expensive and require on-site electric power. But it's not an enormous task to build a solar-heated unit that will take the bite out of winter waterings.

All it takes to furnish cattle livestock with a drinkable supply of water throughout the colder months is to construct a small solar greenhouse over their watering trough. Nothing elaborate is necessary in the way of materials, measurements need not be exact, and only a few tools are required. If you have the trough, a supply of water, and an automatic valve, it's easy to build an A-frame structure with a heat sink. The south-facing slanted side of the A-frame must be glazed, and the trough should project from under one side of the frame. Ideally, the trough will project from the north-facing side of the A frame, as there would be less chance of the glazing being broken by the cattle.

The trough can be anything from an old bathtub to an oblong galvanized watering trough, but it should be situated with its length on a north-south axis. If an old bathtub is used, the drain hole should be well plugged, opened only for cleaning. To keep the tank full, a live-stock-tank float valve needs to be installed and connected to the feed line, which should be buried deep enough to prevent its freezing, or protected with a heat tape.

Set the tank on a foundation of railroad ties or other heavy timber extending about 3' out on either side of the tank and parallel to its long dimension. Between the timbers and the sides of the tank, cover the ground with rocks or some other dense material to absorb heat when the sun shines. This warmth will be released throughout the night, keeping the water in the trough from freezing during the coldest hours.

To make the A-frame, nail a 2 X 6 to either end of each railroad tie, angled so that two boards and the tie form a triangle. Spike each pair of 2 X 6s together at their apex, and connect the two triangular frames by nailing several 2 X 4s across the side that will not be glazed. When positioning this structure, make sure that about 10" of the trough projects beyond it into the feed lot.

The south face of the A-frame can be glazed with discarded storm windows, plexiglass, or clear plastic sheeting with framing provided as necessary. Fill in any open spaces between the sheeting and

(continued on page 217)

the ground, or around the trough, with sheathing or polystyrene foam panels. It's a good idea to stretch plastic sheeting over the top of the sheltered part of the trough.

Next, frame in the triangular sides of the shed, allowing for a small doorway so you can get to the trough for cleaning and maintenance. When all this is done, use plywood to sheathe the sides and the back.

The inside of the structure, except for the glazed area, needs to be insulated. This can be done with either foil-faced fiberglass insulation or rigid foam insulation board, though the rigid board is better because it won't absorb water the way the fibrous material will. The inside surface of the insulation, whatever material is used, should be painted black so the structure will absorb all the heat it can. After that, build and hang the door, and turn on the water.

Though this setup should work well and keep the water from freezing throughout the winter, there are at least two refinements that might be made. All the seams can be caulked to keep the wind from

blowing away the heat you gain from the sun, and an electric line can be run to the greenhouse so a heater can be put inside to provide warmth during extended cloudy spells.

If the trough must project from the south-facing panel, it may be necessary to erect a grid work of steel bars between the drinking section of the tub and the glazed portion to keep animals from breaking the panel. ■

The solar water trough

have been domesticated for a long time! A modern goat enthusiast, however, might wish to add to Solomon's wisdom, noting that over and above its ability to produce healthful dairy products, the "poor man's cow" can be a pretty danged amusing and lovable animal to have around.

Furthermore, the milkers are exceptionally easy to keep, each requiring only half (or less) the barn space that their "competitor," a cow, needs, and they're able to forage nutrients from practically barren land if necessary. Sadly, goats are often taken for granted and looked down upon as mere "lawn mowers." Yet, unlike many other animals, if they're treated with care and affection, these lively and temperamental characters can provide any homestead with plenty of milk and cheese, and a great deal of pleasure.

Raising Feeder Pigs

If you'd like to enjoy pork that costs only pennies a pound and tastes far better than the plastic-wrapped meat available in the supermarket, consider raising your own pigs. Just one of the chunky animals can produce a great deal of premium, inexpensive meat for a homesteading family, and the beasts can be fattened on a diet that consists of little more than garden by-products and kitchen leftovers.

If you begin, as many folks do, with already weaned piglets, you'll avoid the task of hog breeding and find that rearing the animals is downright easy. If you harvest more meat than you can use, many folks will be willing to buy or trade for some of the surplus pork.

At purchase, a four- to eight-week-old feeder piglet should weigh any where from 20 to 50 pounds. If you care for the animal for about five months, or until it weighs 200 to 220 pounds, the butchering-size hog will yield approximately 135 pounds of meat products consisting of roughly 24 pounds of ham, 20 pounds of bacon, 17 pounds of pork roast, 16 pounds of picnic shoulder, seven pounds of pork chops, eight pounds of sausage, seven pounds of miscellaneous cuts, five pounds of salt pork, and 31 pounds of lard.

It's best not to raise your animal beyond the prime butchering weight of 200 to 220 pounds, because at that size the hog has reached the optimum stage of growth. Beyond that weight, additional gains will be little but lard.

In addition to providing food for your table, each porker you raise to maturity will produce a large supply of manure (about 1.6 pounds per 100 pounds of pig per day) for your garden. It doesn't smell despite what "everybody knows," is firm, and is easily removed. The animals will choose a corner of their pen as a latrine. If you maintain a good layer of dry litter, clean up daily, and mix manure and urine-soaked litter into a living compost heap, the pigs will produce nothing but a mild, slightly sweet odor that won't get beyond your property; pig-people actually like it. "Pig perfume" they call it. However, if you contain the pigs in small quarters, fail to clean up daily, let them root in mud, and let feed get mixed in, they will produce the characteristic rotten-garbage stench associated with old-time, garbage-fed hog yards.

Build Your Animal House Well: There's only one really difficult chore associated with raising weaned piglets: keeping the young animals at home. Restricting a small swine may sound like a simple enough task, but every pig sports a snout that's perfectly designed for assaulting barricades. Any fence you build will have to be strung tighter than a banjo, especially where the barrier is closest to the ground, if you expect to keep your stock from prying their way out.

You can construct a taut welded-wire fence, a sturdy wooden enclosure, or a two-stranded electric fence consisting of a bottom cable six to eight inches above the turf with a second line eight inches above that. None of your restrainers will need to be more than 32" tall, though, because pigs can't jump very high. You might also want to dig a trench under your barricade and fill that ditch with old logs or rocks to discourage any of the beasts from tunneling out of the pen.

In addition to fencing, you'll need to construct a shelter for the animals and provide them with a way to cool themselves off. Just about any three-sided, roofed house will protect your livestock from storms and winter winds. However, since pigs don't pant very effectively and don't sweat at all, you'll

Barnyard Livestock Requirements

REQUIREMENTS:	FEEDER PIGS
Housing	10 sq.ft shelter/hog
Furniture	Feeding tough
	Ice-free waterer
Fence	32"-hi "hog tight" welded wire, panels
	or 2-strand elect.
Water	1-3 gal/day/hog
Feed	230 lbs to 500 lbs
Harvest	at 4 to 6 months for 135 lbs meat
	per 220 lb pig
Feed/meat ratio	3:1 or better

need to be absolutely certain each animal has 15 to 20 square feet of shade with the shadow-casting object located at least four feet off the ground. It's also wise to provide a mud wallow or a sprayer so that any overheated pig can cool off during especially sultry weather.

Buy the Best Animals: If you're not going to try to raise the finest-quality pigs available, you'd be better off, as far as both your time and your wallet are concerned, not to rear any swine at all. It may take a little practice before you can recognize a premium porker when you see one, but you can gain any needed instruction by attending county fairs or local livestock shows and listening closely when the judges explain why they select one hog specimen over another.

Once you learn how to pick out the best looking pigs in a litter, do so. Never buy the runts of a piglet crop even if the price sounds like a bargain deal. Too many runts never grow worth a hoot.

You'll probably find that the best time to acquire a young barrow or gilt is at the beginning of your garden's growing season. You'll have plenty of leftover crop pickings for the hog around then, and in most cases, you can expect to end up with a ready-to-eat adult pig by fall or early winter. This, conveniently enough, is the time of year that provides the best butchering weather.

Feed Your Animals Well: Water is the most important food you can give to your swine. A fattening pig will drink as much as three gallons of liquid a day, and the beasts will consume a lot of solid food, as well. Fortunately, since they will pack away almost anything, including vegetables, fruits, milk, meat scraps, spoiled eggs, garden clippings, weeds, and more, they can pretty well balance their diets by themselves.

Still, a 160-pound shoat can handle around 50 pounds of this food a day, so you'll probably need to supplement its diet with grain or a commercial ration containing 20% to 25% protein. The grain also helps the pig reduce paunchiness and produce firmer, leaner pork. In addition, you may want to keep a steady supply of vitamin and mineral supplements available.

Pigs will grow adequately on restaurant and institutional garbage that you can contract to collect. However, you are required by law in most states to boil the garbage before feeding—a major undertaking for a few hogs. You can collect fresh vegetable leavings from grocery stores and feed them as is.

Help Your Animals Prevent Their Own Disease: Pigs are extremely hardy beasts, as demonstrated by their ability to revert rapidly to the feral—gone wild—state, but like all animals they can get sick. A good vaccination program will prevent most illnesses: Check with your local veterinarian so you can inoculate against the diseases prevalent in your region. Hog cholera is a particularly serious threat and is regulated on a national scale.

Since too-close-kept animals have no choice but to root around in their own manure, penned pigs have a never-ending opportunity to acquire internal

Breeding Pigs

If you've raised a feeder pig or two and may be thinking of going whole hog and raising your own, you should know that rearing newborn piglets can be risky. In fact, 30 percent to 40 percent of commercially raised baby swine die shortly after birth.

However, a homesteader can provide better care than a large enterprise, so you should be able to save most of your curly-tailed porksters and raise an average of 16 hogs per sow each year (keep 2, sell 14 for $80 apiece = over $1000 cash/sow/year.) Hmmm. All it takes is a genuine affection for the species, a little knowledge, and help when you need it.

Mating the Sow: A gilt (a young female hog) should reach sexual maturity at five or six months of age and be receptive for two or three days of each subsequent 21-day cycle. You can be sure that a sow's in estrus (heat) if the female has a swollen vulva. She also may have a slight mucus-like or bloody vaginal discharge, act restless, urinate frequently, twitch her tail, hold her ground when you press down on her hindquarters, or try to "ride" other sows. She will also do her best to get out to find a mate, so will work constantly at the fences and gates.

Keeping a daddy pig—a boar—is uneconomical unless you run a dozen or so sows, which means you'll have to haul your gilt to the boar. This is discussed elsewhere.

You should mate gilts on their first day of heat and older sows on the second day. Both young and old sows should receive a second mating 24 hours after their first.

For best meat production, choose your boars carefully. You want them long, lean, meaty in the loin and hams, and proven sires of large litters of robust piglets.

As for the male, an 8- to 12-month-old boar can usually service 12 females in pasture, or he can be "hand mated" (matched individually in a barn) with 24 gilts or sows. A yearling or older boar can service 50 sows in stalls or 35 to 40 pasturing females.

Preparing for the Big Day: The gestation period for your pregnant sow will be approximately 113 days, or as an old saying goes, "three months, three weeks, and three days." However, there are some important preparations to be made before that magic moment of birth arrives.

For one thing, you should take steps to help keep disease from striking the fragile newborns. So be sure to worm each sow and spray her for lice about two weeks before her due date. You should also immunize an expectant mother against erysipelas to strengthen both the sow's and offspring's resistance to this most common, and usually fatal, swine disease. Likewise, good sanitation is a vital part of preventive health care, so

(continued on page 222)

thoroughly clean and sterilize the farrowing pen and keep it clean. Wash the pregnant sow with a mild detergent and warm water before you pen her for delivery.

The Farrowing Pen: Another important pre-farrowing job is building a proper birthing nest with ample space for mother and litter plus a creep where piglets can go but the mother can't. Little piglets need a very warm environment. The baby porkers will thrive at 80°F to 90°F, suffer at 60°F to 70°F, and die if the mercury dips to around 50°F. The mother, on the other hand, has 3 to 5 solid inches of lard insulation around her middle, so she's more likely to suffer from overheating!

The different temperature needs of sow and piglets can create quite a problem. While the little pigs will try to cuddle up against the mother to stay warm, the parent will just as likely be trying to cool off by continually standing up and sitting down. And every time the mother settles back down, she runs the risk of squishing the piglets.

To avoid such a calamity, the farrowing pen should incorporate a separate heat source for the piglets. With their own source of warmth, they won't need to scramble up to their mother till she is lying down to let them feed. Most folks use electric or gas powered heat lamps for this purpose, although a few innovative individuals have taken to building solar-heated farrowing pens.

The heat source should be high enough above the floor to maintain a constant temperature of 90° just under a section of floor separated by sturdy guard rails that stand 8" to 10" off the floor and extend 8" to 12" out from the farrowing pen walls or a corner under the heat lamp. By crawling under the rails and into their "creep" the piglets can sleep safe and warm, and scuttle out to the mother only at mealtime. The sow can't get past the rail and has no reason to jump over, so attrition should be minimal.

The Farrowing: A few days before the piglets are due, you'll want to move the expectant sow into her new quarters so she can adjust to the change. Be sure, though, to let her out for at least two 10- to 15-minute periods of exercise every day that she's in the farrowing pen. This helps her ward off constipation and nervous stress.

Around that same time, you'll need to gather your nursery items such as iodine, clean rags, and plenty of bedding. Also, keep a pitchfork or shovel around so you can keep the farrowing area clean.

You'll know that the sow is ready to bear her young when she gets restless and tries to make a nest in her farrowing pen. She'll usually do this at nightfall, so you can expect to lose a night's sleep. Hogs seem independent and aloof, but they appreciate attendance at the birthday party. Once the mother actually starts giving birth, you can help events proceed smoothly by talking to the sow reassuringly (especially if this her first litter) or

(continued on page 223)

if you feel foolish conversing with a pig, by giving her small hand-feedings of laxative bran meal. As each baby is born, dry the new arrival with clean rags before it hits the ground, if possible.

Also, coat the piglets' navels with iodine by either spraying the disinfectant on each youngster's severed cord or by firmly placing the tot over a wide-mouthed bottle of iodine so that its naval cord hangs down into the container and then deftly turning both bottle and pig upside down.

While the mother delivers, it's probably best to keep the newborn piglets in a heated corner or box, away from her. Once they're all born and you've disposed of the afterbirth, make sure each newcomer has the chance to nurse and obtain some of its mother's precious colostrum. Hand-hold them to the teat if need be. This first milk is high in nutrients, vitamins, minerals, and antibodies. You might even milk some extra colostrum from the sow to store in ice cube trays in case you later encounter a mother who won't allow her piglets to nurse.

Finally, after you've cleaned out and replaced the soiled bedding and made sure that both the new mother and her piglets are comfortable, you can go back to bed and try to make yourself comfortable. Don't expect to get much sleep, though, because farrowing inevitably finishes just in time to begin your morning chores.

Infant Care: A sow's milk is naturally deficient in iron, so one of your first piglet caretaking tasks will be charging the newborns' supply of that mineral. If your youngsters are starting out life on a dirt-floored pen, or if you provide a boxed supply of soil in the nursery, the little ones may get all the iron they need by rooting in the earth. However, if like most folks you choose to raise the piglets on a more sanitary concrete floor with a litter covering, you'll need to give your one- to three-day-old animals either an injection of 150 to 200 milligrams of iron or a feed that contains about 36 milligrams of iron per pound.

Though the piglets' main diet from birth until they're weaned at four to eight weeks of age will be their mother's milk, beginning in the first week, you should also provide the youngsters with an at-hand supply of feed, given to them in a creep feeder so that the sow can't get at the goodies. The feed should contain at least 18% protein and all the essential amino acids, vitamins, and minerals.

Most pig raisers will want to remove the tips of their piglets' eight needle teeth on the same day the young hogs receive the iron supplements. (You can be sure that Mom wants them removed!) The tips of the teeth are nipped off with wire cutters or with special tooth clippers. If left unclipped, the little pigs can use these mini-tusks to injure other youngsters or accidentally harm their mother's teats.

(continued on page 224)

parasites. They need to be wormed every four to six weeks with the anthelmintic your vet recommends for your locale.

External parasites like the anemia-causing hog louse can also be debilitating, so periodically apply a spray, a dust, or a pour-on insecticide to ward off the blood sucking pests.

The best single measure you can adopt to guarantee healthy, happy hogs is to give them plenty of well-treed, naturally watered land to wander over and root around in. They'll obtain soil-borne minerals that are essential (but must be provided in feed to hogs kept on concrete). Free-range hogs will not smell, and—lacking trees—all they need for shelter is a simple lean-to to protect them from the mid-day sun (though it must be built like a fortress to withstand their rooting.)

When October comes around, your darling little piglets have become hogs: chops, bacon, and sausage-on-the-hoof. Unless you want to learn home-slaughtering and meat-cutting or know a butcher who slaughters on-site, you'll have to get the animals to the slaughterhouse. Hogs don't lead unless trained to halter from piglethood. So, they must be driven or coaxed with a

---

(continued from page 223)

Any males that are not going to be raised for breeding stock should also be castrated while young to prevent uncontrolled mating and to keep their meat from developing an "off," or "boarish," flavor and odor. If you perform this operation when the piglets are around two weeks of age, the task will be relatively easy and non-traumatic for the young animal. It requires a pair of small incisions, and you must remove testicles and attached tubing...so get expert instruction or have the vet do it. Young shoats squeal, but don't seem to suffer long; indeed, most return to normal piglet behavior the second they are released.

Raising pigs from scratch definitely takes more commitment, work, and know-how than fattening up some purchased weaned piglets. Along with careful handling of the mating, and the infants' upbringing, you'll need to keep complete records of each sow's productivity and the weights of her piglets when weaned. These records will enable you to cull the poor producers from your herd and promote overall breeding efficiency. You should also keep track of vaccination and worming dates and all other medications used.

All in all, though, breeding your own pigs can provide the opportunity to start a worthwhile homestead stock-raising business. Converting one or two free piglets into full-size freezer-fillers each year and selling the rest as feeder-pigs to others will take you one step closer to self-sufficiency. ■

---

trail of grain…down a fenced chute or up a high-sided ramp and into the back of a sturdy truck. It is best to find an experienced "pig person" who has a truck for hire and such as the breeder who supplied your piglets, the butcher, or a neighbor farmer. The next time you see Porky and Penelope they'll be cutlets. Yumm!

☙

CHAPTER 8

Alternative Energy

Living Without the Power Line

Scott and Nancy purchased 31 remote acres in the Missouri Ozarks with the full knowledge that they would never be able to hook up to the electric power grid. A national wilderness area borders the property on three sides, and the nearest accessible electricity was more than a mile away from the fourth side of the property. There were numerous vertical rock ledges and a year-round stream between their home and that lone pole, and they didn't wish to destroy the beauty of the glades and brook with a big, cleared power line right-of-way.

Unnecessary Conveniences: A year and a half after their land purchase, the couple moved into an octagonal, square-beamed home built from prefabricated components and assembled on site with hand tools, featuring a huge center fireplace and flue mortared up from local stone.

Just before moving, they held a garage sale at their town apartment during which they parted with their television, iron, hair dryer, toaster, blender, and various other gadgets they have long since forgotten and have never missed since that day.

To those who wonder how the couple can get along without such "conveniences" they say, "It's not complicated at all!" They have replaced electric lights and appliance and oil heat with kerosene, propane gas, wood, a car battery, and the heating and cooling properties of thermal mass in their house.

Brilliant mantle-type kerosene lanterns provide illumination for evening reading and work. Five of these—two in the living room and three in the kitchen—give off plenty of white light, which is easy on the eyes and necessary for doing close work. Throughout the rest of the house, standard kerosene wick lamps produce a soothing yellow glow. Their lighting system probably isn't much less expensive than electrical lamps would be, but it does create a mellower atmosphere and isn't subject to brown outs, blackouts, and the pricing whims of the power company.

During the day the home's windows and two skylights provide plenty of light; in designing the house, the builders were careful to base the placement of the openings on the daily and seasonal positions of the sun. The kitchen, which is the center of most household activity, stays bright and cheerful all day long as a result of its southwestern exposure. There is no problem with excessive summer heat buildup, because the dwelling is nestled in the trees, and their leaves filter the sun during the hot months.

Central Heating: The family heats with wood, using a fireplace with an airtight stove-insert built in. Most such arrangements are fitted with electrical fans to move the warm air, but the owners wisely built the fireplace in the center of the house and built vented air shafts into four sides of the massive rock chamber. This system opens into the living room, bedroom, bathroom, and kitchen. Each of the rooms has a floor vent near its outside wall to return cool air to the fireplace, and natural convection keeps the indoor air circulating.

The fireplace's mass acts as an indirect heating and cooling system. In cold weather the 400-cubic feet of rock heats up after about the first 36 hours of continuous fire. With a continual small fire or periodic hot ones, the stone mass remains warm to the touch all winter. In the summer the rock—with its feet deep in the cool earth—stays much cooler than the outdoor air and helps keep the inside temperature agreeable even in the dog days.

One of the home's skylights is also used for cooling purposes in the summer. The rooftop window is opened at night, and the cool outside air pours into the lower half of the opening as the warmer air rises out through the top half. During the day, as the roof heats, cool air is drawn in through the doors and lower windows. Such thermal conditioning doesn't cost any money or make any noise.

Kitchen Needs: For about eight months of the year, all the cooking is done on a woodstove. However, when the weather is too warm for comfortably firing up the range, propane is used to operate a small two-burner stove. The same gas is used to run the water heater and (believe it or not) a Swedish-made ammonia absorption refrigerator, an extremely efficient unit that operates on nothing but a little 600-Btu pilot light.

The cold and hot water tanks are in a closet in the loft area. Water from the stream is lifted up to the elevated tanks periodically with a gasoline-operated pump. The house has complete plumbing, operated by gravity flow, and water pressure is perfectly adequate!

The house was wired for DC current in the hope of someday producing a useful quantity of electricity with wind or water. At present, a car battery powers two car lights, which are mounted under a shelf and pointed down to illuminate the kitchen sink, and the same unit runs an FM car radio that is tucked away on a bookshelf. The battery gets boosted about once a week with a gasoline-powered battery charger.

The fact that this couple gave up most of their powered appliances doesn't mean that they lack for kitchen tools. A hand beater, chopper, food mill, and ricer take care of most food preparation and preservation chores. An 1890s-model meat grinder, which can be used to mince edibles other than meat, and a grain grinder also provide assistance. Such devices may not be as fast as their electrical counterparts, but they do the job.

These homesteaders are proud of an alternative garbage disposal system that is definitely more efficient than conventional methods: Twenty Australorp laying hens do a splendid job of gratefully gobbling up kitchen scraps and give a bounty of eggs in return.

Other Alternative Energy Devices: During the winter months, sewing with an old and treasured treadle machine is a productive pastime. The only time Nancy irons is when she sews, and she uses a flatiron (the type that usually serves only as a doorstop these days) that's heated atop the stove. It isn't a joy to use, but it works well.

Neither Scott nor Nancy miss the convenience of a hair dryer. They spend a few minutes combing their hair in front of the fire or in the sunshine and have found that they enjoy such silent, meditative times in contrast to performing the same task, usually in a frantic rush, with hot, dry air and a noisy motor roaring in one's ears.

The truth is that a nonelectrical house is wonderfully quiet. There's no refrigerator or furnace clicking on and off, and peaceful evenings are enhanced with books and making music, instead of being dominated by a blaring television set.

Scott and Nancy readily admit that they went to extra trouble and expense for independence from the power company, but they have found a deep satisfaction in living this way. It is especially rewarding when someone complains about the power being off for hours during a storm, and the couple can nonchalantly respond, "Oh? We didn't miss it a bit!"

Making the Move to Wood Heat

Rising prices and dwindling supplies of finite fossil energy used for home heating have inspired a large number of people to seek alternatives. Some turned to solar heating systems, which often require major remodeling, and even larger numbers turned to the space heater of bygone days, the wood stove.

However, using wood as a source of home heat requires a great deal more than just turning up a thermostat or flicking a switch, and those who made the move to using the renewable energy source from the forests found themselves needing to learn about not only ash removal and chimney cleaning but also wood lore in general.

Making the shift to wood heating several years ago, a couple in northwestern Wisconsin found there was a great deal to learn and a lot of work involved, but they also got a great deal of pleasure from their newfound heating method.

When they bought their Wisconsin farm, they found the toolshed filled with quaint memorabilia: a two-man saw, a six-pound maul with rough-hewn handle, a rusted Swede saw, several wedges, and a sizable double-bitted ax. They hung the items on the toolshed wall as museum pieces and proceeded to install an oil furnace and forced-air heat in the house.

For the next five years they continued using the oil furnace and paying the fuel bills that might be expected in an old, not-so-airtight farmhouse.

Allergies: About the time that snow flurries began blowing in from Canada, their son developed allergies related to fumes from their oil heating system. Although they have come to know and love wood heat as an efficient source of warmth for their house, they were chagrined at making the initial switch in October, which meant a lot of scrambling before winter set in.

The couple started by stoking up the old country home's fireplace and a small woodburning stove in the kitchen. There was enough dead wood out in the pasture to feed both without their having to face the task of cutting down a tree, but the stove's fire would burn out in the middle of the night, and the fireplace with its serious heat loss was no match for the winter wind.

Then they cried for help in their local paper and located a big, secondhand woodburning heater for $100. With it and the aid of a neighboring old-timer, they not only survived but also enjoyed their initial winter of heating with wood.

The heart of their system, the heater, is located in the center of the kitchen where it provides the family with atmosphere, a handy meeting spot, and warmth. It's a great help if you want to take some of the stiffness out of your hands and feet after a frigid taste of the outdoors or if you just need to stop yourself from shaking on a chilly morning. The couple's sons use the stove to dry their mittens, and it's ideal for keeping food and cocoa warm.

The special warmth of wood heat permeates the house and gives a sense of accomplishment, because the owners have personally completed the cycle of finding, cutting, and splitting their own logs and providing warmth for both family and home.

The crackling of the fire in the stove is in itself a basically cozy sound. The steady, subtle murmur of burning logs casts a comfortable feeling around the kitchen and encourages long, lazy daydreams when you tilt back in the old rocker with your stockinged feet stretched out toward the warmth.

Efficiency: An airtight firebox and a well-designed draft system are essential if a stove is to be efficient, and an ash door helps in cleaning the woodburner. In the couple's stove, air for combustion enters the heater's firebox at the top, is warmed by the blaze as it passes through a down draft stack, and is then distributed evenly along the length of the burning logs by an intake manifold. An automatic thermostat, with which they dial the degree of heat wanted, opens and closes the damper at the top of the downdraft stack to admit just enough air to maintain the desired level of combustion.

The Wisconsin couple found their stove to be highly effective even on the days when temperatures dropped to 30°F below zero and the wind came up to give a chill factor equivalent to 60° below. The family conserved fuel by putting blankets over the kitchen door ways and kept more comfortable than their neighbors, who had their oil burners' thermostats set on high and still couldn't get really warm unless they stood in front of their kitchen ovens. That's the real advantage of a wood stove over modern heat: You can get close to the source and toast comfortably, yet still have warmth evenly distributed to the rest of the house.

Anyone using a woodburner should be aware of the inflammable wastes that can build up in the chimney. A roaring flame could ignite the creosote in the flue and possibly trigger a serious house fire.

Although the chance of such a flare-up is remote, it's wise to be conscious of the hazard. Some old-timers prefer to close the air intake and let any chimney blaze burn itself out, while others keep a large bag of salt handy to dump down the flue to extinguish the flames.

Preventing the Best Cure: The best answer to the problem of chimney fires, of course, lies in preventing the buildup of inflammable residue in the first place. Just look down your flue now and then and clean off the creosote with an appropriate cleaning tool.

If this sounds terribly complicated or dangerous, it's not. Any kind of equipment should be kept clean and in good operating condition, and doing the same for your chimney will lessen the chances of its catching fire.

A close look at your home's water pipes is also in order if the house has wood heat. Any line that runs along an outside wall can be wrapped with insulation to protect it from freezing. If you leave the house for any length of time, it's most important to have a dependable friend drop in and reload your heater. The better models hold 100 pounds of wood at one filling and will burn up to 18 hours unattended. If you plan to be gone several days or more, it's best to drain the water pipes.

Last winter gave the homesteaders an education in fuel gathering, and before graduating, they'd mangled three axes, one chain-saw bar, and a six-pound maul. Their mistakes were their teachers, and when the temperature plummets to the below-zero mark and stays there, a student learns fast.

Spring and fall are the best times to cut fuel, as there are no bugs, no weeds, no burrs, and no prickly heat. If possible, the wood should be left out to dry for a season.

Which timber makes the best fuel? The hardwoods are denser than soft-woods, and oak, birch, and maple are generally the favorites. Elm is good, too, but it's tough to split. The Wisconsin homesteaders were lucky enough to have their own stand of oak on their property, the same stand from which their house and barn were built before the turn of the century.

Other Sources: It's handy to have your own source of fuel, but it's not a necessity. A little scouting around can turn up many possibilities: neighbors who want a tree taken down, telephone and electric company prunings, out-lying farmers or county dump locations with groves to be cleared, or new construction sites where you might be paid to haul away timber.

To handle the wood, nearly any old-timer will tell you, "First thing you need is a chain saw, and don't buy a used one. Get it new, so there won't be any mysteries about how it's been treated." Chain saws, you see, have to be cod-dled. They dislike sand and dirt and need regular cleaning and maintenance checks.

When you begin to use your new tool, remember that its power-packed cutting action deserves a lot of respect. Work slowly, and follow the good and sensible precautions listed in any good chainsaw handbook. Many old timers say that two woodsmen should always work together, with one clearing twigs and branches from the ground to give the other open space to do his sawing.

When attacking a tree, make certain your chain saw is properly oiled and filled with gas. Then give an eye to which way the tree leans and gauge your cuts to let it fall in that direction. If the tree is straight and doesn't lean, check which side holds the most, and the heaviest, branches. Unlike the tall pines, thick oaks with massive limbs won't give you much cooperation if you decide to go against their natural inclination. Whenever possible, let the branch weight of a tree be your guide to where it's going to fall.

Your initial cut into the trunk itself should be horizontal and should con-tinue about halfway through. It should be made on the side toward which you want the tree to fall. Next, saw diagonally downward to the deepest point of the first cut.

Timber!: Make your third and final cut opposite and slightly above the first. When the tree begins to fall, remove the saw from the cut and step well away. However, if the blade wedges in the wood, forget it. Get out of the way. When the great mass crashes to the ground, the branches act as springs and can cause the trunk to kick back.

Begin trimming your fallen tree by cutting away the small branches. Cut the bigger limbs and the trunk into convenient lengths for your stove or heater.

Thick chunks of wood are a little more difficult than smaller pieces, but they can be handled. First, examine the face of the wood for any existing cracks that might serve as splitting guides. Then, with a maul, start swinging away at the center. Sometimes the piece splits open quickly; other times, it won't.

Wedges are excellent tools for a woodsman. If a log refuses to be split with an ax or maul, place a wedge along the grain and drive it in with the maul's flat end or a sledgehammer. You may have to use two, or even three, wedges on a stubborn chunk.

What about kindling? Automatic heaters that burn all night don't need it. In fact, one fire built at the beginning of the season can be kept alive all winter. If you're using a fireplace or smaller wood stove, gather your small fuel early and keep it from getting damp. The drier the sticks are, the easier it is to get a fire going on a chilly morning.

Dry twigs make good kindling, but for a real tried-and-true fire starter, split some of your logs two or three times, let the pieces dry well, and split them again into thin strips. Another first-class kindling source is the log trimmings pile at a local lumber mill. Some operations give trimmings away, while others charge a small amount for a pickup truck load.

Satisfying Labor: Does all this sound like a lot of work? It is, but it's labor of a very satisfying kind. Starting the day with 15 minutes of ax work on the woodpile helps keep a person in shape and the wood box full. Ax swinging is a safe, nontoxic tranquilizer, and it's a surefire way to get lots of fresh air into your lungs in a hurry.

Perhaps it's those moments between ax swings, however, that are the most valuable benefit of all. Many of us have forgotten the delight of examining in close focus the small things around us, and the chopping of wood offers its practitioner a chance to pause and look.

While resting between blows, it's easy to find oneself counting the rings in a large oak, watching a squirrel scamper down a branch, comparing the bark of a hickory to that of a birch, or examining the way a branch grows from a tree's main trunk.

Smells, too, take on a new importance when you heat with wood. The job makes you get outside in the snow in spite of yourself, and you find that you love it. When you're sawing or splitting fuel, the outdoors has a fragrance all its own, a fresh, clear sharpness leavened with the pungent scent of inner wood newly opened. Inside the house, the soft odor of burning logs greets you like incense and wraps you with warmth and comfort.

Using a woodburning stove for heat may require a bit of work, but not really much more than the labor a person has to perform in order to be able to pay a staggeringly high fuel or electric bill. The difference is that the labor involved is direct; it is a personal involvement in the human need for shelter and warmth.

Heat an Entire Home with a Single Wood Stove

Heating with wood can be a real energy-bill saver for a homesteading family, but it often has the shortcoming of providing a great deal of warmth in one area of a house while other sections of the same dwelling remain cold.

One couple, when planning to build their own house in Maine, were determined to sacrifice neither space nor comfort in coping with the long, bitter winters. They were also convinced, though many longtime residents tried to discourage them, that they could heat all 1,360 square feet of their home with one woodburning stove.

They attacked the problem of designing and building an energy-efficient yet spacious house from many different angles. Among the factors considered most carefully were sheltering the structure from the wind, building materials, the number of windows, achieving adequate air circulation inside, what stove to buy, and where to install the woodburner.

Wind Protection: Because they'd been warned repeatedly about Maine's stiff winter gales, the couple wanted to build their home where it would have as much protection from the wind as possible. However, they didn't want to put the building near a windbreak that would block either the view or the sun's warming rays. Ultimately, they cleared a small site in the midst of an evergreen and hardwood forest and built the dwelling so that it would be surrounded by timber on the east, west, and north.

The air around the house is considerably warmer than the air on fully cleared sites nearby, and even on particularly gusty days, the trees successfully block the wind at the site.

Design and Construction: The home is a single-story structure and rests on a gravel base that extends to the depth of the region's frost line. The family protects the dwelling's 16-inch crawl space from winter winds by wrapping the entire base of the house with polyethylene plastic sheeting and then packing snow against the plastic after the first good storm of the season.

Four- to six-inch-thick cedar logs planed on one side and rough on the other serve as the structure's primary building material. These timbers provide a durable and attractive wall, and since cedar is a very porous wood, they furnish several inches of insulation too.

The hip roof with four sloping sides that meet at a ridgepole is insulated with three-inch polystyrene plastic foam boards nailed to one-inch sheathing. This arrangement probably doesn't prevent heat loss as well as would a conventional roof with three to six inches of rolled fiberglass, but it seems to work well enough, while allowing the family to enjoy an open ceiling.

Windows: To give the sun every possible opportunity to enter the house, three homemade skylights and as many windows as the budget could stand were installed. Thus, the home receives passive solar heat during the day. At night, all the windows that are double-paneled are covered with heavy, insulated curtains to keep the stored warmth from radiating back out into the cold darkness.

On chilly, overcast days when the family doesn't want to draw the curtains but does want to keep heat from escaping through the windows, they pull down special shades. These blinds were fashioned from a thin, light weight, metallized plastic sheeting of the type that's often carried in survival kits by skiers and backpackers. They can be rolled up or down and allow some sunlight to enter the house while letting little heat escape.

Air Circulation: In order to allow air to circulate as freely as possible inside the house, and to avoid having the cold corners so common to homes in the north, the builders decided to limit the number of floor-to-ceiling walls. Where partitions seemed necessary for reasons of privacy, they put up fence-like room dividers instead. Thus, the two baths and bedrooms, the study, the art studio, and the utility area are separated from each other and from the rest of the house by seven-foot tall partitions built of weathered pine boards, cedar slabs, or perforated fiberboard. The kitchen, dining room, and living room share the same open area and are separated only by the placement of furniture and rugs.

A Solar Cordwood Pile

Here is how to stack your fuel wood to dry best and, if needed, build a solar heat-collector to bake it dry in even the foggiest climate.

The best fuel for your wood-burning space heater or cook stove is [1.] a good hardwood (maple or oak rather than pine or other softwood) that has [2.] been felled, stacked in 8'-long "ricks," and left to age in the woods for at least six months—12 months is better. It should then [3.] be trucked to a wood yard where it is [4.] cut to stove-length and [5.] split in halves, thirds, or quarters if the log is well over 6" or 8" in diameter.

All this work—hard work that must be accomplished largely by hand—is done for a single purpose: to section and season the wood, or dry it from a natural water content of up to 50% (by weight) to a better-burning 20%, the average water content of the atmosphere. Wet wood burns "cold", wasting a great deal of its energy evaporating the water, which condenses on the inside of your flue and stovepipe, depositing its smoke content as creosote that can ooze out all over your floor or dry into a flue-fire-causing substance.

Even well-dried wood loses a fifth of its heat energy burning off what water remains...but that water content moderates burn rate, so you have a calm and manageable fire. Under-10%-water-content "tinder dry" splinters and small sticks that have been stored under cover or heated so water evaporates out are good to have in small quantities to initiate a blaze. But if all your wood is tinder your fires will want to burn fast and hot. Then, to keep from wasting wood and overheating the stove or your living quarters, you will damp down the air-flow regulators that control the supply of oxygen in the draft-control openings, and the openings that control the smoke exiting at the back of the fire—the smoke dampers. But, the damped-down tinder can generate as much creosote as wet wood.

Its good to bring wood inside for a day or two to warm and evaporate surface moisture. But, season wood to be the kind of fuel your stove was designed to burn: normal air-dried hardwood.

All tree barks are water resistant and some like white birch are waterproof enough to have served the Indians as water bowls and boat hulls. So cordwood dries only from cut ends, limb scars, and split faces. For fastest drying, section and split your wood as soon after it arrives in your yard as possible to increase barkless, good-drying area. Sectioned, split, and left exposed to the rain in a pile, a green log that would take a year to dry in the woods will be burnable in about eight months.

(continued on page 236)

(continued from page 235)

A 2-cord solar wood pile

If stacked properly under this solar kiln, that same wood will make a good fire in six months. More to the point, supposing you take delivery of a load of semi-seasoned firewood (cut the prior winter—so not a full year off the stump) during the summer. Left in a heap it will not be fully dry by fall when you need it. But, cut to length, split and stacked properly in the kiln, the wood will make prime firewood by October.

A Proper Stack: A conventional cord of wood is a cheesebox-shaped pile of 8'-long whole logs stacked 4' high and 4' deep. That's a volume of 128 cubic feet and is the way cordwood is stacked in the woods by loggers. It is also the way firewood is sold—or the way it is supposed to be sold. Some rural scalawags do bring their wood to town and try to foist off a "face cord" (2' x 4' x 8') or even less true cord, though there are laws being written to discourage the practice.

A reputable cordwood dealer will dump a stove-length wood with the larger-bore logs split. For best drying and easiest use during the winter, its best to split any chunks that won't fit easily into your stove. Then, build your stack.

First, figure out the direction of prevailing wind. Find a location in full sun, where air flow is not blocked by a build-

(continued on page 237)

(continued from page 236)

ing or dense thicket. Line the stack up with its long dimension facing flat into the wind. Plan the stack so your logs will be piled with their long dimension perpendicular to the wind flow.

Put down a ground cover of plastic sheeting—a double thickness of black plastic garden mulch will do fine. Roughly grade the soil beneath it so water will not pool on the sheet, but will drain off. This way, soil moisture will not migrate up into the wood, and even the bottom layer of logs will make good firewood.

To be sure that a loose stack will not collapse, sink a trio of stout poles into the ground at each end and every 8' along the pile. Make them stout enough to hold a nail in their top end and long enough that they will extend a good foot above the finished pile.

Start the pile, making the bottom tier or two with all full round logs. Then, pile every quarter and half-split log with its barked surface facing up so that rain or condensation will drip down and not tend to soak into the exposed wood. Pile logs loose in the stack with the maximum amount of air built in between sticks. That way more air will move through, carrying off wood-moisture with it. Pile all logs in the same direction—all with cut surfaces facing into the wind. Try to build so that air channels extend clear through the stack from face to face of the pile.

Make a Kiln: In climates that see more fog and drizzle than sun, you can keep the wet off the wood and heat it at the same time by rigging a cover. A covering of black plastic will absorb sun heat even if the sky is overcast, continually heating the wood and evaporating its moisture content. Wind will whip thin plastic mulch to shreds. So, invest in a better grade of "plastic tarp" with hemmed edges. The kind with fabric molded in lasts the longest.

Some wood burners build a roof frame over the pile by [1.] trimming the poles supporting the pile to even height [2.] nailing flat boards front-to-back over the pile atop each trio of support stakes [3.] nailing or wiring well-trimmed saplings in three pile-long lines between the poles. Then, a tarp or black plastic cover is draped over the roof and down both faces of the pile—but pulled out at an angle from the faces of the pile to let air circulate—then stretched tight and held down with logs.

You may eliminate the roof and just drape black-plastic sheeting over the pile and weigh down the edges against wind. But, it is important that the cover be loose and open enough that it permits damp air to flow out, so don't enclose the ends of the pile in plastic. And, whenever prolonged rain-free weather is promised, roll it up and let the sun bake the wood. ■

The space above each of the fenced-off rooms is completely unenclosed. The only areas of the house that are covered with ceilings are the clothes closet, to protect its contents from settling dust, and the pantry. This room is completely insulated from the rest of the house to maintain the steady, cool temperature that is ideal for the storage of food.

The Warm Floor: The heart of the air-circulation system, and perhaps the single most important factor in the successful heating of the house, is the enclosed, insulated air space under the floor through which warm room air is blown.

When the house was under construction, a false floor consisting of one-inch lumber, chicken wire, and three inches of commercial fiberglass insulation was nailed to the underside of the structure's main eight-inch support beams. A single layer of aluminum foil was placed shiny side up over the insulation and that was covered with a layer of polyethylene sheeting. The wooden floor people walk on is almost 13 inches above the polyethylene, since it rests upon eight-inch joists.

Warm air is drawn under the floor and through the insulated air space beneath by a pair of inexpensive, kitchen-type exhaust fans set into the floorboards between two joists and on either side of the house's center support beam. An eight-foot-tall plywood column stands over each fan, so the blowers draw warm air down from the building's open ceiling and through the columns, and direct it under the floorboards. The air is then vented back into the house through four two-inch-wide, six-foot-long openings set into the floor near the structure's corners. This creates a continuous flow of warmth from the highest, and warmest, parts of the house, down under the floor, and back up through the coolest parts, the corners.

Another Fan: In addition to the two fans in the floor, which run almost continuously throughout the winter, a 14-inch exhaust fan was placed above the divider that separates the bedroom from the utility room. This blower is tilted slightly toward the floor, so that when it operates, it pushes warm air down into the bedroom.

When the bedroom fan is running, which is just on the chilliest days, not only is the bedroom's temperature increased, but the whole house becomes cozier.

The Heater: The woodstove sits right in the center of the house, next to a simple chimney built of eight-inch flue tiles surrounded by mortared C-shaped concrete chimney blocks. This is only a few feet away from the pair of plywood columns that conceal the floor-mounted exhaust fans. Thus, the two fans are able to draw into the floor the warm air that collects directly over the stove. The woodburner's fire blazes all the time during the winter, although on clear days the sun provides the house with a great deal of warmth. At night the stove is packed with as much wood as it will hold, and the front vent and the flue are closed almost all the way, leaving just enough draft to keep the fire alive. This way, the house temperature automatically drops to about 50°F overnight. In the morning the vents are reopened, and the fire quickly flares up again, thereby raising the building's temperature to somewhere between 65°F and 70°F.

Chief among the points in favor of this heating system are simplicity, economy, and reliability. No part of the setup can break down except the fans, and even if they should malfunction, or stop because of a power failure, the stove will still put out enough heat to keep the family reasonably warm. Since the homeowners aren't dependent on maintenance men or fuel oil deliveries, they needn't fear an interruption of service due to foul-ups in those departments or to increases in labor or petroleum costs.

In short, a relatively large and comfortable house can be simply and inexpensively heated, even in Maine, with a single woodburning stove.

Energy-Saving Beadboard Shutters

When the mercury drops to the subfreezing zone, and the winter chill oozes its way inside in any way possible, it suddenly becomes apparent that regardless of how draft-free you've made the roof and walls of your snug little dwelling, a bone-chilling cold can still make its unpleasant presence very well known through that heat-losing culprit: glazing.

Even though your home's portals may all be covered with storm doors or windows and even though those barriers may use double-strength or insulated glass, the fact remains that the panes that bring warmth in during the day can just as easily let it out at night, during a spell of cloudy weather, or because they face north.

Probably the biggest offender in this theft of energy is the sliding glass door typical of many homes and apartments throughout the United States. Fortunately, though, blocking this heat leak is perhaps one of the simplest and least expensive steps you can take to save a few bucks on your heating bill. The same procedure described here would naturally apply to windows you'd like to be able to cover.

You'll need a piece of 3/4' X 4' X 8' beadboard for each glass door panel you plan to protect (this cellular polystyrene insulation is available at lumberyards and paneling centers), 36 six-inch-long magnetic strips (these can be salvaged from the self-sealing gaskets in junked refrigerators) to hold each breadboard sheet in place, and a tube of weatherstrip adhesive, which can be purchased at a hardware or auto parts store. It's a good idea to test a small piece of your polystyrene block to see whether the adhesive affects it, and if disintegration should occur, use some other glue.

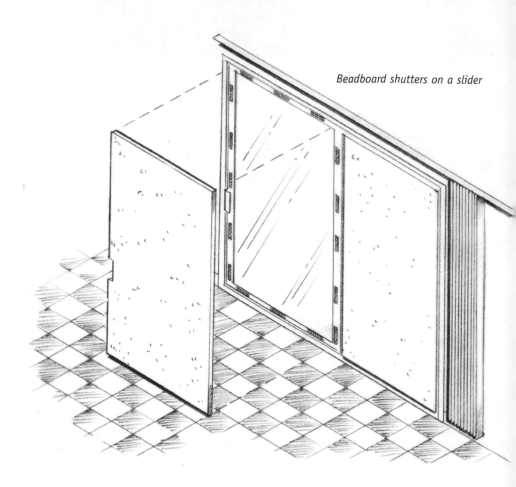

Beadboard shutters on a slider

The idea is to cover the door panes with the foam-like boards when they're apt to leak out warmth and to remove the opaque panels when the sun is shining and can contribute to heating the home.

To begin the project, measure the height and width of each glass door frame right to the edges and cut the insulation boards to these dimensions. It's important that you cover not just the glass itself but as much of its aluminum casing as possible, since the metal transfers heat well also. If you have a wood-cased door or window, you should also plan to cover the frame because the dead-air space formed between the panes and the beadboard adds to the cover's insulative effect.

Once the panels are trimmed to size and snug cut-outs are made for handles, latches, or anything else that would prevent the sheet from fitting flush against the frame, glue the salvaged magnetic strips to the door's framework, six on each side of each large glass pane and three each at the top and bottom, all evenly spaced.

Next, take a soft-leaded pencil and coat the face of each strip with graphite. Position the polystyrene sheet back over the frame so the board picks up the pencil marks at each magnet's location. Using a single-edged razor or a small blade, cut a channel at each smudge spot large enough to allow you to insert and cement in place the remaining 18 magnetic strips to mate with those on the frame. In order for the panel to fit flush against the frame, the channels must be twice as deep as the thickness of a single strip.

Your heat-stopping shutter is now ready to install. If you want to cover the panel with a decorative fabric to jazz it up a bit, be certain the glue you use won't melt the foam, or if you should decide to paint the polystyrene shutters to match your room, use a latex-based product.

That's all there is to it. This winter will find your dwelling more snug than ever because you'll be keeping the warmth inside, where you need it.

Thermal Shades to Cover Windows

Thermal window shades can reduce heat loss through and around windows by acting as barriers to drafts and moisture. Ready-made shades are costly, but you can make comparable window coverings that are handsome, efficient, and inexpensive.

There are three different approaches you can use in assembling a window shade, depending upon your sewing skills and the materials you have available. Any of these will be practical for covering window units up to 4' X 8'. Excluding the time spent in acquiring materials, a single shade should take less than three hours to complete.

The Preliminaries: Begin by measuring the inner dimensions of the window to be covered, adding two to three inches to the resulting figures to provide for seam allowances. With this information, you can now buy the amount of fabric you'll need.

Up to a point, you'll have the same shopping list for any of the thermal shade designs. A pretty, chintz-like cotton-blend fabric that is already quilted with a layer of polyester filling and has a backing of thin cloth is recommended. Such piece goods are customarily used for bed spreads and are readily available, reasonably priced, and easy to handle. By judiciously shopping for materials, you may further reduce the cost of the project. Muslin, for instance, may be used to back some models, and it can be bought by the pound at fabric outlets, as can the quilted cloth described above.

The Various Options: Before you start cutting and stitching, pick out one of the designs listed below, and obtain the other components and the sewing notions you'll need to construct your window shade.

Model 1: This option consists of a layer of batting-backed quilted material, a layer of polyethylene (a drop cloth or a plastic garbage bag will make an

Limiting the Flow of Your Shower Head

When weather forecasters start intoning warnings about below-average levels of precipitation, and the well begins to send up hollow echoes instead of a steady stream of water, you know it's time to pay attention to your family's water-consumption habits. Whether you live in an area where cutbacks are mandated from time to time, or ever-increasing water bills are simply forcing your household to economize, it's a good idea to conserve this limited resource.

You can significantly affect household use by merely regulating the amount of water that runs down the drain when you shower. If you live in a house that was built recently, your bathroom may already be equipped with a water-saving shower head. For older homes, however, there is an inexpensive option you can use to modify your shower head so it will use about 75% less water.

First, remove the existing shower head, using an adjustable wrench. Pad the jaws so the chrome doesn't get scratched. Then rummage through your workshop odds and ends or visit the local hardware store or plumbing supply house. Find a rubber washer without a hole in the middle, about the same diameter as the inside of the pipe that connects with the nozzle.

The next step is as tough as this project gets. Using a pair of snips, cut a number of little wedges all the way around the rubber disk, from the outside of the circle and not quite to its center.

Insert the saw-edged washer into the shower head as far as it will go and refasten the whole affair to the connecting waterline. Try out your modification and if the flow is too constricted, disassemble the fitting and deepen the notches in the washer. If the flow has not been reduced enough, however, start over with another washer and remove smaller slices this time.

With a retrofitted shower head, the water flow will be about 25% of what it was before, and the spray will have the same force regardless of how far the faucet handles are turned. So enjoy! Now you can shower twice as long while using only half the water. ■

adequate vapor barrier), another layer of polyester batting, and finally, the muslin backing.

Model 2: This window cover consists of a layer of quilted fabric, a polyethylene bubble sheet (the material, which will provide a vapor barrier and an additional air space, is used to wrap items for shipping), and a muslin backing. Enough bubble packing for this project should cost less than a couple of dollars.

Model 3: The third design consists of quilted fiberfill backed by a nonporous reflective material such as that used in the heat-retaining "space blankets" carried by many backpackers. A twin-size space blanket and some Velcro-brand fastening complete the necessary purchases. This is perhaps the least efficient model because it lacks the bulk to thoroughly block air drafts, but it's definitely well suited to applications in which lightweight is of primary importance.

In assembling these window shades, do not puncture the vapor barrier, except at the edges where it's necessary to attach the Velcro; otherwise the layer will not offer maximum resistance to moisture and airflow.

Construction Techniques: After the windows have been measured, the materials for the shade selected, and the pattern pieces cut out, it's time to pay close attention to the assembly of the thermal "sandwich." Place the quilted fabric right side up on a table and then lay the backing layer (either muslin or reflective) directly on top, right side down. Next, add the other components to the top or bottom of the stack. (When you use this method, you can be sure that you won't wind up ripping out seams because you've gotten a wrong side facing inward.)

Once you've added and pinned the polyethylene, batting, packing bubbles, or whatever, thread your sewing machine, using a large needle, and set it for a fairly long stitch (this adjustment will keep the polyethylene and batting from becoming bogged down in the machine's feed dogs). After making absolutely certain that your backing material and quilted fabric are right sides together, sew along the outer edges of your window quilt. You'll probably find yourself taking wide seams to insure catching every layer in the stitching, so it is strongly recommended that you cut the components with large seam allowances (at least one inch).

Continue sewing around three sides of the shade, leaving a generous opening on the fourth edge. Turn the whole bulky package right side out, being careful to square the corners, and then finish up by slip stitching the open edge closed.

Putting Up and Shutting Out: With the sewing done, it's time to attach the Velcro. It's a good idea to separate the nubby Velcro strips from their fuzzy "mates" at the outset, as they tend to tangle while you're trying to attach them to the slippery thermal shade.

The following Velcro-application idea works really well, but it does call for quite a few yards of the expensive fastener. Sew the fuzzy side of the tape along the top and halfway down each side on the rear of the shade. Then attach the gripper side of the tape to the remaining edges. Next, staple the corresponding strips of Velcro along the edge of the window frame. This method allows the shade, when not in use, to be folded into either a pillow cover or a child-size sleeping bag, and the technique is so satisfactory and versatile that the cost of the Velcro is justified.

There are, however, other methods of fastening the thermal quilt to the window casing that would considerably reduce the cash outlay. One way would be to attach continuous stretches of Velcro only at the corners, with tabs of the material strategically placed along the edges. Another, less flexible, idea calls for attaching cloth casings along the top and bottom edges of the rear of the shade. Thread lath through the casings and then staple or tack through the wood into the window casing.

The Velcro technique described works pretty well, and it looks good because it allows you to place your shade behind even a close-fitting window treatment like shutters.

These shades may admit enough light so that you will feel no need to remove them during the day. Some folks will undoubtedly desire more sunshine, though, and if you've attached the quilts by means of Velcro, you can easily peel them off or reposition the shades at half-mast to let in more light.

Those who decide to leave the coverings constantly in place should be forewarned that moisture may condense on the windows and run down into the wells, although the inclusion of a vapor barrier in the shades alleviates this problem somewhat. The best way to deal with this annoying situation is to check frequently behind the drape, wipe away any condensation, and then replace the shade. Mold may form where moisture has been allowed to collect. In this case prevention is the best cure: Periodically wipe the window surfaces and wells with a rag dipped in diluted liquid chlorine bleach.

The Outcome: There are many steps homeowners can take to cut down on heat loss throughout a house: increase the insulation in walls, ceilings, and floors; seal cracks around windows and doors; install storm windows; wrap the hot water tank; and so forth. Many of the procedures are not cost-effective for renters or for buyers who will not be living in their home long enough to realize a financial benefit from their investment. Even renters, though, can put a stop to substantial heat loss by using insulated shades in the right places at the right times. In winter, it's best to keep northern windows covered at all times, but to uncover eastern and southern windows to the morning sun. Then lower the shades on those exposures late in the day. Let late afternoon sunshine warm the house through western windows, too.

Properly constructed thermal shades will halt the icy blasts of wind that whiz through cracks and chill your back as you're toasting your toes in front of the fire. Homemade draft stoppers are about a 10th as expensive as ready-made thermal shades, and you can individualize them to add decorative appeal to your rooms.

Construct a Solar Entry

Imagine a cold, windy midwinter day, and picture yourself basking in the sun on your front steps and enjoying the first daffodil of the season. A solar entry to the front door of your dwelling can turn this make-believe scenario into a reality. For about a hundred dollars' worth of materials, concrete blocks, 2 X 4s, and window sash, you can construct an entrance that is enclosed in sun-heat-admitting glass and includes a planting bed. No longer will you need to pick your way up ice-rimmed steps and be ushered into your living room by a howling draft.

If your doorway faces south, you can garner extra sunshine for gardening, but regardless of a home's orientation, this air-lock entry can effectively reduce the amount of cold air actually penetrating the interior of your dwelling.

Design: First, build a raised bed of concrete block, which can be made more attractive by facing it with brick or some other veneer. Construct a framework of 2 X 4s, and space them to correspond to the size of the available sash. Then secure the uprights of the framework in the concrete blocks and fasten the cross pieces to the eaves. Once the glass is put in, the winter air is shut out.

Extras: You might consider making the entire addition detachable. The section of ceiling over the planting beds can be made to swing back under the eaves, and the steps will remain covered. The rest of the glass sash can be removed from the framework and stored. That way, the biggest part of the entrance is open to the pleasant weather of spring and summer.

Benefits: Daily temperature readings taken before sunrise during the month of January show that the thermal mass provided by the raised planting beds in this sun-powered portico holds the heat quite well. A consistent 10° to 20° temperature difference exists between the inside of the vestibule and the bone-chilling outdoors. (Sealing the joints of the addition and using double paned glass will make it even more draft proof.)

These readings were taken before the morning sun hit the glass enclosure, but the temperature difference on a bright midafternoon, when the portico is really gathering in the solar heat, can be much more extreme.

Other positive results of glassing in the entrance include planting areas that never freeze, steps that stay dry, and reduced fuel consumption. Moreover,

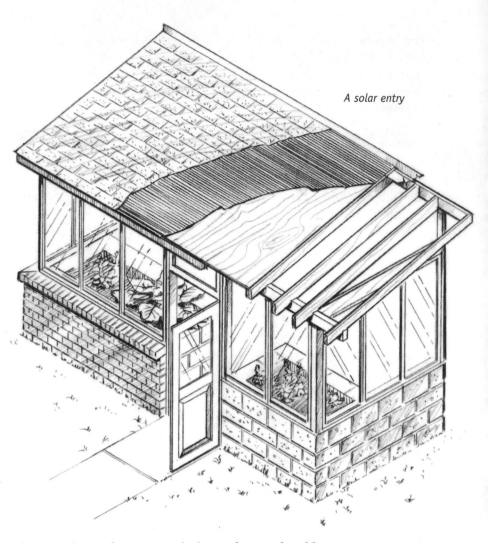

A solar entry

the greenhouse foyer is an ideal spot for comfortably removing soggy winter outerwear.

Still another benefit that will warm any gardener's heart is the possibility of starting many types of bulbs and seedlings early and conveniently. Around the first of March, whether the bitter cold of winter has ended or not, the solar entry makes a large and effective cold frame. Not only daffodils and crocuses, which are fairly hardy, but carnations, camellias, jasmine, cyclamens, and other flowers as well as a variety of vegetables can survive in this solar entry.

One of the finest features of such an entrance is the surprisingly minor amount of maintenance it requires. Fifteen minutes in the spring to take the glass out and 15 more in the fall to install it again. Except for the pleasant responsibility of selecting the next plants to try, that's all there is to it. So consider a solar entry for your home. The benefits are mighty attractive.

Homemade Power from the Wind

Anyone living where there is a relatively constant source of wind can take a substantial bite out of the power bill by installing a wind plant to generate at least part of the electricity used in the home for lights and appliances.

A home-generating system needs to be designed to meet the requirements of the area and the household it serves, as a man named Marshall Price found when he designed and built his own wind plant, which has been meeting most of his electrical needs for more than nine years. The investment Price made in time and money has long since been returned in lower power bills and the satisfaction of having his own independent system.

Make Do, and Make It Work: Price's story really began after he and his family built their residence on the shore of Lake Erie about 15 years ago. The constant breeze blowing off the water served as an ever-present reminder that free energy was going begging, but it wasn't until Price started collecting information on wind machines that he found the answer to the problem that had been keeping him from building his own plant: the need for information concerning the design and fabrication of the wooden blades. Once he'd uncovered that information, the rest, for the most part, was a matter of locating parts and fitting them together so they'd be compatible with one another and with the nature of the lakeside breezes.

"One thing about wind, it's darned unpredictable," says Price. "It can be blowing nicely at a steady 18 miles per hour, and then all of a sudden it whips up to 30 knots without as much as a 'how do you do.' On top of that, it changes direction just as erratically...and that can play the devil with your equipment. A rotor spinning at 200 rpm or so and scribing a 12' diameter circle has tremendous inertia and doesn't take easily to being reoriented."

It was critical to plan for these contingencies before beginning the construction of his plant. He first located an ambulance alternator that was capable of putting out 147 amps at about 15 volts (about 2,200 watts) in a very strong breeze. After reconditioning this component, the do-it-yourselfer started working on a governor system that would allow his three six-foot-long blades to feather by pivoting on their mounts when wind speeds got dangerously high. When feathered, the blades are less effective as airfoils, and this keeps the rotor's rpm within safe limits.

According to Price, this hub-mounted control setup is similar to the type Marcellus Jacobs used on his well-known wind machines. "I'd read stories about Jacobs, and I wanted to know how his governor worked. Well, I finally located a copy of a drawing from an old service manual, studied it, and then built my own version. It acts on centrifugal force and uses lead weights, linkages, and springs to control the blades' pitch. I knew I wanted a top speed of about 230 rpm on the power shaft, so I just used the trial-and-error method to set up the governor correctly. During the winter I made a little testing stand in the basement and mounted the hub on it. Then I drove the unit with a belt connected to my garden tractor's engine, took rpm readings off the hub using a tachometer, and experimented with the governor until I got it right. I've been using it ever since, and by gosh it works."

If the alternator is to generate usable electricity, it must spin a good deal faster than 230 rpm, so Price set about making a gearbox that would step up the driving speed considerably. To accomplish this, he welded a housing out of 1/4" steel plate and mounted two salvaged Chevrolet gear sets inside. The 8.2-to-1 ratio thus created means that for every one turn the power shaft on the hub makes, the alternator shaft spins 8.2 times, or at about 1,800 rpm in near-gale winds.

The power shaft itself was recycled from an old Datsun: "I bought the whole car for $20, then sold the body to a junkyard for $30. That left me with the entire drive train and with a profit of $10. I stripped out the swing arms from the independent rear suspension, used one bearing and all for the wind plant, and kept the other as a spare."

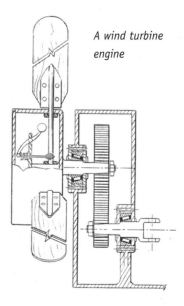

A wind turbine engine

Having taken care of governing the high-speed performance of his generator, Price had to consider control at low rpm. Specifically, he used a centrifugally activated microswitch to energize the alternator's field windings when the shaft speed reached approximately 750 rpm. Translated, that means that the alternator doesn't start charging until the breezes reach seven or eight mph. Below 750 rpm, the alternator is ineffective anyway, so there's little use in allowing battery power to drain into the field circuit when the breeze isn't strong enough.

Finally, to protect his equipment from inevitable heavy blows, Price hinged and loaded the windplant's tail frame so it could be turned to parallel the plane of the blades. A small cable winch mounted at the base of the tower keeps the tail perpendicular to the rotor path under normal conditions, making maximum use of the wind, but when that cable is released, the vane swings to one side, and the tips rather than the faces of the blades are then presented to the breeze. This protects the rotor against overspinning.

This method of restraint is commonly used in up-wind-type machines, but in this case, Price again took a tip from the Jacob's design and set the tail springs so they'd shut down the wind plant if the cable broke, rather than open it to the full force of a storm. Price also points out that he can take advantage of his machine even in strong winds, simply by unwinding the winch partially and allowing his blades to face the breeze at an angle, so they'll spill off a good deal of wind yet will continue to turn rapidly enough to generate power.

A wind turbine

Handmade Redwood Blades: Obviously, a knack for foraging, coupled with the ability to understand the potential of each "junk" component, aided Price immeasurably in bringing his project to completion. However, he knew from the start that he'd have to fashion the blades from scratch.

"I went and handpicked three straight-grained redwood 2 X 8s from the lumberyard, then cut and shaped them according to the specifications I wanted. Because a wind-plant blade is driven by the wind, its contour must differ from that of a standard propeller if it's going to work correctly. After I'd formed and sanded the wood, I protected it with fiberglass resin and matting, coating it evenly to maintain proper balance at speed, then roughed up the glass lightly and gave each blade a second coat," Price said.

"Now, those redwood airfoils aren't just bolted to the hub. Each spar coming off the governor pinions is seated on a 7/8" diameter cold-rolled steel spike that extends a full 20" into a socket that's been bored into the end of the blade. Furthermore, these internal spines are pinned through the wooden shoulders, and I've also got the blades sandwiched on the outside with 6" X 6" metal plates. This way, I can have my feathering feature as a governor, and still feel comfortable about the integrity of those redwood blades at higher wind speeds."

The Weak Link: After fabricating the blades and working out the best method of mounting them, Price had only to erect a tower and place the plant atop it. Since the source of wind is generally from the lakeside quadrants and thus doesn't suffer interference from trees or hills, it wasn't necessary to build a fancy pivot or to rely upon altitude to catch the best breezes. Price simply sank a length of well casing into a concrete footer, leaving about 18 feet of the casing projecting above the base. Then he mounted the generator and gearbox on a frame and set that into the tower so it would pivot on a vertical axis. Double-ought copper cables, purchased at scrap prices from the local power company and in stalled with plenty of slack to allow for yaw, carry electricity to the battery bank.

According to Price, energy storage is the weak link in his system. "There's

Using Wood to Preheat Water

While working in his basement, a homeowner noticed that the water heater was giving off, and therefore wasting, a surprising amount of warmth. He patched that heat leak by wrapping the tank in a blanket of insulation, but he kept thinking that there must be more he could do to reduce the gadget's appetite for electricity. When he pictured the wood stove upstairs, quietly producing plenty of comfortable, economical heat, it occurred to him that perhaps those low-cost calories could preheat the family's water: maybe the incoming liquid could be piped to a storage tank set beside the log burner and then channeled to the water heater in the basement. He figured that by reducing the the number of degrees the water had to be heated, he could reduce the amount of time the water heater was on, and thus cut electricity costs.

The following spring, he scavenged for a suitable used storage container but eventually gave up when the best he could find was a heater that had rusted inside. So, splurging a bit, he bought a new 40-gallon, glass-lined model for just under $200. Before wrestling it into place upright beside his woodburner, he gave the tank a coat of high-heat-tolerant black paint.

To this homeowner's dismay, the addition stood much higher than the stove and looked very cumbersome and unattractive. The solution, obviously, was to lay the tank on its side, but in order to do so, he would need to support it. Without this, the tank would tend to roll, and the weight of 40 gallons of water (about 332 pounds) might warp, and then crack, its glass liner.

After pondering the problem awhile, the homeowner decided to build a concrete base contoured to fit the tank.

(continued on page 251)

absolutely no problem at all in making the power; that's the easy part. If I need more juice, all I have to do is build another wind plant, or several if I want to set up a full-scale wind farm. But decent storage, something that's affordable and can still take the abuse of constant charge and discharge, is hard to come by."

Price could have avoided the storage problem by generating alternating current and then either using it on a separate line or feeding it back into the utility grid, but he decided against both those options because he wanted a system that would allow him to be somewhat independent of the power companies and that would be working even when the wind failed to blow.

As his setup stands, the outsized alternator generates alternating current,

Before starting the project, though, he had to put an extra brace between the floor joists in the space where the base would rest to accommodate the additional weight of water, cement, and container.

When that was done, a rectangular form was built for the base, using pieces of scrap eight-inch-wide lumber. The box was filled to within three inches of its top with mixed concrete. After brushing the lower surface of the tank with oil so it wouldn't stick, he positioned the cylinder and pushed it part way into the mix. Once the concrete had set, he lifted the tank and lined the perfectly indented base with a sheet of plastic to allow it to cure.

After a week, the homeowner stripped the wood forms from the hard block and set the tank in place, locating both components so that the vessel would rest about 2" from the wood stove.

Installing the plumbing came next, and because much of the new tubing would be exposed to intense heat, galvanized pipe was used to connect the tank to the existing PVC system with special plastic-to-steel couplings.

On your own pre-heater, be sure to connect the cold-water line to the lower portion of the tank, so that already-warmed water won't be cooled by the incoming liquid, and to position the hot-water outlet pipe at the top to set up a natural circulation out of the tank and into the conventional heater. Also, don't forget to install a pressure-relief valve on the outlet pipe, and it's a good idea to run a length of pipe from the valve to a small basin to catch any water that might escape if the relief mechanism opens.

The three-line valves in the system are essential, too, and be certain to place them so they are readily accessible, so that when you want to use the preheating tank, you can simply open valves 1 and 2, and close No. 3. Shutting the tank down at the onset of the summer months will then be a matter of reversing the process. ∎

---

which is rectified to direct current through diodes and is then stored in a mixed bank of batteries composed of two-volt and six-volt components. The batteries are wired in a combination series/parallel circuit to achieve 12 volts total. Power from the batteries is fed through an inverter that converts the storable DC back into AC for use throughout most of the house.

Price doesn't use a voltage regulator on his system, because when the batteries are depleted, they require a good three days of steady wind to even approach the overcharging point. In fact, he simply uses his appliances as indicators of his storage bank's state of charge: "I can tell by the way the lights burn. If they're too bright, I know I'm getting 13 volts instead of my usual 12 to 12.5, so I shut down the plant. On the other hand, if the batteries are low, the picture on my color TV gets distorted in the upper right corner, and that tells me it's time to crank the tail out straight again. A few years back, we had a nine-day spell without any appreciable breeze, and the cells were able to handle that, so I'm not too worried about my storage capacity."

Of course, batteries do lose their effectiveness, especially when they've seen a good deal of service. But Price stresses the importance of maintaining a cost effective approach to buying and replacing these essential pieces of equipment.

A Sound Investment: This brings us to the all-important bottom line: Has Price's investment both of dollars and of time been reasonably rewarded? Interestingly enough, he admits that at first his main objective was simply to have one wind-powered light source over his reading chair. As he made improvements in his plant and added more lights, he boosted his storage capacity. Seeing that the generator kept up with his power usage easily, he installed the inverter and then tied other appliances, including the color TV, into the line. Eventually, he reached the point at which everything in his house except the dishwasher, the washing machine, and the refrigerator was powered by the wind.

At one point, Price had installed a resistive heating element in his furnace boiler to make supplemental hot water when the battery bank was fully charged. A switch allowed him to divert power directly from the wind plant to the element, which required no power regulation. This permitted him to make even further use of available winds, because he never had to shut his generator down. That simple load-management system, though effective, was dismantled when Price replaced his leaky boiler tank with a new model.

In summary, Price is an example of someone who, with the help of his welding and metal-shop skills, turned a few hundred dollars' worth of scrap parts into the equivalent of a several thousand-dollar investment, one that demands little more than an annual checkup and a battery replacement effort every so many years. It doesn't take a very sharp pencil to make sense of economics like that.

CHAPTER 9

❧

Home and Hearth

A Cherry Pit Bed Warmer

Folks in the Swiss Alps still practice a warm and delightful household ritual on cold winter evenings: pillows filled with heat-absorbing cherry stones are popped into the kitchen's warming oven, and, come evening, each family member retrieves a pillow on the way to bed. The warmers work wonderfully well for taking the chill off icy bed sheets in the traditionally unheated bedrooms of mountainside chalets.

Because many people in North America these days are heating their homes with wood and trying to rely less on fossil fuels and whole-home central heating systems, the unheated bedroom is no longer a quaint, foreign, or old-time custom. With a little stitchery, cherry stone pillows could be your own family's perfect bed and foot warmer. With three times the heating capacity of pebbles and much lower conductivity, cherry pits provide a steady, soothing warmth for considerable periods.

The little bed warmers are simple to make. The hardest task seems to be saving a sufficient quantity of cherry pits throughout the year. During the balmy days typical of cherry season, it's easy to forget about those long, cold winter nights. Collecting the seeds is no easy task, either. In fact, if you're the ambitious sort who plans to make several pillows, you'd do well to contact a cannery. It takes 30 to 40 pounds of good ripe cherries to supply enough stones to make one pillow!

Cherry stones must be be thoroughly cleaned and dried before they can be sewn into pillows. First, pile the pits in a large pan or in the kitchen sink and cover them completely with fresh, cold water. Rub and squeeze the stones together to loosen any remaining pulp. When that's done, rinse them and repeat the process several times.

Once the cherry seeds are clean of pulp, simmer them in a pot of water, stirring occasionally, for about 15 minutes. Then dump the cooked stones into a sink full of cold water and rub them again. Rinse the cherry pits a few more times (it's essential to remove all the pulp) before draining and placing them on clean dish towels to dry.

Next, dry them thoroughly in the sun if possible. You can finish the dehydration process by spreading the pits in one layer across a shallow pan and baking them in a warm oven. Stir now and then so they'll dry thoroughly. The pits will be evenly colored and much lighter when "done," and can then be stored indefinitely in jars, plastic bags, or paper sacks until you're ready to make your bed-warmers. (The last are the best choice, because they'll permit continued drying and will even absorb any moisture that may still be present.)

To make the pillowcases, use a sturdy natural-fiber material such as denim or sailcloth. (Avoid any kind of synthetic material that might melt when exposed to heat.) Cut two rectangles measuring 8" X 11" or use a single 16" X 11" piece. Put the pieces together face-to-face or fold the double-sized rectangle in half and stitch around the edges, leaving an opening large enough to let you turn the bag right side out to conceal the stichery. Do so.

Then fill the sack full, but loosely packed, with the dried cherry stones.

Sew up the hole. Now, you're ready for the next nippy night.

To use the bed warmers, begin by heating the pillows in an oven set to a very low temperature, in front of the fireplace, or on a high-legged rack over a cool wood stove. Take care with any of these methods that the warmers are not exposed directly to a glowing oven element or an open flame that might ignite the fabric. When the cherry stone cushions are toasty warm, take them immediately to your bedroom and place them between the cold sheets.

By the time you're ready to turn in, your bedding should be just the right temperature.

(Note: Lacking pounds of cherry pits, dried homegrown beans or whole peas will do almost as well. Lacking beans, you can buy 100 pounds of whole corn and feed what isn't needed for the warmers to your daughter's horse or the chickens. Wash each pillow-full of grain—quickly so it won't absorb water—to remove milling dust. Dry well.)

Braid a Rug from Fabric Scraps

Back when great-great-grandmother made most of the family clothes, braided "throw" rugs were a feature of every country home. That's where the last of her sewing scraps went. The rugs were colorful and thick enough to warm a cold floor in front of the kitchen sink or beside the bath tub. They were washable, so good for doormats. And, they were practically free.

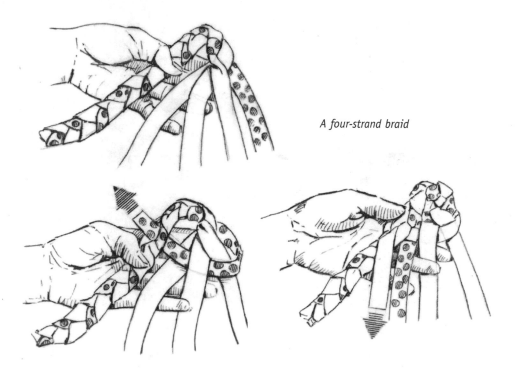

A four-strand braid

The four-strand braided rug described here can be made from inexpensive synthetic or cotton scraps you can buy these days for almost nothing. Interlocking the rows of braid is a modern innovation that eliminates the traditional need to to sew the ropes together, as well as giving the rug maker greater control over the colors.

If you'd like to braid a rug, you'll need a pile of fabric scraps, a pair of scissors, four medium-size safety pins, a needle, and thread. (A sewing machine makes the job of preparing the scraps easier, but you can get by without one. It just takes time and patience.)

To begin, cut your rags on either the lengthwise or crosswise grain—but never diagonally—to make the longest strips possible. The strips should be two inches wide and anywhere from three to five feet long. (Tear the strips when you can to save time, and sew the short pieces together to get the right lengths.)

Next, fold each strip's raw edges into the center, and then refold along the middle of the strips to hide those turned-under edges. If you do have a sewing machine, stitch the folds closed as you go, to make a permanent crease. If you don't own a machine, you will need to baste or iron the folds in place. Each strip will now be four plies thick, which will add strength and durability to the finished rug.

After that task is done, sort the strips by color into bags or boxes. You don't have to fuss too much over the design unless you want to, but even a random pattern will look sharper if a particular color (usually a dark one) is saved for the outer border. Set aside a small amount of another dark hue to form the center of the rug.

It is best to plan the design in advance. If you wish to make an oval rug, you'll have to decide its length and width before you start it, because those dimensions will dictate the shape of the central medallion that defines the shape of the rug. As a rule of thumb, the length of the center can be found by subtracting the proposed width of the rug from its length. A 2' X 3' rug, then, will need a foot-long center medallion, while a 3' X 5' rug will require 2 feet. A round rug, as you'll see, needs only a few inches of center braid.

Until you get the hang of four-strand braiding, don't attempt a really large rug. A 2' X 3' rug, which is a good size for your first project, requires three to four pounds of scraps.

To make the center medallion, choose three strips of cloth and sew them together at one end. Make sure that each of these pieces is a different length. Continue to vary the lengths as you sew strips onto those that are braided in, because three stitched connections if too close together will produce a weak spot in the rug.

While it is certainly possible to do the braiding by yourself, you'll find the going easier if you can persuade someone to hold the sewn ends while you braid (as you would hair) the center piece. Lacking a helper, weight the beginning end with a brick on floor or a table. With the sewn end held while you work, you'll produce a straighter, more even braid.

For an oval rug, make this central "rope" an inch longer than you determined by the length-minus-width formula above, as the end will have to turn back on it self when you begin to work on the next layer of rug. To start a round rug, just braid two or three inches, and fold this center braid over to form a "core."

When you have completed the center, sew a fourth cloth strip under the last crossover formed by the original three. This will give you the four strands that are needed for the interlocking method. Then, fasten a safety pin to use as a "needle" to the end of each strip.

If you're right-handed, hold the working end of the braid in your left hand (vice versa for southpaws), and fold back that extra inch so that the four strands lie side by side to the right of the braid.

Now, imagine that the strips are numbered one through four from right to left. Take strip No. 1 and "weave" it over strip No. 2, under strip No. 3, and over strip No. 4. Then, using the safety pin as a needle, pull strip No. 1 through the adjacent loop of the center braid. Strip No. 2 (the new "outside" strand) can then be woven over No. 3, under No. 4, over No. 1, and through the next loop of the center braid.

This process of weaving the outer strip over, under, and over the other three and then through the succeeding loop of the adjacent braid will continue (with some variations...see below) until the rug is finished. Keep sewing new strips to the unbraided ends as you go and remember to vary the lengths of these new strips to avoid weakening the rug.

Keep It Flat: Every time you round a corner, your rug will have a tendency to "pucker." To prevent this, braid more than one strip through each center braid loop as you round these turns. For example, on your first row around the ends of the center braid, you may have to weave through one loop five or six times. When you go around the same spot the next time, however, braiding twice through every other loop might be sufficient. It's nearly impossible to provide strict rules here, except that fewer of these "extra" passes through one loop will be necessary as the rug grows and the end-curves become less tight.

Keep your work on a level surface so you can keep the rug flat. Braid two or more strips through the same loop more often if the center starts to pucker. If the edges of the rug begin to look frilly, on the other hand, use fewer of these extra "corner" weaves. Expect to make a few mistakes until you get the proper feel for the corners.

Finally, when your rug is the right size, trim each strip to about an inch long, weave the tips under a loop, and stitch all of them in place.

That's all there is to it. After exhausting you own supply of old clothes and sewing scraps, scout out what garage sales, thrift shops, remnant counters, and neighbors have to offer. You'll have the satisfaction of recycling remnants into bright and colorful floor coverings that are durable, will go anywhere in the home, and are easy to make.

Color Your Hair Naturally

Many of us have the urge from time to time to change or enhance the color of our hair, perhaps to remove a few years by tinting the encroaching gray. But, some are reluctant to drive to town and spend half a day in a hair salon or pay the price for expensive over-the-counter products. Others are unwilling to use the harsh chemicals found in most commercial dyes and rinses.

Such folks will be glad to learn that you can quickly, safely, and inexpensively achieve results similar to those possible with beauty shop products. Just as women (men too) have done for thousands of years, you can change your basic hair color, put new highlights in your locks, or naturally darken gray strands...using safe, natural herbs.

Although there are a few especially potent exceptions such as henna and walnut hulls, most herbal dyes act progressively, and must be used repetitively over a period of time until the desired shade is achieved. While no herb is harsh enough to bleach your hair, there are plant-based colorants that will highlight, darken, lighten, or cover the gray.

Despite their versatility, herbal preparations cannot match the strength of commercial products, and unless you decide to dye your curls black, an organic rinse won't totally cover your present shade. The best idea is to enrich your natural color of your hair and avoid drastic changes such as turning blond tresses to a very deep shade or dyeing gray hair darker than it was originally. You should also keep in mind that herbal dyes aren't permanent and will fade unless renewed consistently.

If you've recently used commercial dyes, color rinses, or straighteners on your hair, you'd be wise to test any herbal mixture before applying it, since chemical residues make it impossible to predict the outcome of the natural treatment.

To perform the evaluation, save some snips of hair from your next trim or cut a lock from the nape of your neck and prepare a small amount of whatever recipe you intend to try. Following the instructions for that particular mixture, apply it to the sample of hair, rinse thoroughly, and let dry (in direct sunlight, if possible). Observe the result under strong natural light, and if you want more or less color, adjust the number of rinses and/or the timing accordingly. After a couple of trial runs, you should be able to produce the shade you want.

Here are several preparations that should serve as an introduction to herbal hair coloring. Though the possibilities are almost unlimited, these few formulas will allow you to produce some of the most frequently used natural rinses and dyes. No matter what shade your hair, you should be able to find something here that will give you safe, attractive results.

Chamomile is probably the most popular herbal hair colorant among blonds. A weekly rinse with this herb tea will brighten dull tresses and remedy the streaking that results from overexposure to the sun.

To prepare a chamomile rinse, steep half a cup of the flowers in a quart of boiling water for half an hour. Strain the mixture and let it cool while you shampoo. Then pour the brew through your towel-dried hair at least 15 times,

Growing Chamomile

The delightful heirloom herb chamomile has been grown for generations for its soothing effect on the nerves when brewed as an herbal tea, as a companion plant that benefits cucumbers, onions, and most other herb plants, and as a gold-tone rinse for the hair.

The German cultivars *Matricaria recutia* and *M. chamolilla* grow about 18" high with small daisy-like flowers. The Roman chamomile: *Anthemis noblis* is only 6" to 9" high with lacy foliage and all-gold flowers that makes a good ground cover—a lawn even if kept mowed. A double-flowered variant: *Chamaemelum nobile* flora-plenta is covered all summer with round white flowers that are used in potpourris.

It can be bought as seed or plants and is grown as an annual. The German variety self-seeds and regrows in the same spot year after year.

Start seed in growing medium indoors or in finely-sifted soil outdoors. Keep evenly moist until seed sprouts. It must have full daylight to germinate. Like most herbs, chamomile produces most aromatic oils and richest flavor in spare soil and full, hot sun. It needs moderate water and 80 days to harvest.

Chamomile spreads. In a small herb garden, each variety should be surrounded with edging to prevent one from taking over the space of another.

Harvest flowers when fully open. Dry on a screen in open air. When dry, store in a paper bag.

To make an infusion for tea, crush a heaping tablespoon of dry flower heads and steep in boiling water till desired color is attained.

Breathing the steam is beneficial for head and chest congestion. Tea has been used for centuries as a nerve-settling and calming concoction and to encourage sleep. ■

---

catching it in a basin between each rinse. Wring out the excess moisture and leave the solution in your hair for a quarter of an hour before rinsing your hair with clear water.

Don't limit your herbal experiments to chamomile, however. Just about any yellow-blossomed flower or herb can be used on blond hair, including calendula (pot marigold), mullein blooms and leaves, yellow broom flowers, saffron, turmeric, and quassia chips.

Lemon is also a time-honored hair lightener. Strained into a quart of water, the juice of two fruits makes an excellent rinse that can be used in the same way as the chamomile preparation. In order to get the most from the treatment's lightening effect, try to dry your hair in the sun after using a lemon rinse.

Another native dye favored by blonds and prepared from rhubarb root will also add attractive honey gold tones to light brown hair. To put those glints in your locks, pour three cups of hot water over four tablespoons of chopped rhubarb root and simmer the concoction for 20 minutes. Strain the liquid and pour it through your freshly shampooed hair 15 or more times. Rinse your hair in clear water and, weather permitting, dry it in the sun to strengthen the effect of the dyeing agent.

For more than 5,000 years, Egyptians have used a dark powder made from the henna shrub to give their hair and beards an auburn tint. Today you can buy henna powder at many herb supply houses and at some health food stores. It's known as a safe, healthful dye, and since it coats the cuticle layer of each strand, it'll make your hair feel thicker. However, be warned that henna tends to produce an almost brassy orange-red shade when used alone, so it's best to mix it with a lightening herb like chamomile. Since it is so strong, henna shouldn't be used at all on white, gray, or very light blond hair. Always try a timed test swatch first, too, to insure that you don't end up with an unexpectedly bizarre orange head.

One favorite recipe that can put reddish gold highlights in a dark mane calls for putting together one part of powdered chamomile and two parts of powdered henna water to make a thick paste. Then a tablespoon of vinegar is stirred in to help release the plants' colors, and the blend is cooled for a few minutes.

When the paste is lukewarm, put on a pair of rubber gloves (henna can stain your palms and fingernails) and massage it into your clean, wet hair. Comb it in with a wide-toothed comb to insure even distribution of the dye. Next, pile up your hair, fit a plastic bag over it, and wrap a heavy towel around your head to hold in the heat.

You'll need to leave the dye and towel turban in place for anywhere from 30 minutes to two hours: The darker your natural hair is, the longer you'll have to wait for the henna-chamomile to do its work. When the time is up, remove the towel and the bag, and rinse your hair until the water runs clean. Then allow the newly colored tresses to air dry, in the sunshine if possible. Any stains that the dye might leave on your hands or around your hairline can be removed by rubbing them with lemon juice.

Should you prefer a simpler, slower-acting procedure, make a weaker henna solution and use it as you would any of the previous color rinses. Mix together one tablespoon each of henna, chamomile, and vinegar, and steep them in a quart of boiling water for 15 minutes. Naturally, you should cool and strain the liquid before using it.

Sage is one of the oldest and most effective colorants for use on dark brown or black hair. A brew made from sage leaves can be used to deepen any brunette shade, and it will also effectively cover gray in dark hair.

A sage rinse can be made by steeping a handful of the dried herb in a quart of boiling water for 30 minutes or more. The longer it steeps, the darker the tint will be. Cool the tea, strain it, and pour it through freshly shampooed hair 15 or more times. Then wait ten minutes before washing the liquid out with clear water. Because a sage rinse is a progressive dye, you'll have to apply it weekly until you produce the shade you want and continue using it once a month or more frequently to maintain that color.

Tag alder bark is another popular hair-darkening botanical. However, it generally produces a lighter tone than sage, so it's best used to darken blond hair or to cover gray in locks that are light to medium brown. To make a tag alder rinse, simmer an ounce of bark chips in a quart of water for about half an hour. Then cool and strain the solution, and use it exactly as you would the sage rinse.

A very dark, sable-colored dye can be obtained from walnut husks, but this one is tricky, since the nuts' outer casings (also used to stain wood) tend to stain everything they touch. Because of this, it's a good idea to wear gloves throughout all the stages of the process and to avoid rubbing the mixture into your scalp. To prepare the dark juice, first crush the hulls in a mortar, cover them with boiling water and a pinch of salt, and let them soak for three days. Then add three cups of boiling water and simmer the hulls in a nonmetal container for five hours, replacing the water as it steams away. Strain off the liquid, place the walnut hulls in a cloth sack, and twist it tightly to wring out all remaining juice. Finally, return the liquid to the pot and reduce it by boiling to about a quarter of its original volume. This will be the base for a rich walnut dye.

Add a teaspoon of ground cloves or allspice to the prepared extract. Allow the dye mixture to steep in the refrigerator for about a week, shaking it periodically during that time. When it's ready for use, strain the liquid through a piece of cheesecloth and pour it at least 15 times through freshly washed hair before rinsing thoroughly.

By experimenting with these formulas, you'll be well on your way to achieving just about any hair shade you'd like without resorting to expensive, unsafe chemical dyes. You'll not only be saving money by using easily gathered materials, but you'll also be protecting the health of your hair.

Low-Cost Skin Care Products

You may be surprised to learn that there are safe, inexpensive, and readily available substitutes for many of the personal care products that you are accustomed to buying at cosmetics prices. These alternative preparations, many of which are household staples, will not be elaborately or expensively packaged as drugstore toiletries usually are, but have been demonstrating their usefulness for years.

Common cornstarch is a good substitute for talcum or bath powder, and it's especially valuable to those whose skins are sometimes irritated by the perfumes in commercial products. (In fact, a paste made of cornstarch and mineral oil is often used as a soothing mixture for dry skin.) You might also try patting on a thin layer of cornstarch the next time you need a colorless face powder to take the shine off your nose.

On those hectic days when your schedule calls for a quick dry shampoo, just sprinkle a generous amount of cornstarch into your hair, distribute it evenly, let it soak up the dirt and oil for a few minutes, and then vigorously brush it out.

It's commonly known that hydrogen peroxide is a fine first aid antiseptic for the treatment of minor cuts and abrasions, yet few people realize that this product can also serve as a mouthwash and gargle. Simply mix a teaspoonful in a glass of water and swish.

Rubbing alcohol is another useful product. Indeed, many store-bought astringents (also called toners, tonics, or fresheners) are usually half-and-half mixtures of alcohol and water. Besides saving money, you can reap an added benefit from preparing your own astringent: It's easy to adjust the proportion of water and thus control the solution's drying effect.

Many aftershave lotions are based on astringent formulas, too, so try an alcohol-water blend in place of your usual "bracer," fellows. If you prefer a scented astringent, just add one teaspoon of extract (vanilla, peppermint, almond, lemon, or what have you) to a pint of rubbing alcohol before adding the water.

Witch hazel, an alcoholic solution containing extract from the bark of the witch hazel bush, is another household product that can be diluted with an equal amount of water to make a pleasant astringent, or that may be used full strength as an aftershave.

An application of witch hazel will alleviate the pain of bruises, bites, stings, sunburn, and minor scalds: Splash it on freely, cover the area with a soft cloth, and keep the bandage saturated. A witch hazel rub can ease stiff muscles, though several applications may be necessary to bring about the desired results, and if you happen to stray into a patch of poison ivy, just make a paste of witch hazel and baking soda and spread it on the affected areas for quick relief.

Witch hazel can be a boon for tired eyes, too. Soak cotton pads in the cooling fluid and place them on your closed eyelids while taking a 10-minute rest.

For a sweet, clean scent, use it after shampooing as a hair-setting aid.

One of the most versatile home cosmetic ingredients is common mineral oil. If that lubricant seems too heavy, substitute a light vegetable oil: cottonseed, safflower (Canola), light corn, or refined olive.

Any of these can be used to replace a number of the oil-based products probably found in your bathroom. Baby oil, for example, is often no more than mineral oil with added scent, but you'll pay several times more for the leading brand of baby oil than you will for plain mineral oil!

Mineral or vegetable oils can also stand in for high priced bath oils and skin softeners. If you pour two or three tablespoonfuls into your tub, the beauty aid will float on top of the water and coat you with a fine, velvety film. If you'd prefer the oil and water to mix, combine 1/2 teaspoon of clear shampoo with 1/4 cup of mineral or vegetable oil and pour the mixture under the running tap.

Mineral oil can take the place of your cleansing lotion as well. Just smooth it on with your fingertips, wipe it off with cotton, and follow the application with a splash of astringent. It can be an especially gentle but effective eye makeup remover.

Many thrifty folks use vegetable oil to replace expensive hair conditioning treatments. (Mineral oil may affect the color of blond or gray hair.) Comb a small quantity of the natural lotion through your hair, keep your head wrapped in a very warm, moist towel for 30 minutes, and then shampoo thoroughly. (Another good conditioner, one which combines the benefits of oil and eggs, is mayonnaise. Spoon it directly onto your head, rub it in, wrap as instructed above, and wash the hair well.)

You can even soften whiskers by using mineral oil in place of regular shaving cream! If the oily residue bothers you after you've finished, a mild astringent will readily remove it. Apply a tiny amount of oil to your lips as a combination gloss and moisturizer. To make a lip salve, heat one part beeswax and six parts olive oil and pour the mix into a cleaned-out lipstick container. Put the tube in the refrigerator to harden the mix.

Baking soda (also called bicarbonate of soda) is another kitchen standby that can be utilized in any number of ways.

It works well as a tooth powder, used either plain or mixed half-and-half with salt. To make such a cleaner easy to dispense, put a supply in a small salt shaker. Soda also makes an effective mouthwash if you stir a teaspoon of the powder into a glass of water and gargle.

If your area is afflicted with hard water, you'll be glad to know that baking soda is a good substitute for bath salts. Pour two or three teaspoons under the running tap and enjoy.

Baking soda is a fine body deodorant, too. In fact, it's currently a primary ingredient in several commercially formulated deodorants. To apply it, just pour some in a shallow dish and pat it on with a powder puff or a piece of cotton.

To prepare a facial mask for oily skin, combine one tablespoon of baking soda with three tablespoons of unprocessed bran (an abrasive). Add just enough water to make a paste and apply the mixture to your face. Leave it on for 15 minutes, and then wash it off, using either lukewarm water or a weak astringent.

More and more people have begun to question the wisdom of paying exorbitantly for convenience, gimicky packaging, and excessive promotion. It's a step in the right direction to replace some of the overpriced, specialized preparations in your medicine chest and on your dressing table with a few basic ingredients that work safely and well and have a variety of uses.

Nature's Own Suntan Lotions

Most of us are aware that the sun's ultraviolet rays can harm your skin, especially if over exposure causes a serious burn. A gradual tanning routine is the best approach to sunbathing or achieving the inevitable tan that comes to those of us who farm, work outside, or garden during the summer. Sun blocking lotions are widely available, but are expensive; they wash off if you work up an honest sweat, and can give an outdoor worker a sense of overconfidence that can result in a worse burn than if they weren't used at all.

Your skin has a natural sun-protection system…that you can augment by increasing your consumption of vitamin C and the B vitamins, all of which are depleted when your body is regularly exposed to ultraviolet rays. Summer's delicious harvests of fresh cantaloupe, strawberries, tomatoes, green peppers, broccoli, and collard greens provide excellent sources of vitamin C, as do citrus fruits and juices. Foods rich in B vitamins include eggs, liver, poultry, wheat germ, unrefined cereals, milk, bananas, tuna, salmon, spinach, peas, and dried brewer's yeast.

Other natural protective aids in the form of lotions and salves are readily and economically available from your kitchen, bathroom cupboard, pharmacy, or health food store. When using them, as with all sun-care products, it's best to avoid application in the eye area.

Sesame oil is reportedly very effective against UV rays. Another natural suntan lotion can be made by peeling and mashing one large cucumber, straining the liquid through cheesecloth, and adding one teaspoon each of rose water and glycerin, both of which you can buy at your local pharmacy from a retail or mail order health food or natural-vitamin and food-supplement outlet.

For a minty suntan cream that's soothing and helpful while it soaks up the sun's rays, drop a handful of fresh mint leaves in a blender containing a couple of tablespoons of water. Add 1/2 cup of sesame or coconut oil, one egg yolk, and one tablespoon each of wheat germ oil and lemon juice. You might want to put in a drop of peppermint oil for extra fragrance before blending the ingredients. Keep this lotion refrigerated

When all precautions fail and you get a whale of a sunburn, there are many effective home remedies that can bring relief. Some folks find that if they break open vitamin E capsules and apply the oil to the skin, the burn will often disappear overnight. The same vitamin packaged in ointment form offers similar results. As alternatives, you might try applying sunflower, safflower, or cottonseed oil, all of which are rich in the healing nutrient.

Herbalists and natural beauty experts also recommend compresses made with tea from comfrey leaves or roots, black tea, or the juice of a grated raw potato for the treatment of painful sunburns. You can also dilute apple cider vinegar with water and pat it on the burned area or use it in a compress. A cloth or bandage that's kept saturated with witch hazel, or with equal parts of vinegar and olive oil, can also be beneficial.

Some additional homemade sunburn remedies include the following: sesame, peanut, corn, or some other vegetable or nut oil mixed with vinegar; a solution of equal parts of witch hazel, olive oil, and glycerin; the gel taken directly from the succulent leaves of the aloe Vera plant; a paste made of baking soda or laundry starch and water; a tub bath in water to which a cup of baking soda has been added; lemon juice and yogurt combined to a spreadable consistency; witch hazel mixed with a beaten egg white and honey; plain cucumber slices laid directly on the burn; and mashed cucumber pulp or juice strained through cheesecloth and used either alone or with witch hazel for a cool, soothing compress.

Finally, old-fashioned barley paste is recommended to soothe burn discomfort from the sun or other sources. To make the paste, grind or blend three ounces of barley and mix the powder with one ounce of raw honey. Blend the ingredients into a smooth paste and add one unbeaten egg white. Rub the concoction gently into the reddened skin and leave it on for several hours, preferably overnight, for slow but sure relief.

Fireside Fun with Folk Games

Anyone who grew up in the country before television remembers how rainy days and evenings could get pretty dull for the youngsters unless someone thought of playing a game.

A game! As if by magic the age difference between the grown-ups and children would melt away, and everyone would play together in a spirit of excitement and goodwill. Though competition would occasionally bring a few tears or brief temper fits among the smallest and huffing among those who were old enough to know better, the closeness and constant compromise created life-long good feelings.

Years may have passed, but when today's diet of passive, spectator activities starts to rankle and you feel restless and uninspired by the usual entertainment, remember what fun real participation can be! Try playing together as a family, the way you did years ago—and invite some kindred souls to share your evening of games and conversation.

Be choosy. The right game is important—especially during that most dreaded of times: bad weather on vacation with the kids! The most enjoyable fireside games are not the traditional card games or Monopoly-style board games where the objective is to win, win, win.

The best are really a type of folk recreation. More cooperative than competitive, they focus on the process rather than on the final outcome or score. All the players participate—often having to cooperate rather than compete—and the rewarding interaction just naturally produces smiles, friendly laughter, and

---

More Beanbag Projects

The cherry-pit pillow is a delightful modification of the beanbag: a fabric sheath stuffed with small but relatively weighty dry pellets that will roll over one another so as to conform to any shape, but that are heavy enough to retain shape and position.

Try making these variations:

Doorstop/Draft Reducer: Make a "sausage" of fabric stuffed with dry corn kernels. Cut a rectangle of sturdy cloth a foot wide and a yard long. Fold in half lengthwise. Stitch closed at one end and down the long edge. Turn inside out and fill loosely—don't pack tight—with dry, cleaned whole corn. Close open end with concealed-seam stitch. Use to hold door open or, when temperatures drop, place it snug against sill to keep out those wintry blasts.

Heat/Cold Collar: To relieve headaches, sore neck or shoulder, make a "sausage" as above, but 10" in width and 30" long. Use a softer fabric: velveteen or corduroy in a bright print. Fill with corn, packing tight enough the collar will bend easily into a "U" shape. Heat in low oven or chill in freezer and drape around your aching neck. Sitting in a high-backed overstuffed chair, you can press the back of your neck against the collar and move from side to side slightly to roll the kernels over one another under the cloth and give yourself a pleasant corn-kernel neck rub. ■

---

a positive feeling about oneself and the others involved. When several generations may be snowed in or rained out for days at a time, folks of all ages and abilities should be able to join in without feeling inept or embarrassed.

Choosing the right game is only one step; leading it is another. The role of host or hostess is very important. Without at least one person to think about the group as a whole, the action can fall flat. The leader needs to set the tone, lend encouragement to those who are shy, notice difficulties and attend to them, pay attention to the flow of activity, and be ready to step in with innovations or changes when needed. Remember to be flexible. If a game doesn't seem to be "going over," move on to another one.

The following games may sound mundane and even tedious when written down. Don't be fooled; they spring alive when played. Some favorites described below are mildly competitive (which is fine if the sides are balanced, the spirit is playful, and winning isn't the only goal), while others are of a wholly cooperative nature. All of them can be enjoyable.

Dots and Lines: Here is a two-person game for which you'll need only a piece of paper and two pencils. The paper should be prepared with a grid of 100 dots (10 X 10), and one dot—any will do—in the top row should be crossed out. The players take turns connecting any two adjoining dots with a straight line. You can draw lines vertically or horizontally. Along sides is okay. Diagonals aren't. Whenever someone completes a square, that player initials the box and is then entitled to draw another line. When the grid has been filled in, the player who has the most boxes wins.

Dictionary: This word-game (sometimes called "Fictionary"!) requires from four to eight people. You'll need a dictionary appropriate to the age group, and each player should have a pencil, several pieces of paper or a pad, and an active imagination.

To start, one person reads (out loud) through the dictionary for a really big word that's unfamiliar to everyone else. Without showing anyone, that individual writes the definition or a simplified version of it on a piece of paper while each of the other players makes up a definition and, keeping it hidden from the others, writes it down. All the "ballots" are then folded, collected, and placed in a hat.

Now, the player who chose the word from the dictionary draws out the papers and reads them aloud, one by one. Each of the other players makes a note of the definition that he or she thinks is correct. A tally is made of the choices, and if you want to keep score (although you may think it's just as much fun to play without scoring), a point may be given to every player who voted for the correct definition, and to any player whose incorrect definition got a vote from someone else (one point for each vote). Needless to say, if you're going to keep score, the player who selected the word in the first place can't vote on the definitions.

Progressive Story: Here is a good game to play while supper's settling. From three to eight people sit in a circle, each with a large sheet of paper and a pencil. To begin, each person starts a story by making up and writing down the answer to the question "When?" One phrase will do. This section is then folded under so it can't be seen, and each paper is passed to the person on the left. Next, each player continues the story by answering the question "Where?" The papers are again folded and passed to the left. Every time the papers are passed, the players answer another question: "Who?", "Did what?", "How?", "Why?", and "What's happened since then?" The real fun comes at the end, after you've passed your last contribution, when each person reads aloud a completed story. The results are delightful and often hilarious! One of the beauties of this game is that it can be played in the car or anywhere else.

In the Manner of the Word: This pantomime game can be played with as few as three or as many as twenty people. One person volunteers to be "It." He or she goes out of earshot while the other players choose a descriptive adverb, such as "smoothly." Upon returning, "It" asks a player to perform some action "in the manner of the (chosen) word": to shake hands, to put on a shoe, etc. "It" then tries to guess the adverb and may ask as many players as necessary to pantomime until "It" guesses correctly. The game is then repeated with another person being "It."

Jenkins Up: This game requires about a dozen people and a long table. Half the participants sit on one side of the table and half on the other, making two teams. Each team selects a captain.

One team is called the Spotters, and the other the Passers. The Spotters watch carefully while their opponents pass a quarter secretly from one to another under the table. When there has been plenty of time to pass the quarter, the captain of the Spotters calls out "Jenkins Up!" At this, the Passers close their fists tightly, put their elbows on the table, and in unison thump their elbows three times. On the fourth count, their hands come down hard and flat on the table, concealing the sound of the quarter hitting the table top. The captain of the Spotters, in consultation with his or her teammates, can either eliminate hands that don't have the quarter (leaving the hand with the quarter until last), or can "spot" by immediately identifying the hand with the coin. If the captain makes a wrong call, the game is lost, and the original Passers get to pass again. If the Spotters are correct, the game's won, the quarter changes sides, and the office of captain is given to another member of each team. Jenkins Up is particularly good as a leveler, making differences in age and ability unimportant.

I'm Thinking of a Word That Rhymes With...: Anywhere from eight to thirty people can play this one. All are seated in a circle, with one player as "It." This person thinks of a one-syllable word, such as "plow," and says aloud to the group, "I'm thinking of a word that rhymes with 'cow' (or any other appropriate rhyme). The group must now identify the secret word, but the guessers are not allowed to speak and must use dramatic action instead.

Any player who wants to guess raises a hand and, when called upon by "It," acts out the word. If "It" recognizes the pantomimed guess as being incorrect, "It" says for example"No, it isn't 'sow' " (or what ever). If "It" doesn't recognize what the mime is trying to "say," other players can help the actor with additional dramatizations (confirming in whispers that they've correctly identified the guess) until "It" finally determines the word.

The game has a two-part objective: The players must guess the word "It" has chosen, and "It" must understand the players' guesses. If someone identifies the word correctly, that player becomes "It" for the next round. Of course, if a reasonable length of time has passed and "It" still hasn't guessed the players' actions (or if they haven't guessed the word in question), common sense dictates that the word be revealed aloud and the game be continued with another word!

Actually, there are many similarly enjoyable pastimes based on informal dramatics, from the simple guessing game of Pretend (you're a fairy princess, an auto mechanic, a gardener, or whatever) to Charades with its array of hand signal clues. Of all recreational activities, these games combine some of the most exciting and satisfying elements of cooperative play.

The Bean Game: Start this contest by giving each player 10 or so dry beans (any number is satisfactory, so long as participants start with the same amount). The object of the game is to see who can acquire the most beans in a given length of time—say, 10 or 15 minutes. The game can also be played until someone gets all the beans, but this can make the game longer and less exciting.

A group may prefer to play the Bean Game while seated around a table, so each cache of seeds can be manipulated undercover. The transfer of treasure takes place in the following manner: Player A holds any number (or all) of his share, in a closed right hand, and shows this fist to player B. Player B must then make a guess as to how many beans are in that fist. If player B guesses correctly, he or she receives the beans in question, but an incorrect guess results in player B giving the number of beans guessed to player A. Regardless of the action, player B then goes on to hold out a fist of beans to player C, and the process is repeated around the table, with the last person turning to player A.

The direction of play can continue the same way until the game ends, or it can be reversed with each round to add variety. The rules are flexible; just be sure to define them before the game begins.

An interesting offshoot is Build a Machine, a group effort that can be enjoyed many times with both children and adults. You'll need about 10 people. Draw numbers from a hat or "count off' into groups of three or four. Each group goes off to a separate corner or room and decides on a machine to portray together, using their bodies for the parts. Each machine is then acted out in front of the other groups. Guessing the identity of the machine is as much fun as acting, and a clock will never be just a clock again, once you've been the pendulum!

After such a gathering, participants often feel as if something significant has happened, and indeed it has. Cooperative games have been refined over the years to a beautiful and deeply human simplicity, cutting across centuries and cultures to appeal to something basic in all of us. They are strengthening and positive: Someone may feel beset by problems, but after such activities, that person gains a sense of hope and enthusiasm generated by the spontaneous fun and joy that's been shared. This kind of play with one's fellow humans is pleasurable and nourishing to the spirit, and all participants are able to experience a special sense of triumph.

CHAPTER 10

3~

Out In
The Community

Bargains at a Farm Auction

"Sold!" bellowed the auctioneer, "to the man in the blue jacket for $8. And that, sir, is one fine bargain."

The item purchased by the fellow in blue was a pretty fair buy. For his $8 he got a used, but perfectly serviceable, pitchfork—an old-time farm tool of better quality than he could have gotten for several times that much in a store.

And there's no reason why anyone else couldn't duplicate (or better) this luck. The next time you decide to buy almost any kind of homestead equipment, try visiting a local farm auction. You too might well latch onto a really first-rate bargain.

If you don't know what you're doing, however, you can drive away from your first farm auction with a truck load of trash, and you might even pay more for a used article than you would for the self-same item brand new in a store. There's a real danger of catching "auction fever," an uncontrollable urge to pay too much for something you don't really want or need as a result of getting caught up in the excitement of the moment.

At an an auction, goods are spread out on tables, on the lawn, or around the barnyard where they can be examined—and in the case of powered equipment, started and run—by potential buyers. Bidding begins promptly at the advertised time: after supper on workdays, as early as they can get up a crowd on Saturday mornings, and after church (in small country towns) on sunny summer Sundays.

Buyers gather around the auctioneer who is usually a friendly and flamboyant individual, but who nonetheless is a shrewd business person, long in the trade, and must be licensed to collect state and local sales taxes. From a raised dias or standing in a tractor footwell or on a wagon bed, the auctioneer will present each item and its opening price, then rattle off price rises with the familiar running banter between bid, pointing at each bidder till a certain time goes by without a new bid. Then, you hear the call " Sold…at $20 to the lady with the white hat by the post on my right".

Most auctions are cash-on-the-barrel for casual customers; some accept credit cards or checks on local banks if you have photo IDs. Auction regulars or dealers may have a charge account with the auction company. For big-ticket items—especially when a bank property-foreclosure or FHA or other government agency is involved—you must have a cashiers check for a certain percentage then and there, and pay the balance in a given time.

Items at an auction can come from anywhere: from the owner of the items or of property where the auction is held, from the auctioneer's own firm, from other dealers, or from concessionaires. All must agree (in writing at a large affair) that the auctioneer will take payment, then remit to the owner a given percentage of the cash received in-hand (or once a check clears) for each item, or they may agree on another lump-sum, escalating percentage, or other arrangements. The fee can range from a thin dime to 90% of a disappointing sale. If bidding takes experience, its nothing compared to dickering with an experienced auctioneer who is selling off your great-aunt's spoon collection. Keep your wallet inside your shirt and your shirt buttoned up to the chin, or you can lose them both.

Learning the Lingo: Like the law, medicine, and most other organized activities, auctions have a peculiar set of terms with which the beginner should become acquainted. ("Auction" itself is derived from the Latin word *auctionem*, a process by which Roman soldiers bought captured booty on the battlefield by topping each other's offers for the plunder.) Once you've cracked the code, you'll be able to follow the fast-moving auction action with ease.

A "bid" is the amount you offer to pay for the merchandise, and "increments" are sequential jumps in price. There's usually a round-number minimum jump of 10% or so.

"Opening bid" refers to the sum at which the offers start. Sometimes the opener is set by the auctioneer; sometimes it comes from the crowd—including paid "ringers" who start high and keep the bidding going to raise excitement but quit just before the price reaches a peak.

Just how high the initial sum should be is often a source of great debate among auction buffs. Some bidders prefer to open low, hoping that buyer interest will be minimal so they can waltz away with the object for a song. Others—especially those who are really keen on owning a particular item—

will start a little high to discourage rival buyers. Still others believe it's best not to bid at all until the action slows down a bit toward the end.

A "lot" is a number of pieces that are sold as a unit, such as a set of dishes or a matched pair of chairs. "Knocked down" is the auctioneer's term for "sold." For example, "That table was knocked down at $30." A "reserve" is the lowest price the owner will accept for an article. While most farm auctions will not include a great number of reserve items, an expensive piece of farm machinery or the like may have a reserve price, and a conscientious auctioneer will generally tell you so before the bidding starts. "As is" means that you're buying the object complete with nicks, cracks, burned-out motor, and all.

Many auctions assign buyer's numbers. To obtain one, you simply register with the event's secretary, who will give you a card with a number that's recorded each time you "bid in" an item. This simplifies bookkeeping, since the secretary can then run a tab for your purchases, and you can settle your bill when you leave. Buyer's numbers also provide bidders with a certain anonymity. Often the number is printed on a large lapel sign or a paddle you wave to indicate or confirm a bid.

Helpful Hints: While you're learning "auctionese," you'll also be gaining assurance in your ability to recognize, and bid on, bargains. The following list of tips should help a novice avoid misunderstandings and expensive mistakes.

[1] Before the auction, read the "sale bills," which are long and detailed, small-print ads in local newspapers, or fliers that describe the merchandise being offered. By doing so, you'll know which things you're interested in and be able to check their retail prices. At the same time, you should note the terms of the sale and work out your own financial arrangements.

[2] Thoroughly inspect any merchandise you want to bid on prior to the opening of the auction. Arrive early enough (or attend the preview day if the goods are exhibited to the public beforehand) to pore over the loot. You should, for example, plug in electrical appliances to see if they work, crank the handles of mechanical items to make sure the gears aren't frozen, and check bureaus or chests for missing or mismatched hardware.

[3] Make a list of the items you want and stick to it to avoid compulsive buying (if you can). Many auctions place convenient little number stickers on each article or lot, and these are announced as the objects are put up for sale. Jot down the numbers of any goods you're interested in, with a brief description of each and the maximum you're willing to pay for the privilege of owning it.

[4] Antique books, knowledgeable friends, and comparison-shopping at used goods and antique stores can help you find out what an object is worth. If you've done your homework, you won't get so carried away that you pay more for a broken-handled pitchfork than you would for a new one. On the other hand, don't let the fact that an article is used affect your judgment. You

can find real bargains in merchandise whose only fault is that its owner no longer needs it.

[5] Know how you're bidding. Suppose there are four chairs in a lot: Is the auctioneer selling them one at a time or all four at once? If the sale is announced as "one money," you're bidding on all four chairs. "Times the money" means that you're bidding the price of one chair, and if the lot is knocked down to you, you'll get all four chairs at four times your final bid. "Choice of chairs" means that your winning bid will buy you first pick among the four. (Most auctioneers will then let you or anyone else in the audience take any or all of the remaining chairs for the same price, but if there's no interest, the bidding starts anew.)

[6] Be sure you understand the spiel. As a good auctioneer chants in a singsong, he or she is telling you what's being sold and how, plus both the current bid and the price that's being sought. Listen carefully until you're certain you're following the action. It's a shock to find out you bought a hammer for $12.50 when you thought the bid was $2.50.

[7] Stop the show if you have a question. An honest auctioneer won't object.

[8] Secure your goods. As soon as the auctioneer says "sold" and hands over the merchandise, it's your responsibility. One of the biggest problems at auctions is thievery. Watch your goods. Or lock them in a theft-proof locker or alarm-equipped vehicle.

[9] If you go with friends, stay together and decide—in advance—who'll do the bidding on which items. It can be embarrassing to discover that the "stubborn pest" in the back who keeps topping your offer is your spouse.

[10] Watch your hands. You've likely heard the horror stories about auction-goers waving at a friend and suddenly finding themselves the proud owners of a moose head. While some such tales are so old they ought to have whiskers, it is probably safest to control your hand movements until an auctioneer becomes familiar with your bidding mannerisms.

[11] Fit your pickup truck with a lockable, alarm-fitted cap. As mentioned before, your new property is your responsibility, and auctions often aren't equipped to hold the merchandise until you can pick it up. If you have plenty of room to stash and transport your goods, you'll also avoid paying hauling charges, which can add considerably to "bargain" prices.

Farm auctions are far more than just sales. They're social gatherings. There's no better place to spend a leisurely day in the country or to get an education in old-time comparative shopping than at a rural auction. Many offer delicious homemade meals and baked goods and fresh produce to take home. And while you're stuffing on homemade K'lbasa and kraut and learning the auction business, you just may walk away with the "bargain of a lifetime."

Set Out a Country-Plain Mailbox

When you move into your new country place, the first thing most of your new neighbors will see of you is the rural route mailbox you set out at the foot of your drive. What it looks like and how well it is set in place will tell a lot more about you than you may realize.

If you try and get by with the battered, rusty old wreck of a mailbox that comes with many old country places, the locals may admire your frugality. But the postal driver won't (and, there's nobody who can pass around a less-than-favorable impression of a newcomer better than the mail driver).

Setting out one of those fancy boxes—fiberglass with game animals on them or conventional tin with cows or other country-cute images painted on—may get you branded as a show off.

Your best bet is a standard tin box on a competently built wood-post stand. You can buy mailbox stands of wood or

(continued on page 276)

A mailbox for snow country

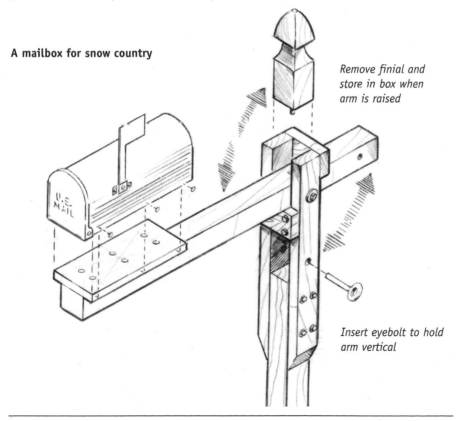

Remove finial and store in box when arm is raised

Insert eyebolt to hold arm vertical

metal, but you'll get more respect if you build your own from scratch. Introduce yourself to the driver first chance you get and ask which side of the road the box goes on, how high it should be, and what kind of post is best for the local weather conditions. Ask if you have a number to be painted on the front of the box and which side your name should be printed (in the largest, easiest-to-see letters you can manage.) The name is so that substitute mail drivers, the UPS driver, and first-time visitors can find your place.

The post can be sunk into the berm or set into a 5- or 10-gallon plastic tub that is filled with concrete or stones. A tub-mount is probably best until the box finds its own place along the road side...as a movable post can be hit by a cordwood truck cutting the corner too close and not break off. Be sure to punch a good-sized hole in the bottom of the tub so that rain water will drain out and not fill to harbor mosquitoes in summer or freeze and crack the tub in winter. ■

Swapping Your Way to a Great Vacation

We all need a respite now and then, but taking a vacation most often means scrimping and saving to meet the expenses of room, board, and travel while away from home. However, by living lean, negotiating trades, and turning a vacation into an adventure, it's entirely possible to make that break from routine not only pay for itself but be profitable and fun as well.

A Canadian couple with two small children had their summers free (of both work and income), as one was a teacher and the other finishing up graduate school. Cash was short, so they decided to swap the use of their apartment in a coastal university town for a big old two-ton truck, and spend the summer camping and following the crops in the agricultural Okanagan and Similkameen valleys of British Columbia—the healthy and carefree way they'd spent summers when in college.

With an open-minded spirit of of adventure, hard trading, and plenty of welcome physical activity, they managed to exchange enough labor and produce earned in-lieu-of-cash to support themselves and their kids for an entire three months—and they actually came out money ahead.

A college friend had taken up organic farming in the valley, and they arranged to help him with summer work in return for parking and tent space plus water from the house and a reduced price on produce at harvest time. They also agreed to bring him a load of seaweed for fertilizer when they came in from the coast—where the trace-nutrient-rich algae is storm-tossed on the shore, and freely available to anyone willing to gather it.

Foraging and "beachcombing" along the shore was a favorite pastime for the young family. They all pitched in (literally) and began toning their muscles for the summer's work by filling the truck with repeated loads of wave-shredded giant kelp, eelgrass, rockweed, and dozens of other varieties of algae—all of it heavy (99% sea water) and seasoned, so to speak, with sand, shell particles, fine-wood debris, and (sadly) plastic refuse that was picked out and recycled. They spread the kelp out to dry in the sun and be washed by rain (their farmer-friend felt that fresh seaweed is too salty for use as fertilizer). Turning it to dry like hay, they eventually had most of a truckload of choice, dry, nutrient-rich fertilizer to take to their farming friend.

When the couple, their just 6-year-old son and 3-year-old daughter arrived at the farm, they found their friend way behind in his hoeing. The grass, pigweed, and nightshade were choking his soybeans, squash, corn, and tomatoes so badly that he couldn't keep up with it by himself. He immediately offered them a credit of $8.00 per hour to hoe his fields for him. This was all the excuse they needed to pick up their tools and get to work.

After gently prodding their pal with, "How long have we been hoeing so far?" and "What d'ya think the kids' work is worth?" the couple came right out and asked whether they could swap the whole family's efforts for produce rather than cash money. Further bargaining resulted in a deal that was satisfactory all around: The family would keep certain fields hoed clean during the fast weed growth of early summer and be paid in September with twenty 40-pound boxes of tomatoes.

Then came the question of the seaweed. "What do you figure all that fertilizer's worth?" the farmer asked.

"Well, " said the husband, "we've put so much love and labor into the weed that it's beyond price, so we'll just have to give it to you."

The farmer chuckled. "You know, that's exactly how I feel about my vegetables. So while you're here, you just take all you can eat."

With this informal trade, the farmer got quality fertilizer for his land and many hours of quality labor, and the family wound up with as many onions, new red potatoes, cucumbers, kohlrabi, and ears of sweet corn as they could eat as well as a truck load of fresh tomatoes to sell or barter in town later in the year.

Next, they discovered eight damaged fruit ladders ranging from 8 to 18 feet long in an old ladder-and-bucket shed—left over from when the farm was an orchard. After a quick huddle with the farmer, they had another deal. Using the tools they'd brought along plus scraps of lumber and odd hardware from the farmer's shed, it took the couple only a day or two to put all the ladders back into prime condition. The farmer selected four for himself, and the couple kept the others and a good supply of picking buckets equipped with rung hooks.

The equipment was most useful too. Later in the summer, when negotiating to earn cash by picking fruit for local orchards, they could say, "We have our own ladders and buckets." And they'd get the job.

Both the farmer-host and our vacationing family liked to dry fruits and vegetables. The farmer had an unused plastic-covered dome-greenhouse that proved to warm up fast when it was set out in the summer sun. So the vacationers arranged a third deal: Their friend would provide screening, a staple gun, and free access to his scrap lumber pile, and they would construct eight drying racks covered with fine fiberglass screening. Then everyone would share the use of these frames.

After they'd built the racks and dried some early cherries on them, the couple didn't feel that they had really come out even on the exchange. As luck would have it, this imbalance was corrected at a later date.

The family moved on—following the crops—and after picking in different orchards, they ended up with 1,200 pounds of cherries and 1,000 pounds of apricots and peaches to take home as a supplement to cash wages. These were trucked to the city and sold at a farmer's market.

Another time, as they were driving to a new job at three o'clock in the morning, the tractor-trailer truck just ahead began to rain 50-pound sacks of chicken feed along the freeway. They flashed the trucker, who stopped in time to save most of his load. While the kids slept, the husband helped reload the sound feed sacks. In return, the trucker let him keep the sacks that were split.

In no time they found a homesteading family that could use the feed. However, the homesteaders' hens weren't laying many eggs at the time, and their goats weren't giving much milk, so the travelers gave them the feed, with the promise of "whatever" in return at a later date. They stopped over on the way home at season's end. That feed had given the homesteaders a boost just when they needed it, and when the family went on their way the next morning, they carried four beautiful rounds of goat-milk cheese. Plus, they swapped winter squash for enough fresh eggs to last a month.

After their summer of traveling and trading, the family returned to their first stop, only to find their farming friend burdened with a field of luscious, ripe, organically-grown tomatoes that he couldn't sell. The local market was glutted, and those tomatoes wouldn't sell at even a few cents a pound. Yet, 200 miles away, over the mountains, lay the city of Vancouver, where people were paying dollars a pound for tomatoes of poor quality shipped all the way from Mexico.

The couple's truck was the answer. So, after agreeing to split whatever proceeds might eventuate, they all spent the next three days picking and packing tomatoes. Then, the husband started for the coast with nearly 4,000 pounds of perfect fruit and high expectations.

Ten days later he returned, dejected. It had been the sort of disaster we all experience now and then—where people don't keep their promises and containers unaccountably collapse; where market-opening hours and vender fees and ferry ticket-takers and food co-op buyers all seem to conspire against you; where nothing goes as planned. The husband had sold tomatoes, traded tomatoes, dumped tomatoes on friends' doorsteps. He'd thrown away rotten ones, and had even taken the time to return to their apartment and can 400 pounds of the pulpy fruit before it spoiled.

He was able to give the farmer enough cash to cover the value of the goods that survived the journey. Still, the family had not only failed to make wages on the deal; they'd actually lost money. Their friend had accepted the risk of this venture along with them, however, and he compensated their loss with an 800-pound field of acorn squash on the vine.

During the husband's absence, the wife and children had begun drying and pressure-canning the twenty 40-pound crates of tomatoes they received as part of their early-season hoeing swap. They continued to work on the fruit for more than a week, cutting off tops and bottoms of the juice-filled tomatoes to cook and bottle as sauce, and slicing the meaty centers into thin wheels, which after four days on the drying racks under the dome became tissue-thin slivers of potent flavor. It was then that the drying-racks swap finally balanced out.

By the time they'd finished with the tomatoes, it was late-season grape-picking season, so they bade farewell again to their friend on the farm and headed for a vineyard, where the owner allowed them to camp on his property in exchange for helping with harvest. In addition, they dickered a deal to keep a pound of grapes for every 15 pounds they harvested.

Grape picking is interesting work. You get to eat a lot of the sugary-tart little fruits (which slows you down), you quickly develop purple hands, and occasionally get buzzed off by the yellow jackets that seem to savor grapes, too.

The "vacationers" continued to barter for things they needed. They discovered that the vineyard owner had a number of old plastic crates. Designed to stack, and invaluable for shipping wine grapes, they were now cracked and too weak to be reliable. But the husband mended 10 of them with a drill and scraps of thin wire. The owner was so pleased that he gave them five of the handy containers as payment for the work.

About this time, they decided to begin packing up for for home. They already had more squash, bottled tomatoes, fresh tomatoes, corn, onions, cull plums, and cull apples than they knew what to do with, and some of the grapes they'd harvested for themselves were wilting. So, borrowing the owner's grape press, the family pressed 500 pounds of muscats and gave the mash (the pulp left over from the pressing) to the vineyard owner for "second wine."

Print Your Own Money

Barter is mankind's oldest (friendly) way of exchanging goods and services without having to exchange cash. And it is coming back in many communities—rural areas in particular, where money of any sort is hard to come by. Staffers from *Mother Earth News* visited one example of a thriving community barter-exchange in Ithaca, New York.

The currency is a "scrip"—a private paper currency denoted in HOURS—one hour of honest work, valued locally at an average of $20. Notes of 1/4, 1/2, 1, and 2 hours bannering the slogan "In Ithaca We Trust" were printed at a local shop and distributed among cooperating members of an association established by some of the same community-minded individuals who founded the weekly Farmers' Market. Negotiating values among themselves, members may exchange garden produce for clothing,

mechanic's skills for a fine meal at a local restaurant, or trucking services for legal advice. All is paid by exchanging Hours. Like conventional currency, Hours remain in circulation—but cannot be saved or used outside the town. Sales tax is due on commercial goods and services exchanged, and income tax is due on gains made in commerce. Payment is up to the individual.

Here is how to go about setting up a local currency-based barter exchange in your own community.

First, determine if there is a body of supporters who are more interested in establishing a community economy based on real value rather than advertising, middlemen, and salesmanship. As one Ithaca resident observed, "You've got a lot of old hippies here."

Gather a core group of supporters

(continued on page 281)

In the meantime, the family realized that they had kept a crate or two grapes more than they'd earned. The owner at first agreed that they could make this up the following year, but before they left he came beaming to their truck to say that the muscat mash they'd given him was well worth the overrun. Thus, the accounts were balanced after all.

As the family departed the Similkameen Valley, truck groaning with tent, tools, and late-season produce, yet another exchange occurred when they stopped overnight at a hostel. There they happily traded plums, tomatoes, and one crate of grapes for their supper and breakfast.

And finally upon arriving home, they still had an abundance of grapes and

you can count on to distribute flyers, drive when needed, and provide small amounts of financial help if needed.

After organizing the cooperative:

1. Design a currency that is entirely different in size, color, and design from legal tender.
2. Show it around town—to individuals and businesses. Say that they get to set their own values; all the association does is maintain the exchange medium. Each member gets a starting amount of scrip, and pays a small fee to print the cash.
3. Design a newsletter identifying participants.
4. Sell ads (for legal tender...to pay for paper and printing.)
5. Print the bills (Ithaca's are printed on local cattail paper with soy ink.) Use bright colors, and consecutively serial-number bills.
6. Print first issue of the newsletter and distribute to participants with their first supply of money.
7. Distribute newsletter to the public to generate more memberships.
8. Promote the plan in all local media.
9. Keep in touch.

Periodic meetings (potluck suppers are good) must be held for participants to air problems and resolve differences. In this sense, the system is an exercise in economic democracy.

The Ithaca program exists in part to empower the economically disadvantaged. If your group shares the goal, they should discuss ways to distribute currency where it would do the most good. Remember, the currency has no value in itself. It is a testament of commitment of neighbor to neighbor—a tangible affirmation of community and our essential interdependence. ∎

---

squash that could be traded for other food stuffs or any number of other items or services.

"What a summer of hard work!" their friends exclaimed when told about the trip. Well, it was hard. But it was also a fun-filled adventure. They returned tanned, healthy, and fit, and they had their children right there with them all the time, learning at a tender age the value of real work. The whole family had made many friends and experienced first hand the tremendous effort and care that it took to produce the food they enjoyed in such abundance.

Bargains Through Barter

For kids, bartering has always been a way to acquire the treasured things of life. What child hasn't swapped school lunch, comic books, or broken a parent's heart by trading an expensive toy for a half-dead frog, a cat's-eye boulder marble, or a broken slingshot? Bartering was abandoned by most of us when we entered the grade-school-age world of high finance, where lucrative lawn-mowing jobs paid actual, instant, no-dickering-about-it dollars. From then on, the importance of the green stuff probably exerted a powerful influence on our lives, inflicting us with the stress, tension, and headaches that go with surviving in a cash-oriented society. However, recession, inflation and hard times have forced folks to seek ways to reduce their living expenses, and a number are reverting to yesteryear's methods, bartering goods and services with friends and neighbors.

For the past few years, a farmer has swapped cash for barter to obtain essentials and nonessentials of life on his 150-acre farm. By using the bartering process, his need for ready cash for ordinary food items and small services has diminished, and he has been able to channel the cash he does receive back into the farming operation. Plus the fun of bartering has relieved some of the everyday financial pressures associated with running a business.

Anyone can barter; it's an acquired attitude toward commerce. This man started bartering after planting two acres of strawberries that he planned to sell on a pick-your-own basis. A neighboring woman who lived on a dairy farm spied them, and the two struck a bargain. For every four cases of his strawberries, her family would manure one acre of his land. This exchange cut his fertilizer bill in half. Later he bartered strawberries for other foodstuffs and for such services as tailoring, knife sharpening, equipment repair, and seasonal promotion spots on the radio. He even traded strawberries for the glass used in a new greenhouse on his property.

That was the start of his produce business.

The barterer expanded his pick-your-own operation by putting in melons, and there was the inevitable surplus—ordinarily let rot in the field. Another farming neighbor wanted the waste to supplement his hogs' diet and offered in return to dress a pig at butchering time for the melon-grower's freezer. Later, the same farmer agreed to roast the pig to be served at a harvest dinner if he could invite a set number of his friends. The greenhouse owner furnished the side dishes and derived a fair amount of free publicity for his fruit farm by inviting people who were in positions to spread the word about his own business ventures.

On another occasion, the bartering entrepreneur hosted a party for 300 guests by swapping various types of publicity. The chamber of commerce in a nearby town approached him about using his farm as the scene of a party for television, radio, and newspaper personalities from across the state with the purpose of obtaining publicity for area attractions.

The money provided for the party by the chamber of commerce was enough to cover only the meat and drinks. The host proceeded to swap promotional exposure at the affair for added goods and services. For example, he asked the chef/owner of a local restaurant to cook rounds of beef (provided by the chamber) over a roasting pit dug at the farm. In return, the restaurateur would get a sign on the skewer, promoting his business. Next, the barterer called a tent rental company and offered similar advertising in exchange for a large open tent. A square dance group and band were offered free food and television coverage of their performance. The dauntless barterer did the same for a skydiving club that added a bit of unplanned (and un-hoped-for) sensationalism when one of the divers landed wrong and broke his leg—requiring a visit from the local volunteer ambulance company (whose members were encouraged to take the occasion to solicit contributions).

A longtime friend who operated a beer distributorship was persuaded to contribute the fireworks for the mere privilege of setting them off. (Appealing to a person's sense of adventure is important in the bartering business.)

Money Saved is Money Earned: Bartering on many levels has cut the labor costs for this farm by nearly 50%. By offering a pay-package of $3.00 an hour and all the vegetables and fruit their families want, the owner is able to attract a crew of teenagers who give him all the help he can use. An adult worker who comes out during harvest time trades a day's labor in return for melons, and a neighbor cans an entire winter supply of fruits and vegetables for the farmer in return for the produce she needs to put up for her own family.

The farm includes a 50-acre woodlot, which has proven a gold mine for barter. With the returning popularity of woodburning stoves, wood is in great demand, and it can be traded for almost anything. The next-door neighbor who raises hogs traded another pig for permission to cut two cords from the woodlot. The farmer bartered the extra pork with a dairy/organic beef operation for a side of beef for the freezer. They also swapped garden produce and melons for eggs and milk.

An average family can employ similar bartering techniques on as little as an acre or two by planting cash crops. Good crops for barter are pickling cucumbers, tomatoes in canning quantity, green peppers, and green beans. Field-ripened melons have a special appeal because supermarket varieties are usually picked green, to ripen during shipping, so they are less flavorful. Many kinds of berries are also especially sought-after during their brief seasons.

Services can be bartered as well, especially in urban areas. Any special skill or hobby constitutes a tradable commodity. One might barter culinary or sewing talents for babysitting or hairdressing expertise. Woodworking skills can be exchanged for produce or labor of another kind. If you own a welder and know how to use it, you may find yourself turning away swaps for lack of time.

As more and more people become interested, trading networks can be established in neighborhoods and rural areas for the benefit of everyone involved. Some groups place equivalent values on services and goods and print up "scrip"—coupons representing equivalent cash value that members can accumulate and swap for goods or services at a future date.

You may find that the quality of services and goods received in barter will be better than that of commercially purchased vendibles. It's a pleasantly curious thing, too. For instance, if you barter produce, you will notice that most people will readily barter for fresh produce at a higher value than they would pay at a supermarket, because of the assured quality and good condition of the homegrown foods.

The law of averages dictates that some swaps won't work out as well as you would like. Not every bartering deal turns out. To wit, the case of the red union suit.

A department store asked our bartering farmer to model for a newspaper ad touting a new shipment of red union suits—the genuine old-time article equipped with a rear trapdoor. The model alleges that the mid-February wind was as cold as a well-digger's destination when he posed out in in the snow, and the trapdoor admitted enough wind-chill that he was frost-bit in a sensitive region of his anatomy. For completing his end of the bargain, he got a plug in the ad (for his farm) and two sets of the scarlet long johns.

After spending a month recovering, this big-time barterer had to admit that he could have easily bought a dozen union suits and a month of ads for much less than he paid in doctors' bills. He offers these words of caution to beginning barterers: Be careful what you bargain for. You just may get that and more!

Despite that caveat, bartering can provide important intangibles. A swap that makes both parties happy establishes a special relationship. The goodwill generated by such a transaction can have far-reaching consequences. As other people learn that there is someone nearby with a willingness to barter, many will initiate contact and suggest working out a deal. And everybody has something to trade. "One person's trash is another one's treasure" as the old saying goes.

Use your imagination and above all, be flexible. No swap is exactly like any other. Enjoy your interactions with other people. Approached in the proper spirit, this age-old practice can give you a great deal of pleasure and many of the material goods and services you need.

Country Fairs

There is nothing more fun for a new country arrival than to discover that uniquely North American version of the traditional Harvest Festival: the fairs that take place at town, county, state, and provincial levels in late summer and early fall.

The town fair may last only a weekend, but it is sure to feature a softball game between the volunteer fire departments of your town and the next one down the mountain, plus a dunking chair where a well-aimed $1 toss will land the school principal in the drink—all to augment the school budget and elicit delighted howls from the assembled student body.

County fairs can go on for a week and state-wide events for a month. With a little driving, many families can spend weekends from August through Thanksgiving…not vegging out on fattening fast foods in front of the tube watching football games…but participating in the definition of good, clean family fun: A Country Fair.

These festive gatherings usually feature a carnival with booth games, a side show, a fairway with rides, and food booths. Some larger fairs will have a circus. Others exhibit the new auto models or have home and garden shows during their run.

You'll often be treated to fiddling contests, folk dancing, and concerts by local and touring professional musicians—most of them country and western or bluegrass groups and solo artists, and in many areas, there'll be a nightly barn dance under the big tent or, weather permitting, under the stars in the racecourse infield. And, there's still a place at most fairs for light-hearted competitions in hog-calling, mud rasseling, frog-jumping, corn husking, hoo-rawing, golly-whomping, and raising the roof in general.

Most feature exhibitions of speed and power. Animals compete in ox-pulls, draft horse-pulls, and horse races (trotters or thoroughbreds—often with pari-mutuel wagering). In the West, rodeo events are featured. In the Northern lumber-jack country, log-rolling, timber-chopping, and pole-tosses are favorite competitions.

The infernal combustion engine cheerily renders most every evening at the fair loud and noxious. Midget racers of various classifications, stock cars, and trucks race the dirt oval. A demolition derby/mud wallow featuring the local gear heads and their "expendable" junkers is a favorite with the lads. Serious competitions are held in tractor- and truck-pulls, monster truck races, off-road and hill-climbing of two- and four-wheeled machines.

But the warm heart of the fair is the ring of sheds, show-tents, and auditoriums around the perimeter of the fair grounds where local folks show their prize livestock, produce, crafts, and cookery. You'll need an event schedule and a walking map to find your way around. One or another agricultural exhibit or competition will be going on most of every afternoon, but if your daughter's new sixth-grade pal is showing her loppy-eared rabbits in Judging Shed #12-A at 3 p.m., you'd best be there on time—and 12-A more than likely is a good half-mile trek from the main gate where you enter.

A new-to-the-country family's first fair visit will probably be brief—or, at least planned to be so. It can be an intimidating to run into all the new neighbors who seem to know so much more about country life than you do. But rest assured that seeing you at the fair—showing an interest in the humble things that are most important to them—will "cut the ice" with rural people who may seem aloof at first…but who are probably more leery of you than you are of them.

There is no better way to gain a talking familiarity with farm tractors, birthing calves, and the livestock and crops raised locally than just to hang around and soak it all in. Country schools often enter individual children's and class projects as exhibits, and your own kids will get a sense of belonging when they spy their art masterpieces in the school-exhibit shed next to the stables holding the cutting horses or the tin-roofed pole barn where the old-time tractors and threshing machines are exhibited.

More and more fairs are following the state of Maine's Common Ground Fair in encouraging sale of healthy natural foods rather than the usual fair fare of hot dogs and cotton candy, so meals at the event can be both healthful and inexpensive. With camping facilities available nearby (even if in the nearest farmer's back field), a visit of several days need not be an expensive proposition for families on a scrimp-and-save budget.

A family's first participation in fair events might well come when one of the youngsters becomes involved in 4-H Club, FFA, or Scout activities, which usually include preparing exhibits for the fair. Those first entries might be in kid-level events in categories such as sewing, canning, crafts, pets, or small livestock. Winning a ribbon or two is the success that can spur a youngster to branch out into more country activities and to enter other areas of competition.

The fields in which family members can enter exhibits cover every aspect of country living: cooking and baking, canning, pickle-making, woodcraft, bee keeping, making jams and jellies, raising small livestock, growing fruits and vegetables, collecting minerals or arrowheads, sewing, knitting or crocheting, needlepoint, painting, photography, leather work, whittling and treen-ware...and on and on.

Preparing a major exhibit such as a beef steer or lamb for the annual judgings is a year-long activity, climaxing only when the prizes and premiums are awarded at the fair.

However, the fair is more than an opportunity to display the fruits of a year's labor. Aside from all the fascination and the fun, a fair can provide an education for the beginning homesteader. It may, for instance, be the place where a person decides to plant a garden just to get in on the fun of trying to grow the biggest pumpkin. Watching the livestock judging has inspired many a family to begin raising chickens, goats, sheep, hogs or cattle. The fair-time spent talking and listening can be an early education in animal husbandry.

Day trips to the fair can be as easy as loading the family and its exhibits into the truck or car and driving a short distance. But staying a few days will make the outing a real vacation, and camping near the fairgrounds can hold the cost down to the expense of gas, meals, and gate charges.

All ages can make new friends around the evening campfire—many proceeded by shared pot-luck suppers with everyone serving up popping-fresh home-raised produce and regional country casseroles: Tex-Mex and chili in the Southwest, gumbo and jambolaya in Cajun country, fish chowder in New England and coastal Pacific Northwest, corn chowder in Kansas, stone soup and macaroni/hamburger/tomato sauce "Glop" EVERYWHERE in endless regional variety. Plus homemade ice cream, cakes, and pies...mmmm, the pies. Ever had Missouri-Ozark yam and marshmallow pie? Or Michigan tomato cobbler? Plus, in time, winning a few premiums can offset the money spent for the fair visit. And, your son's blue-ribbon Black Angus beef steer or your daughter's prize Romney ewe can pay for a whole lot more than a week at the county seat or state capital.

A few days at the fair are hard to beat for a wholesome country-good time you'll want to repeat year after year.